Public Enterprises

Economics and Management

Public Enterprises

Economics and Management

Volume–I

K.R. Gupta

ATLANTIC

PUBLISHERS & DISTRIBUTORS (P) LTD

Published by
ATLANTIC
PUBLISHERS & DISTRIBUTORS (P) LTD
7/22, Ansari Road, Darya Ganj,
New Delhi-110002
Phones : +91-11-40775252, 23273880, 23275880, 23280451
Fax : +91-11-23285873
Web : www.atlanticbooks.com
E-mail : orders@atlanticbooks.com

Branch Office
5, Nallathambi Street, Wallajah Road,
Chennai-600002
Phones : +91-44-64611085, 32413319
E-mail : chennai@atlanticbooks.com

Printed in India at Nice Printing Press, A-33/3A, Site-IV, Industrial Area, Sahibabad, Ghaziabad, U.P

Preface

Public enterprises assume great importance, especially in developing countries like India. These enterprises are considered to be a powerful engine of economic development and an important instrument of attaining the widely cherished goal of a socialist society. These were set up to meet the immense task of facilitating the industrial development in the country in a manner that no region was left behind in the process.

During the period since Independence, public enterprises have been reliable partners in advancing growth in the country. They remain relevant as they have demonstrated the ability to adjust to the changing environment. Many public enterprises have been able to withstand the intense competition that ensued from domestic and global firms since the early 1990s when India began the process of liberalizing its economy. In recent times, some of the public enterprises have emerged as effective players in international markets. The 2010 Forbes Global List of 2,000 companies includes 56 Indian companies; among these 28 were Indian public sector companies.

Public enterprises will continue to be important if they take steps to keep their performance under constant review and strive for efficiency and competitiveness. In order to maintain sustained profitability and consistently give good performance, public enterprises need to adopt best practices of management and keep themselves abreast of market orientation.

India's sustained economic growth requires that all stakeholders, both in the public and the private sector, contribute their very best, so that there is overall development in the country. Public enterprises have a huge responsibility on them to excel in their fields and through their work to serve the national goal of socio-economic development. It should be their endeavour to maintain high level of standards so that these become best practices in the industry, setting benchmarks for other companies to emulate.

The reputation of an organization depends upon the strength and values of its personnel. There should be continuous efforts to upgrade human resources through skill development, attitudinal change and team building, including through more women in the higher echelons of public sector management.

Starting with a modest investment of ₹ 29 crore in 5 enterprises on the eve of the first Five Year Plan in 1956, enterprises in the public sector have steadily progressed to 246 in number with an investment of ₹ 5,29,950 crore till 2009. This rapid growth of public enterprises has given rise to a number of debatable issues like the forms of organization, financing, price policy, governing boards, public accountability, goals and measurement of management, personnel management, financial management, industrial relations, efficiency and disinvestment. *Public Enterprises: Economics and Management* analyses these issues with a detached and scientific outlook and provides suitable suggestions. Although benefit has been taken of, and illustrations cited about the experience of working of public enterprises abroad, the book is written primarily in the setting of working of public enterprises in India. Report of Ad hoc Group of Experts on Empowerment of Central Public Sector Enterprises (CPSEs), Guidelines on Corporate Governance for CPSEs, and White Paper on Disinvestment of CPSEs are given in Annexures.

I had the privilege of working in a large public enterprise (State Trading Corporation of India) for four years which provided me an opportunity to study the problems of public enterprises from a very close angle. This has enabled me to be more realistic, as compared with pure academicians who often have a tendency to be idealistic, in analyzing problems and making suggestions.

I am highly indebted to many top executives of several public enterprises for providing me an opportunity for free and frank discussions and supplying me useful information.

The book will be useful not only to the students of Economics, Commerce and Business Management but also the executives of public enterprises, government officials and parliamentarians deeply concerned with the setting up and working of public enterprises.

K.R. Gupta

Contents

Annexures

Role in Economic Development

1

The philosophy of laissez-faire propounded by the classical economists, which dominated the economic and political scene of the world during the 17th and 18th centuries, started giving way to state regulation and control in the nineteenth century. With the passage of time, it was recognised that mere regulation and control is not enough and to effectively execute its policies, the state must directly participate in business. The recent years have been particularly marked by an increasing intervention by state in the economic field. In the words of S.S. Khera, "The nineteenth century concept that the interests of society are best served by the state interfering as little as possible with the life of the people, has lost its meaning, and, with it, has lost support".[1] He further states, "...the State to-day, far from being merely a passive observer of the economic process, which once it was, has emerged as an active participant, taking upon itself the role of protector, of controller, of guardian of the citizen, and of entrepreneur".[2]

The most important factor leading to an expansion of state intervention in economic affairs was the social evils which accompanied the industrial revolution. The era of industrial revolution saw the inhumanity of man to man and a brutalisation of human nature in those very societies where the greatest advances were being made in the field of science, technology and organisation. In the United States, miracles of industrial revolution co-existed with the inequities of the slave system which were put to an end by the American Civil War of 1861. Similarly, in

Europe, there was a separation of the man from his craft and from his family. Man became just an attendant upon a machine erected with the sole objective of earning money for its owner.

In addition to the social evils which the industrial revolution brought in its train, it created private capitalism. Private capitalism developed a number of undesirable characteristics which damaged man, his security, his welfare, even his whole future. It disrupted the age-old system of independent, self-supporting families carrying on their life's activities within and around the village community. The old family ties and the old fraternities yielded place to the barren realities of the economics of industrial revolution. The old system was destroyed without adequate thought of what would take its place and perform its functions. The result was the operation of the inexorable laws of laissez-faire which led to side by side existence of distress and luxury, starvation and plenty, riches and nakedness. It was these conditions which gave birth to state intervention as a matter of historical necessity. The early attempts of state intervention in economic affairs took the form of formulation of factory laws.

The First World War necessitated a further increase in state intervention. For mobilising maximum resources for war, it was essential for the state to control and regulate the apparatus of production. Towards the end of the First World War, in 1917, there came the Russian Revolution. It led to wholesale management by state of the overall economic life of the people. The Great Depression of the thirties showed the need for greater intervention by state in economic affairs with a view to control business fluctuations. The Second World War gave a further fillip to state participation in economic matters.

State enterprise has become a world-wide phenomenon in the twentieth century. State enterprises have come into existence in all countries, whether capitalistic or socialistic, developed or underdeveloped. Even in a country like the United States, where the state enterprise is looked upon with an eye of suspicion and considered a threat to individual liberties, there is an outstanding example of state enterprises, i.e., Tennessee Valley Authority. In socialist countries, like the erstwhile U.S.S.R., state enterprise dominated the whole economy. The U.S.S.R. Constitution stated, "The economic foundation of the U.S.S.R. is the Socialist system of economy and the Socialist ownership of the instruments and means of production, firmly established as a result of the liquidation of the capitalist system of economy, the abolition of private ownership of the instruments and means of production and the elimination of the exploitation of man by man".[3]

Public enterprise covers a large part of French economy. The list of public enterprises covers electricity, gas and coal corporations, the railways, the national airlines, two major shipping companies, the Paris transport system, the Alsation potash mines, Toulcuse nitrates plant, the greater part of the aircraft construction industry, Renault Motor Works, the four great deposit banks, half the country's insurance business, commercial radio stations on the borders of France, film and cinema companies and many others. During the period 1945-50, the Labour Government in Britain nationalised coal, gas, transport, airways, electricity, iron and steel and the Bank of England.

Similarly, developing countries, like India, Sri Lanka, Pakistan, Burma, Turkey, etc. have established several state enterprises. In Turkey, Agricultural Bank, office of soil products, the Agricultural Equipment Agency, etc. are all state-owned and assist farmers in several ways. In the words of A.H. Hanson, "Both in industry and agriculture the story of Turkish economic development has been largely one of state enterprises".[4] In South Africa, too, state-owned public enterprises play a crucial role in socio-economic development. They are especially dominant in transport, communication, natural resources, financial services and agriculture.

Thus, there is hardly any country where the government does not actively participate in the establishment and management of economic and industrial enterprises. Such enterprises range from transport systems (railways, roadways, air and shipping enterprises), generation and distribution of power, irrigation system, supply of water for industry and for domestic consumption, mining and processing of coal, iron and other minerals, banking and insurance to industrial enterprises like integrated steel plants, machine tools, fertilisers and chemicals, manufacture of aircraft, of locomotives and of transport equipment, etc.

The growth of state enterprise is due to a variety of motives, pressures and purposes which differ from country to country, and from government to government. The factors which in one or the other way determine the extent of state enterprise include the practical needs of a nation, defence considerations, political ideology, social philosophy and the stage of economic development.

In developing countries, it is the public enterprise which has to lay the basis upon which the structure of a dynamic and diversified economy is to arise. In the words of Hanson, "Whatever the ultimate perspective may be, the country anxious to develop economically has no alternative but to use public enterprise on a considerable scale, at the very least in order to 'get things going'."[5] The public enterprise has to provide power, transport, irrigation facilities, etc. To quote Hanson again, "Public enterprise without a plan can achieve something; a plan without public enterprise is likely to remain on paper".[6]

Even when the base has been built and other facilities like protection from foreign competition, fiscal incentives and cheap loans provided, the response from the private entrepreneurs may be very poor. This is particularly likely to be the case in the initial stages of development because of unfamiliarity and complexity of the entrepreneurial function, uncertainty of adequate rewards and superior attractions of commerce, speculation and real estate. Under such circumstances, the major entrepreneurial initiative will have to come from the government.

Most of the countries have introduced planning to varying degrees. For successfully implementing a plan, mere regulation of the economy may not be enough and an active participation of the state in the establishment and management of the undertakings may be required.

Private enterprise leads to vast inequalities in the distribution of wealth which are not desirable on social grounds and also on economic grounds to the extent they are the result of unearned income. It artificially creates 'poverty in the midst of plenty'.

Artificial scarcity exists side by side unemployed workers and unused plant capacity. Producers complain of gluts and surpluses while consumers are underfed, underclothed and undersheltered. There are limits to which inequalities in the distribution of income and wealth can be reduced by fiscal measures because, if carried beyond these limits, they tend to impair the incentives to enterprise, to work and to save and invest.

State participation in commerce and industry is an important instrument of attaining the objectives of social and economic justice like labour welfare. The state enterprises may prove themselves a model for private sector by introducing concepts like "Workers' Participation in Industry".

The functions of the government which were originally limited to the maintenance of law and order have considerably expanded in recent years. The Indian Constitution, particularly in the Directive Principles of State Policy, for instance, holds the state responsible for the total socio-economic welfare of the people. To discharge its increasing responsibilities, the state requires expanding resources. The taxation alone cannot provide resources on the required scale. "By active participation in business, the state has sought to tap the gold mines of industry and commerce for the funds needed to discharge the new and heavier burdens it now shoulders".[7]

Phenomenal increase in the efficient scale of business and industry has narrowed the gap between public and private enterprises in respect of management. In large-scale enterprises, it is no longer possible for the private owner to look into details. Management is primarily in the hands of paid managers and executives. Impersonal management is particularly marked in joint stock companies. Most of the shareholders, particularly the small ones, take hardly any interest in the working of the company in which they have invested their money. The faith in the innate qualities of business leadership is fast disappearing. Imparted qualifications are considered more important than the innate ones. Any person willing and qualified to learn can get training in business administration schools. Failure of public enterprises is, often, not so much because of inefficient management as because of the tendencies of the ruling powers to exploit business enterprises for political purposes. Efficiency of public enterprises can be considerably improved by freeing them from political influences and running them on commercial principles.

Role of Government in Public Sector

State participation in economic activity can hardly be a matter of disagreement. The free play of economic forces, even in highly developed capitalist countries, has often meant large unemployment and instability of the system. Hence, there is a considerable dilution of the laissez-faire principle and the governments are now called upon to intervene in economic fields which were considered sacrosanct, for the private sector. In these advanced countries, state intervention has been invoked to ensure economic stability and full employment of productive resources of the community.

But state action is all the more inevitable in developing economies. Here the state has to play a vital and ever-expanding role to accelerate the process of economic growth. These countries are struggling hard to get rid of poverty and to attain higher living standards. In a developing economy, there is a circular constellation of forces tending to act and react upon one another in such a way as to keep a poor country in a stationary state of underdeveloped equilibrium. The vicious circle of underdeveloped equilibrium can be broken only by a comprehensive government planning of the process of economic development.

It is obvious that high rate of investment and growth of output cannot be attained in an underdeveloped country simply as a result of the functioning of the market forces. Even the operation of these forces is hindered by the existence of economic rigidities and structural disequilibria. Economic development is not a spontaneous or automatic process. On the contrary, it is evident that there are automatic forces within the system tending to keep it at a low level. Thus, if a developing country does not wish to remain caught up in a vicious circle of poverty, government must interfere with the market forces to break that circle.

In the initial phase, the process of development in a developing country is held up primarily by the lack of the basic social and economic overheads such as schools, technical colleges and research institutes, hospitals and railways, roads, ports, harbours and bridges. Provision of these overheads requires very large investments. Such investments will lead to the creation of external economies, which in their turn, will provide incentives for the expansion of private enterprise in the field of industry as well as of agriculture.

Private enterprise will not undertake investments in social overheads, because the returns from them in the form of an increase in the supply of technical skills and higher standards of education and health can be realized only over a long period. Also, these returns will accrue to the whole society rather than to those entrepreneurs who incur the necessary large expenditure on the creation of such costly social overheads. Therefore, investment in them is not profitable from the standpoint of the private entrepreneurs, howsoever productive it may be from the broader interest of the society. This indicates the need for direct participation of the government by way of investment in social overheads, so that the rate of development is quickened.

Investments in economic overheads require huge outlays on capital which are usually beyond the capacity of private enterprise. Besides, the returns from such investments are quite uncertain and take very long to accrue. Private enterprise is generally interested in quick returns and will seldom be prepared to wait so long.

Nor can private enterprise easily mobilise resources of building up all these overheads. The state is in a far better position to find the necessary resources through taxation, borrowing and deficit financing—sources not open to private enterprise. Thus, private enterprise lacks the capacity to undertake large scale and comprehensive development programme. Not only that, it also lacks the necessary approach to development.

The role of government in development is further highlighted by the fact that developing countries suffer from a serious deficiency of all types of resources and skills, while the need for them is so great. In these circumstances, what is needed is a wise and efficient allocation of limited resources. This only the state is best fitted to do through central planning, according to a scheme of priorities well suited to the country's conditions and needs. Until the country has attained the stage of self-sustained growth, the government must make determined and conscious efforts to push the economy through the 'take-off' period of development.

Rationale of Public Sector in Economic Development

The *raison d'être* or a rationale for the public sector undertakings is to be found in the inadequacies or weakness of the price system. The price system, as it actually functions, is far from being an ideal mechanism of the efficient running of an economy—especially, in terms of the three vital considerations of resource allocation, income distribution and employment generation.

(i) **The Compensatory or Substitutive Role:** The participation of the public sector undertakings in the economic activities is called for when it has a compensatory role to perform. The compensatory role, in turn, would be necessitated when there is a need to compensate for the deficiencies or shortfalls of the price system.

When the public sector assumes a compensatory role it serves to provide a substitute for the private sector of the economy. In fact, the public sector enterprises then perform the functions of a corrective activity or device. This in itself provides a rationale for the participation of public enterprises in economic activity.

In the same way, where the price mechanism hinders the full utilisation of resources due to the existence of monopolistic tendencies or externalities, e.g. power sector, the public sector makes up for the deficiency by its direct participation in the productive and distributive activities of the economy.

Again the compensatory role of the public sector becomes necessary where the price system left to itself, fails to achieve some socially desirable objectives. For instance, if education, health and other welfare activities were in the purview of the private sector, it will lead to both inadequate quantity and inequitable distribution of the service. The public sector can compensate for these deficiencies by undertaking these activities.

(ii) **The Adjunctive or Added Role:** The price system may not only fail to function satisfactorily, but also in a number of situation it may fail altogether. And when the market mechanism fails to operate, certain goods and services would not be produced in the economy. Under such a situation, it is necessary for the public sector to undertake to produce these goods and services. These public activities would, in effect, be an addition to the overall level of economic activity of the economy. That is how an adjunctive role is assumed by the public sector undertakings.

In general, the public sector performs its adjunctive role when it aims at producing 'public goods' or things that satisfy 'public (or social) wants'. The market mechanism fails to register the true preferences of individuals for public goods (e.g. roads, bridges, courts, police, etc.). Since no private enterprise can afford to undertake activities aimed at satisfying 'public (or social) wants', the public sector has necessarily to step-in in this direction.

(iii) **The Competitive Role:** Competition between private sector and public sector is very rare. Public sector either plays a substitutive or supportive or adjunctive role. Only when private sector, in case of goods with positive external effects (externalities) resort to monopolist characteristics that the public sector intervene and may play a competitive role. In case of merit goods the public sector plays a role to keep the private sector (or price mechanism or market forces) under check to satisfy the merit wants like low cost housing, education, minimum food, etc. to the vulnerable sections of the society. The government may subsidise the efforts of the private sector in this regard or can directly participate in the production of these goods.

Role of Public Sector Enterprises in Economic Development

It is now recognised that in the developing countries, the vicious circle of underdevelopment can be broken only by a bold intervention by the government in the form of public sector enterprises.

The role of public enterprises both in accelerating development and realising the avowed social objectives of underdeveloped countries can be brought as: (a) achieving socialistic pattern, (b) building industrial base, (c) capital formation, (d) optimum allocation of resources strategies, (e) balanced and unbalanced growth, (f) balanced regional development, and (g) achieving social objectives.

Some other ways in which public sector can promote economic development are diversification of economic structure, enlargement of employment, bridging the entrepreneurial gap, generating foreign exchange earnings, supporting private enterprise, and checking against malefficient tendencies.

Arguments Against Public Enterprise Examined

It has, sometimes, been argued that public enterprise system is not very congenial to experimentation and innovations. "Whatever the merits of public administration, it is not well adapted to the process of woodshed invention, trial and error, experimentation, and risky decision making that characterised the early stages of the industrial revolution".[8] Progress of science in socialist countries like China shows that public administration is not less suitable for experimentation and innovations. It has vast funds and can liberally spend on research and experimentation. Public administration can afford to take greater risks because the cost of risks is widely diffused over the whole society. Under private enterprise system, the cost of risks has to be borne by a single enterprise and, consequently, the tendency to take risky decisions is not so marked. Under private enterprise system, the fruits of research and experimentation are limited to a single enterprise which incurs the costs of research and experimentation. Under public enterprise system, all producing units can freely draw on the results of research and experimentation. Thus, public administration leads to a much fuller utilisation of the results of research and experimentation. Further, experimentation and innovations which played an important role in the development of pioneer countries are not very important in developing countries. The process of development in least developed and developing countries consists primarily in utilising the known technology existing in advanced countries.

In Third World countries, the government machinery is generally corrupt and inefficient. Under these conditions, public enterprise beyond what is barely necessary may do more harm than good to economic development. There are no inherent reasons for the government employees to be more corrupt and less efficient. Corruption is no less rampant in private enterprises. The only thing is that the corruption in private enterprises does not receive publicity because the public is not directly concerned with the functioning of the private enterprises. The superior efficiency of employees in private enterprises is because they can offer better salaries and therefore get more efficient persons. The private enterprises can pay higher salaries because they enter only the most profitable fields while the state has to look after the fields which may not be profitable but are essential for the public welfare. If the state enters the commercial fields also, there is no reason why it should not be able to pay higher salaries and get highly efficient persons. Moreover, the inefficiency in government enterprises receives more publicity than that in private enterprises because of the above-said reason.

Public Sector in Indian Economy

Before the commencement of planning in India, activity in the public sector was confined to sectors like railways, ports, communications, broadcasting, irrigation and power and a few departmental industrial undertakings such as the ordnance factories, railway workshops and P&T workshops. Since then the public sector has grown at a phenomenal rate. Today the public sector covers a vast and varied range of activities, e.g. mining and metallurgy; manufacture of electrical goods, machine tools, chemicals and fertiliser; building of ships, aircraft and locomotives; building and construction; oil exploration and refining; provision of air, sea and road transport; industrial financing and writing of life insurance. The volume of investment in the public sector undertakings has substantially increased since independence. The public sector occupies a dominant position in the basic industries and capital goods industries.

It cannot be denied that the public undertakings in India have served as powerful instruments for achieving social and economic objectives. Serious gaps in the economy, particularly in the field of heavy industries such as manufacture of steel, heavy machine tools, heavy electricals equipment, exploration and refining of oil, manufacture of heavy chemicals and fertilisers and the indigenous production of defence equipment have been overcome through public enterprise.[9] An important economic objective of state enterprises in India, which has come to be increasingly recognised in recent years, is the creation of surpluses required for the execution of development plans. This objective is important in view of the limits to the raising of taxes and to the floating of loans for developmental purposes.

The public enterprises have helped in reducing the regional imbalances through a planned dispersal of new industries. The governments have kept in mind the claims of the relatively backward areas in locating new public enterprises as far as this was possible without disregarding the essential economic and technical considerations. Thus, steel plants have been located in Madhya Pradesh, Orissa, West Bengal and Bihar; fertiliser factories in Bihar, Orissa, Assam, U.P., Kerala, Punjab and Maharashtra; precision instrument factories in Rajasthan and Kerala; and the new machine tools plant in Rajasthan. The growth of investment in public sector has also helped in reducing the concentration of economic power in private hands. The progressive expansion of the public sector means increasing control of the country's economy in the public interest.

To lay the foundation for future growth, heavy investments were required in basic industries. It would have been futile to expect private domestic capital to come forward in an adequate measure for basic industries in India where the prospects of gain cannot be immediate. Foreign capitalists prefer investing in extractive industries which are linked with the home market. Further, the very scale of the investments required deters private capitalists from embarking on such ventures, particularly when they have little difficulty in investing their available resources in ventures involving lesser risks but yielding more lucrative returns. Under such circumstances, the government has naturally to play the role of an entrepreneur.

Sometimes government participation has had to be resorted to in the overall interest of the country. One of the objects of setting up the National Coal Development Corporation, for instance, was to conserve metallurgical coal, and to develop available resources along rational and scientific lines. Similarly, the necessity of producing cheap fertilisers and insecticides to increase food production has resulted in the setting up of the Sindri Fertilisers Company (which was later incorporated into the Fertiliser Corporation of India) and Hindustan Insecticides Limited.

The rapid expansion in public sector has not come about in an accidental manner. It has behind it a definite social and economic philosophy. This philosophy is spelt out in the Industrial Policy Resolutions of 1948 and 1956 and in the various plan reports issued so far. The major purpose of the expansion of public sector has been to stimulate economic growth by setting up enterprises which are basic to economic growth but are not likely to be undertaken by the private sector because they involve investment beyond its resources or because of certain other reasons.

The role which the state has to play in the economic life of the country was defined in the Industrial Policy Resolution of 1948 as follows: "There can be no doubt that the State must play a progressively active role in the development of industries, but ability to achieve the main objectives should determine the immediate extent of State responsibility and the limits to private enterprise. Under present conditions, the mechanism and the resources of the State may not permit it to function forthwith in Industry as widely as may be desirable. The Government of India are taking steps to remedy the situation.... They feel, however, that, for some time to come, the State could contribute more quickly to the increase of national wealth by expanding its present activities wherever it is already operating and by concentrating on new units of production in other fields, rather than on acquiring and running existing units. Meanwhile, private enterprise, properly directed and regulated, has a valuable role to play." It was decided "that the manufacture of arms and ammunition, the production and control of atomic energy, and the ownership and management of railway transport should be the exclusive monopoly of the Central Government. Further, in any emergency, the Government would have the power to take over any industry vital for national defence". The state authorities shall be exclusively responsible for the establishment of new undertakings in coal, iron and steel, aircraft manufacturing, shipbuilding, the manufacture of telephone, telegraph and wireless apparatus, and mineral oils, "except where, in the national interest, the state finds it necessary to secure the cooperation of private enterprise subject to such control and regulations as the Central Government may prescribe". "The rest of the industrial field will normally be open to private enterprise, individual as well as cooperative. The State will also progressively participate in this field; nor will it hesitate to intervene whenever the progress of an industry under private enterprise is unsatisfactory".

On 30 April 1956, the government announced a new Resolution on Industrial Policy. Many important changes and developments had occurred in the intervening period of eight years which necessitated a review and adjustment of the earlier policy. The concept of welfare state as embodied in the Constitution of the Indian Republic and the declaration of socialist pattern of society as the objective of the state's social and economic policy brought greater responsibilities on the shoulders of the state and made necessary greater state intervention in commerce and industry. The Constitution provides that it should be the effort of the state to see "that the ownership and control of the material resources of the community are so distributed as best to sub-serve the common good; and the State is also to see that the operation of the economic system does not result in the concentration of wealth and means of production to common detriment".[10]

The Industrial Policy Resolution of 1956 states, "The adoption of the socialist pattern of society as the national objective, as well as the need for planned and rapid development, require that all industries of basic and strategic importance, or in the nature of public utility services, should be in the public sector. Other industries, which are essential and require investment on a scale which only the State, in present circumstances, could provide, have also to be in the public sector. The State has therefore to assume direct responsibility for the future development of industries over a wider area.... After considering all aspects of the problem, in consultation with the Planning Commission, the Government of India have decided to classify industries into three categories, having regard to the part which the State would play in each of them." The first category of industries includes arms and ammunition and allied items of defence equipment; atomic energy; iron and steel; heavy castings and forgings of iron and steel; heavy plant and machinery required for iron and steel production, for mining, for machine tool manufacture and for such other basic industries as may be specified by the Central Government; heavy electrical plant including large hydraulic and steam turbines; coal and lignite; mineral oils; mining of iron ore, manganese ore, chrome ore, gypsum, sulphur, gold and diamond; mining and processing of copper, lead, zinc, tin, molybdenum and wolfram; minerals specified in the Schedule to the Atomic Energy (Control of Production and Use) Order, 1953; aircraft; air transport; railway transport, shipbuilding; telephones and telephone cables, telegraphs and wireless apparatus (excluding radio receiving sets); and generation and distribution of electricity. The second category consists of all other minerals except "minor minerals" as defined in Section 3 of the Minerals Concession Rules, 1949; aluminium and other non-ferrous metals not included in Schedule 'A'; machine tools; ferro-alloys and tool steels; basic and intermediate products required by chemical industries such as the manufacture of drugs, dyestuffs and plastics; antibiotics and other essential drugs; fertilizers; synthetic rubber; carbonisation of coal; chemical pulp; road transport; and sea transport. All remaining industries are included in the third category.

The state will be exclusively responsible for the future development of industries included in the first category. The second category of industries will be progressively state-owned. In such industries, the state will generally take the initiative in establishing new undertakings but private enterprise will also be expected to supplement the effort of the state. The future development of industries in the third category will, in general, be left to the initiative and enterprise of the private sector. The Resolution, however, made it clear that "The division of industries into separate categories does not imply that they are being placed in watertight compartments. Inevitably, there will not only be an area of overlapping but also a great deal of dovetailing between industries in the private and the public sectors. It will be open to the State to start any industry not included in Schedule A (first category) and Schedule B (second category)[11] when the needs of planning so require or there are other important reasons for it. In appropriate cases, privately-owned units may be permitted to produce an item falling within Schedule A for meeting their own requirements or as by-products. There will be ordinarily no bar to small private-owned units undertaking production, such as the making of launches and other light-craft, generation of power for local needs and small-scale mining. Further, heavy industries in the public sector may obtain some of their requirements of lighter components from the private sector, while the private sector in turn would rely for many of its needs on the public sector."

The Industrial Policy Statement of 1973, inter alia, identified high priority industries where investment from large industrial houses and foreign companies would be permitted. The Industrial Policy Statement of 1977 laid emphasis on decentralisation and on the role of small scale, tiny and cottage industries. The Industrial Policy Statement of 23 December 1977 states, "Apart from socialising the means of production in strategic areas, public sector provides a countervailing power to the growth of large houses and large enterprises in the private sector.... The public sector will be charged with the responsibility of encouraging the development of a wide range of ancillary industries, and contribute to the growth of decentralised production by making available its expertise in technology and management to small scale and cottage industry sectors. It will also be the endeavour of Government to operate public sector enterprises on profitable and efficient lines in order to ensure that investment in these industries pays an adequate return to society. The Government attaches high priority to the building up of a professional cadre of managers in the public sector who would be given the necessary autonomy and entrusted with the task of providing dynamic and efficient management to such enterprise."

The Industrial Policy Statement of 1980 focused attention on the need for promoting competition in the domestic market, technological upgradation and modernisation. The policy laid the foundation for an increasingly competitive export base and for encouraging foreign investment in high technology areas. It states, "Public Sector constitutes a substantial segment of industrial activity in the country and its contribution in terms of generating surpluses and employment for further growth of the economy needs to be improved." These policies created a climate for rapid industrial growth in the country.

A statement of Industrial Policy was released on July 24, 1991 along with the introduction of the New Economic Policy of Liberalisation, Privatisation and Globalisation. The statement adopts a new approach to public enterprises and states that the priority areas for growth of public enterprises in the future will be: essential infrastructure, goods and services; exploration and exploitation of oil and mineral resources; technology development and building of manufacturing capabilities in areas which are crucial in the long-term development of the economy and where private sector investment is inadequate; and manufacture of products where strategic considerations predominate such as defence equipment. At the same time, the statement adds, "the public sector will not be barred from entering areas not specifically reserved for it". Further, the "Government will strengthen those public enterprises which fall in the reserved areas of operation or are in high priority areas or are generating good or reasonable profits. Such enterprises will be provided a much greater degree of management autonomy through the system of memoranda of understanding. Competition will also be induced in these areas by inviting private sector participation. In the case of selected enterprises, part of Government holdings in the equity share capital of these enterprises will be disinvested in order to provide further market discipline to the performance of public enterprises.... The country must be proud of the public sector that it owns and its must operate in the public interest."

The First Plan states, "The scope and need for development are so great that it is best for the public sector to develop those industries in which private enterprise is unable or unwilling to put up the resources required and run the risks involved".[12] The Second Plan goes further and states, "The public sector has to expand rapidly. It has not only to initiate development which the private sector is either unwilling or unable to undertake; it has to play the dominant role in shaping the entire pattern of investments in the economy, whether it makes the investments directly or whether these are made by the private sector.... In a growing economy which gets increasingly diversified there is scope for both the public and private sectors to expand simultaneously, but it is inevitable, if development is to proceed at the pace envisaged and to contribute effectively to the attainment of the larger social ends in view, that the public sector must grow not only absolutely but also relatively to the private sector".[13]

The Second Plan also emphasizes the importance of using the public sector as an instrument for checking concentration of economic power. It states, "Public ownership, partial or complete, and public control or participation in management are specially required in those fields in which technological considerations tend towards concentration of economic power and wealth".[14] The Third Plan states this argument in a more forceful and categorical manner. "As a decisive instrument which the State can employ in preventing concentration of economic power and growth of monopolistic tendencies, the rapid expansion of the public sector serves a two-fold purpose. It helps to remove certain basic deficiencies in the economic structure and at the same time it reduces the scope for accumulation of wealth and large incomes in private hands.... As the relative share of the public sector increases, its role in economic growth will become even more strategic and the State will be in a still stronger position to determine the character and functioning of the economy as a whole."[15]

The Fourth Five-Year Plan states, "A matter of crucial significance will be the emergence of the public sector as a whole as the dominant and effective area of the economy. This will enable it to take charge more and more of the commanding heights in the production and distribution of basic and consumer goods."[16]

The Seventh Five-Year Plan states, "The public sector has initiated and sustained the industrial transformation of India. It shall continue to play its pivotal role in modernising Indian industry and in reducing the concentration of economic power...the public sector has to undergo basic structural changes to conform to the Plan priorities of efficiency and productivity. Only in the measure that the public sector generates investible surpluses can it play its indispensable social role of providing an adequate infrastructural base for the economy, being a vehicle for the introduction and absorption of new technology in critical sectors of the economy, and for achieving balanced regional growth."[17]

By the end of the Seventh Five-Year Plan, however, it was found that many PSUs are making "substantial losses and have become a continuing drain on the exchequer, absorbing resources which are withdrawn from sectors where these are desperately needed to achieve other developmental goals"[18] and "many loss making PSUs do not serve the goal for which they were set up".[19] Clearly, a policy of the government meeting the cash losses of so many enterprises for all times to come is just not sustainable. Hence, it became necessary to address the issue of loss making public sector enterprises.

The Eighth Five-Year Plan states, "The public sector has expanded considerably. Its expanse and its influence may not be measured just by the size of its contribution to GDP or its share in investment, but by the fact that it touches every aspect of life. In the process, it has made the people take the public sector for granted, oblivious of certain crucial factors like efficiency, productivity and competitive ability. This has eroded the public sector's own sense of responsibility and initiative. Many of the public sector enterprises have turned into slow moving, inefficient giants. A certain amount of complacency has set in which is not conducive to growth. While there are several social and infrastructural sectors where only the public sector can deliver the goods, it has to be made efficient and surplus generating. It must also give up activities which are not essential to its role."[20]

The Eighth Plan further provides the following objective principles for the public sector plan:[21]

(i) The public sector should make investments only in those areas where investment is of an infrastructural nature which is necessary for facilitating growth and development as a whole and where private sector participation is not likely to come forth to an adequate extent within a reasonable time perspective;

(ii) The public sector may also withdraw from areas where no public purpose is served by its presence. The public sector should come in where the investment is essentially for preservation and augmentation of basic resources of the country like land, forest, water and ecology, science and technology or for running key infrastructural activities. The public sector will have responsibility for meeting social needs or for regulating long-term interests of the society like population control, health, education, etc.

(iii) In large parts of public sector operations where commodities or services are produced and distributed, unless it is necessary for protecting the poorest in the society, the principle of market economy should be accepted as the main operative principle. It means charging as per cost and costing with full efficiency in operations.

After sixty years of Independence, the situation changed dramatically and an all-pervasive government role was no longer felt necessary at a stage where private sector capabilities were no longer undeveloped and the country has a strong and vibrant private sector. It became clear that industrial growth in future will depend largely upon the performance of the private sector and the government policies must therefore provide an environment which is conducive to such growth.

One of the measures introduced to reduce idle capital stock by the Tenth Five-Year Plan was rapid privatization of public sector enterprises (PSEs), particularly those, which are working well below capacity. The Tenth Plan states, "...the relative role of the public sector as a distinct entity will decline...as the process of disinvestment converts many of the existing public sector enterprises from Government controlled enterprises to non-Government enterprises in which Government may have a minority stake but the units will either become board managed or managed by a strategic investor. In either case, they will not be part of the public sector."[22]

The Eleventh Plan outlines the new priorities for the public sector. These relate to reviving dynamism in agriculture and building the necessary supportive infrastructure in rural areas, expanding access to health and education, especially in rural areas, undertaking programmes for improving living conditions for the weaker sections and for improving their access to economic opportunity. It also includes a major thrust for infrastructure development in general, which is a critical constraint on our development. Due to this changed role of government in the Eleventh Plan "the public sector will increasingly concentrate in areas that lie in the domain of the State governments, and within the States in the domain of panchayati raj institutions. This is especially true of elementary education, health, rural drinking water, rural sanitation, child nutrition, housing for the poor, the national employment guarantee, and schemes for watershed management."[23]

Conclusion

The state enterprise has become a worldwide phenomenon in the twentieth century. State enterprises have come into existence in all countries, whether capitalistic or socialistic, developed or developing. The growth of state enterprise is due to a variety of motives, pressures and purposes which differ from country to country, and from government to government. The factors which in one or the other way determine the extent of state enterprise include the practical needs of a nation, defence considerations, political ideology, social philosophy and the stage of economic development. Phenomenal increase in the efficient scale of business and industry has narrowed the gap between public and private enterprises in respect of management. Efficiency of public enterprises can be further improved by freeing them from political influences and running them on commercial principles.

NOTES

1. S.S. Khera, *Government in Business* (Bombay, 1963), p. 3.
2. *Ibid.*
3. Article IV.
4. A.H. Hanson, *Public Enterprise and Economic Development* (London, 1959), p. 124.
5. *Ibid.*, p. 23.
6. *Ibid.*, p. 183.
7. Khera, n. 1, p. 19.
8. Edward S. Manson, "The Role of Government in Economic Development", *American Economic Review, Papers and Proceedings* (May, 1960), p. 637.
9. Administrative Reforms Commission, *Report on Public Sector Undertakings* (New Delhi, 1967), (Mimeographed), pp. 16-17.
10. The Constitution of India, Directive Principles of State Policy, Article 38.
11. Words within parentheses added.
12. Government of India, First Five-Year Plan (Delhi, 1953), p. 422.
13. Government of India, Second Five-Year Plan (Delhi, 1956), pp. 22-23.
14. *Ibid.*, p. 23.
15. Government of India, Third Five-Year Plan (Delhi, 1961), p. 14.
16. http://planningcommission.gov.in/plans/planrel/fiveyr/4th/4planch1.html
17. Govt. of India, Seventh Five-Year Plan, Vol. I.
18. Govt. of India, Eighth Five-Year Plan, Vol. I.
19. *Ibid.*

20. *Ibid.*
21. *Ibid.*
22. http://planningcommission.gov.in/plans/planrel/fiveyr/10th/volume1/10th_vol1.pdf
23. http://planningcommission.gov.in/plans/planrel/fiveyr/11th/11_v1/11th_vol1.pdf

2 Forms of Organisation

The form of organisation has an important bearing on the success of the enterprise. The right choice would promote good administration which would lead to sound management and efficient production or service. On the other hand, a wrong choice could hinder good administration which would result into uneconomic production, inefficient service and unscientific management.

The forms adopted and methods followed have varied from country to country and also from enterprise to enterprise within the same country in regard to forms of organisation, legal status, operational authority, financial independence, degree of control and the extent of public accountability. The differences in form arise because every country has to seek a solution keeping in view its constitutional system, structure of government, political traditions, economic background and social needs. While the developing countries should take benefit of the experience of advanced countries, it would be dangerous to thoughtlessly imitate the structural organisation adopted by advanced countries for the public enterprise.

The important types of organisation employed for organising public enterprises are: (a) departmental management controlled by a departmental secretariat, (b) departmental management controlled by an inter-departmental committee or board, (c) public trust, (d) public corporation, and (e) joint stock limited company. We briefly discuss below their main features and suitability in relation to various types of public enterprises.

Departmental Management Controlled by a Departmental Secretariat

This is the oldest and traditional form of public enterprise and in the earliest process of nationalisation was introduced in posts and telegraphs, railways, highways, defense industries and some public utility services. In the beginning of the era of public enterprise, in fact, no distinction was made between the administrative functions of the government and the public enterprises run by them. An analytical study of the undertakings under departmental management would show that this form was favourably chosen for those activities which were either yielding revenue to the government or considered strategically important.

It ensures maximum degree of control by politically responsible officials. It works satisfactorily in countries with a stable government and a competent civil service of high integrity. It requires prior approval of the central control agency under specific and rigid rules and as such involves less risk of public money being misused or misappropriated.

Since such enterprises do not possess a separate entity of their own and are a part and parcel of the activities of the government, whenever this applies in the legal system of the country concerned, the enterprises possess the sovereign immunity of the state and cannot be sued without the consent of the government.

The departmental form of organisation suffers from a number of defects and shortcomings. It involves too much centralisation and inadequate delegation of powers. It curbs initiative and flexibility which are very essential for industrial and commercial enterprises. To safeguard against misuse of public money, the government departments have to generally lay down rigid rules for the purchase of supplies, contracts, and so on. Such rules, however, conflict with accepted commercial trade practices and hamper the smooth operation of a public enterprise. The routine working against the background of rules, regulations and procedures drawn from ordinary administration creates disincentiveness. The executives bereft of the power of exercising initiative find little opportunity to grow to a stature and the resultant frustration tempts them to settle down as mere cogs in a huge machine. The usual government procedure is not conducive to quick action which is very essential in business and industry. There are long delays in taking decisions. Every matter has to pass through the hands of several officials who are reluctant to take a decision, their area of authority not being clearly demarcated. In many matters, approval of different Ministries has to be obtained. In the words of R.K. Jain, "The system militates against the initiative and flexibility which are fundamental and basic for the successful operation of a business concern. The bureaucrat's overemphasis on caution, conservative temper and 'through the proper channel mentality' do not leave even elbow room for refreshingly, bold approaches, adventure, and risk."[1] "Under this form of organisation, public enterprises have sometimes become synonymous with red tape, delays, inadequate service and in-sensitivity to consumer needs".[2]

In least developed countries there is generally a shortage of competent civil servants and the available ones are overburdened with the routine work of their Ministry. They also lack training and experience for commercial services. They, therefore, are not very suitable for managing public enterprises. Further, since their fixed salaries are not affected by the level of profits of the enterprise, they have a tendency to obey an order from their superiors rather than hazard a prompt and timely decision themselves.

The departmental type of organisation has to operate under rigid financial and budgetary controls. Such enterprises are required to obtain annual appropriations from the legislature. They are not permitted to utilise incidental revenues or to retain unspent balance of appropriations at the end of the fiscal year. They, therefore, cannot easily operate on a self-sustaining basis. Since they have no power to utilise their revenues, there is hardly any incentive to charge rates calculated to recover all the costs of their operation. Because they can obtain all the required funds without much difficulty, they have no incentive to use funds in the most economical manner.

The departmentally managed enterprises are also exposed to the danger of reckless adventure in order to strengthen and stabilise the ruling party's position, particularly when it is at stake. The industrial power may be misused to fight political battles and the field of industry and trade may be contaminated with the rapidly changing dirty politics which would impair the effective handling of the enterprise with continuity.

A departmental public enterprise is under the plenary control of the minister responsible to Parliament. Every detail of administration can be challenged in the parliament and subjected to undue criticism, scrutiny and investigation. This impairs the initiative of the staff and officials and limits their freedom of action. The minister concerned and his senior officers are overburdened with mass of detailed parliamentary inquiries and defending their own actions and, therefore, do not get enough time to give thought to policy matters.

Speaking against the departmental form of management, Earnest Benn remarks, "We think that Ministers should be directly responsible for commercial operations and the employment of labour to the least possible extent, and that the financial side of these operations should be kept separate from the State Budget to the greatest possible extent. The great Departments of State are not organized for business administration. Nor are Ministers selected for their business capacity".[3] Similarly, a Trade Union Congress study states, "...it is doubtful, according to modern Socialist ideas, whether there is ever any advantage in conducting an industry or a commercial service by the method of direct state operation, i.e. by a Government Department. State activities such as the general supervision and administration of national education, public health, postal service, and trade, as well as the older functions in relation to foreign affairs, finance, and the rest, are obviously different in kind from the operation of services like Transport, Coal Mining, etc. The former are typical Governmental functions which cannot be divorced from the machinery of the State and Parliament. The latter are really commercial undertakings, whose business is production, not regulation and supervision".[4] In the words of A.D. Gorwala, "Departmental management must be the rare exception, not the general rule. In many ways it is the direct negation of the requirements of autonomy. It militates against initiative, flexibility.... For, departmental management means management by one or more Administrative Departments as part of their larger routine, inevitably in conjunction with the Finance Department as part of its own routine, with an attempt in some instances to minimise the routine aspect of the disposal by entrustment to a committee formed of departmental representatives, but in every case against the background of the rules, regulations and procedure inseparable from ordinary administration and of the plenary control of Minister and Parliament, also inseparable from that administration.... Nevertheless, in a few types, departmental management is inevitable. These must be defined, isolated and kept down to the minimum".[5]

The departmental form of organisation fails adequately to take into account certain features which distinguish public enterprises from general government functions:[6] "(i) the government is dealing with the public in the manner of a businessman rather than a sovereign; (ii) individual users, rather than the general taxpayers, are to pay for the cost of goods and services; (iii) expenditures necessarily fluctuate with consumer demand and cannot be predicted accurately, or realistically kept within annual budgetary limitations; and (iv) operations are being conducted within areas in which there are well established trade practices." Sargent Florence mentions five important reasons why Britain never repeated state-departmental experiment with post office. "First, the Minister in charge, the Postmaster-General, was and always is changing, even during the period of office of any one party. Second, there was (and is) continual questioning in Parliament. As one consequence the top executives of the department have had to be skilled in apologetics and the writing of Minister's answers, but not necessarily able in the real business of running the post office. Third, the civil service selected, conditioned, and organised for a different purpose than "running" an industry, stood fast, too deliberative, conventional and "bureaucratic". Initiative counts for nothing against the meticulous observance of regulations which are both made and applied by those who know nothing of the daily detailed exigencies of practical work. Fourth, even if the department showed some initiative, say, in capital development, the Treasury might impose its traditional veto. Fifth and final reason for the business flight from departmental government is that any profits from the business (and they were and are often large) are liable to be used for the relief of general taxation instead of for reduction of prices".[7]

The question arises: Can we not remove the shortcomings of the departmental form of organisation by introducing some modifications into the structures and procedures of departments concerned with the running of public enterprises? Professor Dimock remarks, "if sufficient improvements could be made among the departments in the direction of greater autonomy and flexibility, there would be little or no justification for public corporations at all".[8] In practice, some of the necessary adaptations have occasionally been made in different countries. An important form of these adaptations is the use of a revolving fund under which the revenues of an enterprise are deposited in the fund and may be withdrawn for any authorized purpose without reappropriation. In this way money in the fund is made available constantly. In some countries sometimes specific exemptions have been granted through irksome laws and regulations, though they are not always in accordance with any established policy of the state. General legislation has been enacted to liberalise budget accounting and budget procedures. With a view to mitigating delays in the normal government procedure, in some cases the administrative and financial rules pertaining to these enterprises have been revised.

Many enterprises, though technically under departmental management, are in practice run by the appointed Boards.[9] In India, for instance, the Railway Board manages Railway organisation, the Defence Production Board manages defence industries, the Posts and Telegraphs Board functions in postal organisation, and so on. But these Boards do not enjoy the autonomy that an independent Board should enjoy in practice. Dr. Pranjape's observation on the Railway Board that it has been "relegated to the status of a subordinate executive body rather than a supreme policy-making body"[10] is pertinent and true of other Boards also. Of late, there has been a change in the outlook of the government towards making the Boards more strong and it is encouraging to note that, as a result of dissatisfaction expressed over insufficient delegation of powers to the former Board, an autonomous Board has now been introduced in the Posts and Telegraphs Department.

Bending the departmental organisation to accommodate activities for which it was not orginally designed is, however, usually a difficult task. So long as the enterprise is not clearly distinguished from other types of government activity, strong pressures will be brought to make it conform to standard government regulations and procedures. The emphasis on uniformity being a common characteristic of bureaucratic administration, unless specific legal provisions are made applicable to public enterprises, the effort to apply different procedures often fails. Hanson observes, "Even in a developed country, with an intelligent and adaptable civil service, the operation of making a genuine public enterprise out of a government department is not one to be lightly undertaken; in a underdeveloped country it is often impossible. Special forms of organisation, therefore, are usually necessary".[11]

The trend of thought now has definitely swung to some other type of organisation and the departmental form is visibly on the decline. In the United Kingdom, the Atomic Energy was under direct departmental control, but under the Atomic Energy Authority Act, 1954, it has been brought under autonomous management pattern. In Japan also departmentally run state enterprises are considered a synonym for inefficiency.[12] In India the dissatisfaction with the departmental management is evident from the conversion of the Oil and Natural Gas Commission from departmental management to a Statutory Corporation.

Departmental Management Controlled by an Inter-departmental Committee or Board

So far as overall governmental control is concerned, there is no basic difference between this and the foregoing type of departmental organisation. Some modifications are, however, made in order to introduce flexibility and to remove causes of unnecessary delays. An inter-departmental committee or board is set up consisting of representatives from all those ministries which are concerned with a project or which are required to be consulted in the execution of the plan or taking any decisions. Such a committee is entrusted with the overall management of the enterprise. The presence of the representatives of the different ministries concerned is expected to facilitate quick decisions. But this has not always been true in actual practice because of lack of adequate authority with the members. They often refer matters to their ministry where the matter is dealt with in a routine manner which leads to long delays. Such Boards are expected to take better decisions than individual heads because so many heads are put together. In India, important examples of this type of organisation are Bhakra Control Board, Hirakud Control Board, Chambal Control Board, etc.

Public Trust

This form of organisation has been used particularly for activities concerned with the rendering of services or regulating activities affecting the society in general. It is common for constituting port authorities, e.g. port trusts. It is also found in the monetary field, e.g. investment trusts. This form is not found in the industrial field.

The 'trust authority' is generally an autonomous body holding and operating assets of the state in trust. The principle is largely prevalent in the United Kingdom where public trusts have long and sound traditions. Certain types of trusts like investment trusts in India, however, have been handicapped because of the tendency on the part of the government to have overriding powers over the Boards of Trusts or the Trusts themselves. The members of the Board often include a representative of the government who tends to be less a member of the trust and more an officer of the government with overriding powers.

Port commissions and port trusts have an important bearing on specialised industries and trade, particularly shipping. The administrative authority is vested in the trust with a view to achieve efficiency. The authority is governed by a parliamentary or legal act which defines the powers of the trust regarding the area of jurisdiction, activities in relation to management of the port and regulating the facilities rendered. The executive head of the Trust is generally appointed by the government and the members are, more or less, in advisory capacity.

Public Corporation

For efficient and effective functioning, the public enterprises require such an organisation as may have independence of action within a broad framework prescribed by the legislature. While the organisation should be free in its day-to-day administration, it should faithfully carry out the policies laid down by the Parliament and should be answerable to the people in contrast to private enterprise which is answerable only to its shareholders. The public corporation form fulfills these requirements. "Admittedly, Western opinion has run fairly strongly in favour of the public corporation on the grounds that it provides just the right combination of commercial freedom and Government control".[13] In the words of Morrison, in it "we are seeking a combination of public ownership, public accountability and business management for public ends".[14] At another place he remarks, "a public corporation gives us the best of both worlds" because with it "we can combine progressive modern business management with a proper degree of public accountability...".[15]

A public corporation may be defined as a legal entity created by the government but exterior to the government organisation, hence financially independent, for carrying on specific activities prescribed in the law creating it. Earnest Davies describes it as "a corporate body, created by public authority, with defined powers and functions and financially independent. It is administered by a board appointed by public authority, to which it is answerable. Its capital structure and financial operation are similar to those of the public company, but its stock holders retain no equity interests and are deprived of voting rights and power of appointment of the board".[16]

A public corporation comes into existence as a result of decision taken by legislature of the country which is embodied in the form of an Act. It differs from a departmentally administered enterprise or a government company which are created by the executive without any special legislation. The Act creating the public corporation also prescribes its aims and objects, powers, duties, immunities, the form of management and its relationship to established departments and ministries. It is a corporate entity for legal purposes and can sue and be sued, enter into contracts, and acquire property in its name. The corporations doing business in their own name have been generally given greater freedom in making contracts and acquiring and disposing of property than ordinary government departments.

Except for appropriations to provide capital or to cover losses, a public corporation is generally independently financed. It obtains funds by borrowing either from the Treasury or the public and also from revenues derived from the sale of goods and services. It is authorised to use and reuse its revenues. It is usually subject to taxation in the normal way.

It is generally exempted from most regulatory and prohibitory statutes applicable to expenditure of public funds. Normally it is free from budget, accounting and audit laws, and procedures applicable to non-corporate agencies. In most cases its employees are not civil servants and are recruited and remunerated under the terms and conditions determined by the corporation itself.

It is an independent body, fettered neither to the government of the day, nor, since its capital carries no voting or ownership rights in the enterprise, to a particular group of voting shareholders; it is a functionally constituted body, having a clearly defined and specific piece of work to perform as laid down in the statute of its origin. The fundamental principle and the objective with which the organisation of public corporation is associated have been very aptly brought out by Prof. Robson. "The underlying reason for the creation of the modern type of public corporation is the need for a high degree of freedom, boldness and enterprise in the management of undertakings of an industrial or commercial character and the desire to escape from the caution and circumspection which is considered typical of Government departments".[17]

In the United Kingdom most of the nationalised industries, manufacturing or otherwise, have been given the autonomous pattern of management in the form of public corporations. The same is true of the French nationalised industries. The corporation form of organisation dominates in the American and Canadian public undertaking. The Tennessee Valley Authority (T.V.A.) is the most illuminating example of public corporation in the United States. President Roosevelt characterised the T.V.A. as a public corporation par excellence and modelled it as "a corporation clothed with the powers of Government but possessed of the flexibility and initiative of a private enterprise."[18] In Sri Lanka, the Commission on Government Commercial Undertakings recommended the public corporation form for administration and management of those enterprises about which the state decides that it should be the sole owner but the Joint Stock Company form for enterprises "with varying degrees of Government participation in their capital and management".[19] But the position has substantially changed with the passing of the State Industrial Corporation Act, 1957 and now the idea of public corporation holds the ground. In India several Acts have been passed for the nationalisation of existing enterprises and for the establishment of new undertakings, e.g. Electricity Supply Act (1948), Road Transport Corporation Act (1950), Air Corporations Act (1953), State Bank of India Act (1955), Life Insurance Corporation Act (1956), Industrial Finance Corporation Act (1948), Damodar Valley Corporation Act (1948), Employees' State Insurance Corporation Act (1948), Rehabilitation Finance Administration Act (1948), State Financial Corporation Act (1951).

The corporation device enables a government to waive some of its sovereign immunities within limited and well defined area and to establish an agency which can operate under its own name rather than that of the state. The major benefits of this form are freedom in administration, elasticity in management, autonomy in finance and freedom from government intervention. It is free from rigidity and long delays—usual in government administration. At the same time it functions within the framework of parliamentary control and ministerial responsibility and thus ensures consistency in the national policy. Dr. Gyanchand observes that the "public corporations, as a form of economic organisation, have come into favour because in them is the implicit promise of fulfillment of a social purpose without the handicap of bureaucratic rigidity. They are intended to meet the old and traditional objection to state management of economic undertakings,—red-tape, unnecessary multiplicity of rules and regulations, excessive regard for precedents and conventions, division of responsibility, the resultant conservatism of policy and practice and fear of innovation and experimentation. Their underlying principle is that stereotyped procedure is entirely unsuited to the management of public enterprises and must unavoidably lead to stagnation, thwarting of creative impulses and lack of adaptability to changes in conditions and circumstances".[20] It is free from unsuitable government regulations and controls and with its high degree of operational and financial flexibility, it may follow standard commercial practices in conducting its business. It can finance expansion of facilities to cope with an unanticipated growth in business without undue delay by use of revenues and borrowings.

There have been often complaints of undue interference by the Government Departments in the autonomy of public corporations. A.D. Gorwala observes, "The history of the Corporation [Damodar Valley Corporation] since then appears to have been series of unedifying episodes in which so far as one can make out, the corporation has had to use a great deal of its energies in attempting to maintain its autonomy, and sections of the government theirs, in attempting to reduce the corporation to the position of a department subordinate to the Secretariat".[21] Similarly, the Chagla Commission on the autonomy of Public Corporation remarks, "In my opinion, it is most unfortunate that the wise and sound principle laid down in Section 21 has not been adhered to in the working of the Life Insurance Corporation. The evidence before me...clearly shows that there was a clear tendency on the part of the Finance Ministry to look upon the corporation as a wing or branch of that Ministry and to issue orders to it in the belief that the corporation was bound to carry out those orders. If one thing is more important than any other, it is that the Chairman of the corporation should be an independent official who is conscious both of his own position and the status of the corporation under the Act. But this salutary principle has been completely overlooked".[22] The Commission further remarks, "But the record shows what technically took the shape of advice was in reality an order issued by Government and that is how it was looked upon by the officials of the corporation. In my opinion, it is very necessary that appointments to important offices in the corporation should not be looked upon as merely the transfer of an officer from one department to another. There should be some security of tenure and fairly long duration of office and it should be impressed upon those who are appointed to these posts that they have to discharge their duty to the corporation, irrespective of whether their actions find favour with Government or not".[23] While interference in the day-to-day working of a corporation is undesirable, complete autonomy for it is out of question and would not be suggested by any informed person. In a democratic government, the executive should always reserve the right to intervene in any matter really vital for the country. This has become particularly important now because, with the rapid expansion in their number and field of operation, they are playing an important rcle in shaping the country's economy. That is why there is a recent tendency towards reserving certain rights for the government and vesting them with an overall control over the public corporation—right to ask for any information and veto any proposal, and above all, power to give directive on all policy matters. A United Nations Study observes, "Where extensive use is made of public corporations, the problem of public accountability can no longer safely be ignored. This is particularly true in countries which have assigned to public corporations responsibility for the most significant and dynamic segment of the government's total economic programme. Corporate revenues and expenditures necessarily have a vital bearing on a government's overall financial plan. Corporate programmes frequently overlap or cut across those of ordinary departments and agencies. The theory of corporate autonomy has come into direct conflict with the urgent need for bringing the operations of public corporations into harmony with related actions of the government. Means must exist by which public corporations may be held accountable for their acts to those who bear political responsibility—the Chief Executive, the Cabinet and the Legislature.[24]

An important question is whether each corporation should be created by a separate statute or there should be a general law for this purpose. It would be useful in this regard to study the practice being followed in some countries. In the United Kingdom, the practice is to have a separate statute for each public corporation. The same is the practice in India. But in some countries a general law relating to public undertakings has been passed which governs public sector undertakings. In Philippines, for instance, there is "Uniform Government Corporate Charter", Executive Order No. 399, promulgated by the President, pursuant to the powers vested in him by "the Republic Act Numbered Four Hundred and Twenty-two", otherwise known as the "Reorganisation Act of 1950", Section 21 of which provides that "All corporations hereafter organised by authority of the President for the economic development of the country, except those vested with governmental and regulatory powers, shall be chartered under the provisions of this Uniform Corporate Charter, unless otherwise provided by the President". All public corporations, excepting some finance corporations, in Philippines are now governed by this Charter. Similarly in Indonesia, "there is one master law for state enterprises".[25] All state enterprises in this country are established under the "Indische Bedrijven Wet, 1927". In Sri Lanka, the industrial public enterprises are governed by the "State Industrial Corporations Act (49 of 1957)". Turkey has a central law, viz. Law 3460 of 1938. There is a controlling law relating to public enterprises in the United States as well as in Canada. In India, there is no general law governing public enterprises of the country. The government companies are governed by the

Companies Act, 1956 to which a few Sections have been added relating to government companies.[26]

The views differ in regard to the desirability of having a general law with basic provisions to govern public corporations. The Rangoon Report says that "the creation of public enterprises by special legislative act appears to be clearly preferable to the other alternative methods. It is the only method which provides for thorough scrutiny and approval by the legislature and executive of the objectives and scope of the undertakings and for a clear definition of legal status, obligation, powers and organisational relationship".[27] Prof. Hanson calls this view as convincing but dogmatic and holds that in certain circumstances this practice will prove inconvenient and irksome. "If a whole sector or public enterprise has been made over to a Development Corporation", he observes, "it would surely be unwise to insist that the agency should seek legislative authorisation for every subsidiary it proposes to create",[28] and strongly asserts that a special legislative act is not invariably the best way of bringing a public enterprise into existence.[29] Mohammad Sadli in his paper on Indonesian Public Enterprises offers a practical solution to the problem when he says that "separate laws are perhaps needed to regulate public corporations of a public utility nature, of a manufacturing nature, or a service nature. Of course, it would be cumbersome to require a separate law for each enterprise, but something in the form of a master law can probably be worked out, under which coverage the individual enterprise can be set up".[30] This obviously suggests classification of enterprises. The Estimates Committee also considers it "most desirable to have all the public undertakings to conform to a common pattern or patterns", though "some individual variations are inevitable due to the special characteristics and functions of a particular undertaking. Such variations should not, however, affect basically the overall pattern of organisation and responsibility".[31]

A study of the existing public corporation Acts shows that there are some provisions which are uniformly applicable to all corporations. Important of such provisions are (a) status of *sui juris*, (b) central and executive boards, though number of members vary in different corporations, (c) borrowing powers under the government guarantee, (d) disqualification of directors, (e) powers of the Central Government to issue directives, (f) approval of capital expenditure by the government, (g) audit and accounts matters, (h) rule-making powers of the government, etc. These basic provisions can be easily incorporated in the general law while special sub-rules should be formulated for each undertaking keeping in view its special and peculiar characteristics. The sub-rules for an enterprise intended to be set up should come up before parliament for discussion and approval. This process would ensure parliamentary control and accountability of the enterprise.

Joint Stock Ltd. Company

This is another common form of organisation of public enterprises. It possesses the necessary freedom in finance and autonomy in administration and at the same time permits adequate control by the government.

The Indian Companies Act recognises two forms of companies, viz. (a) private limited and (b) public limited. The formation of a public limited company requires at least seven shareholders while the private limited company can be formed even with two shareholders. In public limited companies there is no restriction on the maximum number of shareholders whereas the number of shareholders cannot exceed fifty in private limited companies. The private limited form restricts the right of a shareholder to transfer his shares. There is no such restriction in the public limited form. For a public enterprise the private limited form is more suitable than the public limited one. This explains why, barring a few exceptions like Eastern Shipping Corporation Ltd., Rehabilitation Housing Corporation Ltd., and Orissa Road Transport Co. Ltd., all state-owned companies are in the private limited form.

As a body corporate, it is a separate entity for legal purposes and can sue and be sued, enter into contracts, and acquire property in its own name. A number of advantages have been claimed for this form of organisation.

This is the only form of organisation which can associate private enterprise, national or foreign. While in other forms of organisation, private capital can be associated in the form of loans, in the joint stock ltd. company form it can be associated as a share holder. The need for such association may arise because the government may not be in a position to provide the entire capital for the undertaking and the private capital, national or foreign, may not be forthcoming in the form of fixed interest-bearing public loans owing to the availability of more profitable opportunities elsewhere.

Sometimes the government enters a field of business just to initiate the process of its development and has no intention of staying in it permanently. It starts public undertaking with the intention of ultimately handing it over to private interests. In such cases the company form of organisation is the most suitable form because it permits the desired change in ownership without the need for additional legislation. In some cases the government acquires share of a private undertaking of national importance to put its finances and management on a sound footing. "The government may have to acquire shares of an existing enterprise in an emergency, in response to financial or employment crisis, or in order to maintain a nationally important production or service which has become unprofitable or insolvent under private enterprise".[32]

The company form is popular, particularly in India, because of the ease and convenience which it offers for setting up an undertaking. It does not need the sanction of the legislature and can be set up by executive decision and action. In several cases the government has provided hundred per cent of the capital required by the enterprise and yet given it the form of a company. Some such examples are the Sindri Fertilisers and Chemicals (P) Ltd., Bharat Electronics Ltd., Hindustan Cables Ltd., Hindustan Antibiotics Ltd., Hindustan Insecticides Ltd., National Instruments Ltd., etc. But the very ease of formation of a government company has led to its criticism. The Estimates Committee, in its eightieth report, remarked that the Parliament should be "fully acquainted with all the aspects of a projected company" and enabled "to express its considered views"; with a view to ensure this, the Committee recommended that "in future before a public undertaking is set up in the form of a government company a resolution seeking the approval of Parliament for the formation of the company may be moved".[33]

The company form offers flexibility in regard to capital and managerial structures. Adjustments in these regards can be made as expeditiously as necessary without legislative amendments required by a public corporation. A company may, for instance, issue different kinds of capital with corresponding dividend differentials to take maximum benefit of the conditions of the money market and to raise the largest possible amount of capital. Loans may be converted into capital if their purpose is found to be permanent and profitable. Similarly, different methods of managerial organisation may be tried as required by the economic conditions or the personnel problems of the company. The number of directors may range from two to fifty in case of a private company and from seven to any number in case of a public company. It is free from intricate financial rules, restrictive procedures and delays which are a prominent feature of the departmental organisation. It is suitable for being run on business principles with prompt action and initiative. The private limited company suits the needs of those who wish to take benefit of limited liability but at the same time keep the business as private as possible.

The actual working of the Joint Stock Ltd. Companies in the public sector has, however, shown that the financial flexibility and autonomy are more a myth than a reality. The undefined and unrestricted powers exercised by the Government Department responsible for the state undertaking have such an all-round control that these companies are reduced to mere adjuncts to the ministries and treated more or less like subordinate offices of the ministry. The Estimates Committee observed, "In the relations between these undertakings and the ministry the former are treated in the same manner as Departments and offices of Government controlled and supervised by the Secretariat. The State undertakings have thus become adjuncts to Ministries and are treated more or less on the same lines as any subordinate organisation or office".[34] The departmental representatives on the Board of Directors are often unwilling or unable to act in their individual capacity and have to refer the matters to their departments for guidance or instructions. In addition, the powers of the Board are restricted in many matters like borrowing, increase in share capital, appointment of General Manager and Managing Director, appointments on salary exceeding a certain limit, placing large orders, entering into contracts, etc. The same is true of finance. Any scheme involving expenditure, treatment of funds, appropriation of profits, maintenance of accounts and audit thereof is subjected to the approval of the Finance Ministry.

The composition of the Board, their powers and area of action show that there can hardly be any flexibility, autonomy, incentive to efficiency, or inclination to economy. The Board consists of (a) Chairman who is normally the Secretary of the Ministry concerned and is responsible for necessary control; (b) one or two officials of the rank of Deputy Secretary from the Ministry of Finance. They have great control over matters concerning finance; (c) officials of any other Ministry concerned with the enterprise; (d) any member from the participating states or collaborators, if they possess such a right; (e) there may be a member from outside non-officials, mainly industrialists; (f) a member with technical knowledge or experience in any particular problem concerning the enterprise may be appointed; (g) there may be a member representing labour interest in general; (h) the Managing Director and/or the General Manager holding overall charge of the concern is appointed, usually though not necessarily, by the Ministry or the President as the case may be and not by the Board.

Thus, the Board is dominated by officials representing various ministries in their ex-officio capacity. Such a Board cannot be homogeneous. It cannot have any consistent and continued policy because the ex-officio members are frequently changed as and when they are transferred or leave their posts or for other reasons. Further, the Managing Director and/or the General Manager is frequently changed which is not very conducive to efficiency. This also affects the sense of responsibility and the incentive for economy.

The powers of the Board of the state-owned companies in India are much restricted in a number of ways. There is a general reluctance to delegate powers from Ministry to the Board and from Board to the Managing Director. This impairs efficient functioning and quick decisions. Above all, the officials lack desire, willingness and courage to act freely even in the area of their authority. They have a tendency to shift responsibility for any decision to their ministries.

The working of various companies shows that the Boards have not been effective, efficient and economic. According to the Estimates Committee, "The Directors...have not been fulfilling useful role...their powers being limited.... Nothing of importance either from the point of Government or from that of the undertaking has been done by them".[35] The Comptroller and Auditor General of India observes, "The purpose of adopting the company form of management was to give these enterprises flexibility of operation and to free them from the application of rules and regulations framed for normal activities of the administration. The purpose has now come to be largely defeated since the control of the enterprise has been placed in the hands of permanent officials who are nominated to the board of directors. A few non-officials have also been appointed to the boards, but they are in minority; they have, further, no financial stakes in the companies and are largely unconcerned with their efficient administration. The non-official directors drawn from trade and industry are not generally in sympathy with the policy of nationalization; they concern themselves mainly with safeguarding the interests of private industries in the same fields of production. The official members representing various ministries look to their ministers for direction, and matters brought up before the Board are often reserved for further consideration by the Government. Nor have the managing directors been given power and authority commensurate with their responsibilities or even comparable to those rested in managing directors of private enterprises. The cumulative effect of these arrangements has been to make these companies move even slower than Government departments, although quick decision and speed are essential for their efficient operation".[36]

Another defect is the dissemination of scanty information about the activities of the company for public knowledge or refusal to supply information about them. For instance, the Minister refused information on the Sindri's on the ground that he, as a shareholder, had no absolute right to obtain it. This provoked criticism in the Lok Sabha that each company "has become an 'imperium in imperio'—small kingdom, completely assigned to, shall we say, the overlordship of the officer who happens to be the Managing Director or Chairman".[37]

Many provisions of the Companies Act do not serve much purpose in the context of public enterprises, e.g. provisions stipulating the holding of annual general body meetings and requiring notices and returns to be filed with the Registrar of Companies. The Articles of Association of the government companies contain a number of provisions for transferring, making calls on and forfeiture of shares, and imposition of penalties which have hardly any significance. In Indian state-owned private limited companies, the entire share capital is owned by the Government of India in the name of the President except where a part of the share capital is allotted to some State Government, or the collaborator supplying the technical know-how, but their share is normally nominal. In addition, to fulfill the legal requirements, one or two shares are held in the name of the officials. Being the sole shareholder, or a substantial shareholder, the President, working through the Ministry concerned, has the right to appoint all members barring a few nominated by other interests, if any. The functions of the shareholders rest with the Ministry concerned. In this capacity, the Ministry exercises the ultimate control over the whole functioning of the company. Thus, the organisation is company type only in form and law, but is sole proprietorship concern in actual practice.

Another example of the asymmetry between joint stock companies in the two sectors relates to the concept of limited liability. This principle has a purpose under the private enterprise. It safeguards a shareholder, whose interest may be limited to a safe dividend and who has neither the time nor the capacity to satisfy himself that the company's affairs are absolutely in order, against the possibility of being called upon to pay towards the defaults or disaster of the company over and above the face value of the shares for which he has undertaken responsibility. If ever the company goes in such a bad position that its available funds are inadequate to fully pay the creditors, the company is declared insolvent and the shareholders are not held liable to the creditors of the company for the losses suffered by them. The principle of limited liabilities does not have much relevance to a public undertaking because it will not be worthy of a government to write off payments to creditors taking advantage of the principle of limited liability.

Under Section 620 of the Companies Act, the government is empowered to exempt any government company from the operation of any provision of the Act. Hardly any use has been made of this Section so far. Full use should be made of this Section to reduce to the minimum the provisions of the Companies Act which are to be applied to the government companies since most of their affairs are in any case controlled by the government. The actual provisions to be applied to a government company would have to be determined specifically in each case.

The organisation of public enterprises "as companies only reduced their accountability to the audit authorities appointed under the Constitution and to the legislature."[38] The Estimates Committee also observes, "the propriety of earmarking separate sums from the Consolidated Fund for a large number of public undertakings in the shape of companies, and putting them out of reach of normal parliamentary control on expenditure on the ground that the undertakings are autonomous is, therefore, open to question."[39] The ECAFE Seminar stated two important reasons against the company form of organisation of public enterprises: "(i) The company device evades the constitutional responsibilities which a state controlled enterprise has, in a democratic society, to the government and to parliament; (ii) The use of company form and of the law regulating commercial companies usually becomes a mere fiction because all or most of the functions normally vested in the shareholders and in the management are reserved to the government by the statute setting up the company".[40] The company form of organisation has been sharply criticised by the Auditor General of India, who remarks, "These Private Limited Companies are in my opinion a fraud on the Companies Act and also on the Constitution, because money cannot be taken away from the Consolidated Fund for the establishment and transformation of certain concerns into private companies in the name of the President and Secretary to Government.... Further, to convert a Government concern into a private company solely by executive action is unconstitutional."[41]

The Companies Act, 1956 has considerably improved the situation and many criticisms originally leveled against the company form have lost their force. It defines a government company as "any Company in which not less than fifty-one per cent of the share capital is held by the Central Government, or by any State Government or Governments, or partly by the Central Government and partly by one or more State Governments".[42] It provides for the power of the Comptroller and Auditor General of India to direct the manner of the Company's audit and to conduct also a test audit.[43] It empowers the Central Government to suspend or modify any of the provision or provisions of the Act as necessary.[44] In doing so the Central Government is to place a copy of the draft notification regarding modification of the Company Law before both Houses of Parliament not less than thirty days before its issue for approval of both the Houses.[45] The Parliament thus gets the opportunity of examining the case.

In fact, there is need for a special Act of the government, as in various other countries like Canada, Sweden, etc. prescribing a code of conduct and providing that all the Government, industrial and commercial, corporations have to be incorporated only under that Act. "What is essential is, not that public enterprises should be fitted into an existing act, but that proper legislation must be promoted for governing the public enterprises".[46] Shri Morarka suggested that "There should be a convention that before a company or a public corporation is actually floated, the Minister concerned or the ministry must come before the House of Parliament and justify why they want to entrust a particular activity of Government to that company or corporation. The House must be taken into confidence and must also be called upon to pass or give its consent by means of a resolution saying that the Minister or Ministry is authorized to float that company and entrust that particular activity to that corporation".[47] This is essential because "the moment a company or corporation is floated, a certain activity and a certain amount of finance is taken away from the purview of the House and the purview of the Comptroller and Auditor-General, and the service people employed in that company or corporation are taken away from the purview of the Public Service Commission".[48]

It is important to note that originally while going in for state enterprise, the Government of India intended to adopt the form of public corporation. The first Industrial Policy Resolution of 6 April 1948, laid down that the "management of State enterprise will, as a rule, be through the medium of public corporations under the statutory control of the Central Government". Although this view of the government was not modified in the Second Resolution on Industrial Policy issued on the 30 April 1956, or in any subsequent declaration, the Government has not made much use of the public corporation form. In fact, most of the public enterprises of the Central Government as well as of the State Governments have been set up as government companies under the Indian Companies Act. Many public enterprises styled as 'corporations' are actually companies and not statutory corporations, e.g. the Fertiliser Corporation of India, the Indian Oil Corporation, the State Trading Corporation, etc.

The Estimates Committee recommended[49] that all wholly state-owned public undertakings should generally be in the form of statutory corporations, and the company form should be an exception to be resorted to only

(i) when the government may have to take over an existing enterprise in an emergency;

(ii) where the state wishes to launch an enterprise in association with private capital; or

(iii) where government wishes to start an enterprise with a view eventually to transferring it to private management.

The government, however, did not accept this recommendation (vide reply given in September 1962) on the ground that the "company form was advantageous in that it allowed the flexibility and autonomy necessary for the successful operation of commercial enterprises and also provided for parliamentary control over the companies under the special provisions of the Company Act".[50]

The Articles of Association of most of the government companies in India do not clearly state their objectives and obligations. The result is that the management is not very clear as to their responsibilities which impairs the efficiency of the enterprise. To avoid a state of confusion and to enable the management to work in the right direction, it is very essential that the Articles of Association unambiguously define the objectives and obligations of government companies.

Sectoral Corporations

An important characteristic of the public sector in India is that more than one public undertaking with an independent legal status have been set up in the same field. Most of these are individual undertakings which function directly under the Ministry concerned and depend on the Ministry not only for all matters of policy but also for the solution of all other problems that arise when more than one undertaking operates individually in the same field. There are, of course, some exceptions to this characteristic, like Hindustan Steel and Fertiliser Corporation of India, in the sense that these undertakings have boards that are charged with the responsibility for managing many units and thus function at an intermediate level between management at the unit level and the controlling Ministry. But the government has not entrusted such Boards with any special responsibility for the development of the industry concerned nor has given them any special status or greater autonomy. There are 14 such undertakings of the Central Government but not all of them have been entrusted with the exclusive general responsibility for the development of its particular sector and new projects have been often set up by the Ministries outside their jurisdiction. In the setting up of the Cochin Refineries, for instance, the managerial and technical expertise of the Indian Oil Corporation was not utilised. A new undertaking named as Machine Tools Corporation of India has been set up as a separate government company in spite of the existence of the Hindustan Machine Tools in the same field. There are cases in which the existing multi-unit undertakings have been bifurcated such as the Heavy Electricals Limited, the State Trading Corporation of India and the Heavy Engineering Corporation. The establishment of a number of individual undertakings of varying sizes operating in the same field of industry has resulted into a fragmentation of the industrial effort in the public sector.

The Articles of Association of the multi-unit government companies show that their Boards have more or less the powers as those of many single unit undertakings. Thus, it is not possible for the units to benefit from the elimination of the need to go up to the controlling Ministry on a range of matters that are not matters of high policy and yet not matters of the day-to-day administration that the unit itself has to handle. This puts the Boards of multi-unit undertakings in an awkward position. They do not have the additional administrative and financial powers which can be of use to the managements at the unit level. They are, therefore, considered to have been unnecessarily interposed between the Ministry and the operating units. While General Managers of units consider them a source of delay in approaching the Ministry and obtaining its approval, the Ministries themselves have been known to deal directly with the General Managers thus reminding both the management at the unit level and the Board at the multi-unit level of the limitations and usefulness of such Boards.

It may be argued that the responsibility for planning and promoting industrial effort in the public sector vests in the government and this responsibility cannot be transferred to any other body. There can be no doubt that ultimately the government is responsible for planning and achieving industrial development in the public sector and for taking all policy decisions that determine the size and direction of investment in the public sector. But the development of an industry does not depend only on these decisions. It also depends on the initiative, boldness, expedition and efficiency with which these decisions on high policy and investment are translated into day-to-day managerial decisions necessary for the success of individual projects and the growth and development of the industry as a whole. In the absence of integral corporations entrusted with the responsibility for coordinating the effort in the industry and for providing direction, supervision and auxiliary services that individual units require, the Ministry itself had to assume certain functions of coordination. The management becomes accustomed to looking for and depending on the advice of the Ministry even on matters which actually fall within their own domain. The controlling Ministry develops the expectation that its views would be sought even on matters that do not fall within the area of powers reserved for the government. There develops a feeling that those who shoulder the responsibility for operations at the project level are directly accountable to the controlling Ministry. This leads to a situation in which Project Managers have to spend a good deal of their time and effort in supplying information and seeking clearance for decision. Such a situation results in an impairment of the operational autonomy of the undertaking.

To safeguard against the dangers of fragmentation of effort and erosion of autonomy, the foreign countries have used the device of integral public corporation entrusted with the responsibility for the development and management of the industry. These corporations like the Coal Boards of the United Kingdom and France, Ente Nazionale Idrocarburi (the great petroleum complex) and Instituto per la Ricostruzione Industrials (Institute for Reconstruction of Industry) in Italy, have functioned with great success and there is no reason why such institutions should not work in India.

The setting up of a single integrated corporation in each major sector of industry will have a number of advantages:[51]

(1) It will avoid fragmentation of the industrial effort in the public sector.

(2) It will reduce the extent of government control as many of the functions that are of a coordinative nature will be taken care of by the corporation.

(3) It will make government control more effective by keeping it confined to a few vital and strategic points.

(4) It will help to achieve the economies of large-scale operations and the establishment of otherwise expensive staff organisations and of common service facilities in the fields of research and consultancy, training of personnel and sales promotion.

(5) It will lead to better personnel management, uniformity in the terms and conditions of service of employees, wider prospects for the managerial and technical personnel and the development of managerial resources in the public sector.

The powers of the government vis-a-vis the sector corporations and the functions of the corporations have been envisaged by the Administrative Reforms Commission[52] as below:

Powers Reserved to Government

(i) to appoint the chairman of the corporation and the government representatives on the board of the corporation;

(ii) to appoint, in consultation with the chairman, other members of the board of the corporation;

(iii) to give directions to the corporation as to the exercise and performance of its functions in matters involving national security or substantial public interest and to ensure that the corporation gives effect to such directions;

(iv) to call for such returns, accounts and other information with respect to the property and activities of the corporation as may be required from time to time;

(v) to authorise the amount of capital to be raised and the terms and conditions on which it may be raised;

(vi) to approve the corporation's five-year and annual plans of development and the corporation's capital budget;

(vii) to approve the corporation's revenue budget in case there is an element of deficit which is proposed to be met by obtaining funds from the government; and

(viii) to approve agreements involving foreign collaboration proposed to be entered into by the corporation and to approve purchases and contracts of a major nature involving substantial capital outlay which are in excess of the powers vested in the corporation.

Functions of Sector Corporations

(i) to advise the government on general matters affecting industry in the public sector.

(ii) to promote and develop industry in the public sector including the setting up of new projects in accordance with the Plan;

(iii) to promote, provide or coordinate activities relating to—

  (a) training of personnel;

  (b) research and consultancy;

  (c) sales promotion; and

  (d) such other common services as the constituent units may agree to be provided by the corporation;

(iv) to evolve a common policy for the wages and salaries and other terms and conditions of service of the employees of the corporation;

(v) to approve the revenue budgets of the constituent units;

(vi) to scrutinise the capital budgets of the constituent units and submit a consolidated budget to the government;

(vii) to make appointments to posts below the board level in the sector corporation;

(viii) to appoint the chief executives of the constituent units in consultation with the government;

(ix) to appoint heads of departments in the constituent units in consultation with the chief executive of the unit concerned;

(x) to call for such returns, accounts and other information with respect to properties and activities of each of the constituent units as the corporation may require from time to time;

(xi) to secure the largest degree of decentralisation consistent with the proper discharge by the corporation of their duties and functions; and

(xii) to set up an effective machinery for the speedy disposal of grievances and complaints pertaining to maladministration and abuse of authority by officers subordinate to the corporation.

Powers of Constituent Units

Subject to the above, all the necessary powers required by the constituent units to discharge their duties and functions should be conferred on the management at the unit level.

Structure of Subsidiary Units

The structure of the subsidiary units can take any of the three forms mentioned below:[53]

(1) The Public Corporation can be set up by an Act providing also for the organisation of subordinate units in the form of public corporations.

(2) The Public Corporation can be set up under an Act leaving the form of organisation at lower levels to be determined by the corporation itself.

(3) The Public Corporation can be set up at the national level and this corporation can hold shares, in full or in part, in a number of sub-holding and operating units registered as joint stock companies under private law.

Examples of the first two types of public corporations are found in the United Kingdom and France and also in India in case of food and warehousing corporations. The third type, has been extensively employed in Italy. The first form has generally been adopted for public utilities and transport undertakings which require a relatively greater degree of legal sanction for carrying on its operations even at the lower levels. This form, however, is not suitable for industrial and manufacturing concerns because of the rigidity involved in such a structure. It would be better if the management organisation at lower levels is left to be worked out by the public corporations so that the requirements of each industry and undertaking at each stage can be fully taken into account. The second form would, therefore, be more suitable for industrial and manufacturing enterprises.

The integral corporations, of course, have to guard against certain dangers. They should not lead to diffusion of responsibility or ambiguity in the respective responsibilities of the Ministry, the corporation and the subsidiary units. They should insulate the subsidiary unit from the deleterious effects of interference in day-to-day administration. But they themselves should not become slow-footed leviathans concentrating too much power, authority and initiative. The success of these integral corporations would, therefore, depend on two factors: firstly, the extent of real autonomy and the amplitude of powers to cover the sub-policy area that is transferred to them, and secondly, the wisdom with which they delegate optimum powers and initiative to the subsidiary units while providing for the need to review or resume the use of these powers in the interest of the industry.

Further the setting up of sector corporations should not result in their functioning as large monopolies in the public sector eliminating competition among units producing a similar range of products or providing similar services. The managerial personality of the constituent units should be preserved by giving each of them a financial framework within which it is to operate and against which its performance is to be evaluated. The budget, accounts and performance data of each of the units should be separately compiled. This would infuse in them a spirit of healthy competition and facilitate a comparative appraisal of the success achieved by different units in reducing costs and increasing productivity.

Conclusions

It is not possible to suggest any form of organisation which is best for administering public enterprises in all fields of economic activity, in all countries and under all circumstances. The choice of the form of organisation for any enterprise will depend on a number of factors, e.g. nature of the enterprise, operational and financial requirements, past traditions, impact on the national economy, resources of the government in skill and experience, special production and managerial needs, general economic climate, etc. The selected form should possess adequate operational and financial flexibility, structural elasticity, suitable franchise and also political sanction.

The joint stock company form is more suitable where the nature of the work is substantially commercial. It is suitable for undertakings which are concerned with the manufacture or sale or where the enterprise is financed by more than one government or in association with private enterprise. It is useful where the organisation of an enterprise in public sector is temporary and the enterprise is likely to be ultimately transferred to the private sector. The need for temporarily putting the enterprise in the public sector may arise out of special conditions like inefficient operation in the private sector, bad industrial relations and regional adversities in the employment situation. Sometimes the state may temporarily enter a new field of activity just to pave the way for the private enterprises which may not be forthcoming till the field is exposed and pioneering work done.

The company form of organisation is not suitable for enterprises set up to perform non-commercial functions. Where non-commercial considerations occupy a dominant place, departmental organisation, under a control board, is more appropriate. In case the commercial considerations are dominant but at the same time there are also non-commercial elements, the public corporation would be preferable. In such cases the corporation acts should clearly demarcate the fields of commercial and non-commercial activities.

In case of enterprises involving special decisions relating to conflicting regional interests or competing consumer-group interests, the parliament is the competent body to take decisions. For such enterprises the corporation established under an act of the Parliament is the most appropriate form of organisation. "...the organisational and managerial structures most appropriate for effectuating parliamentary decisions may have to be given regular statutory form that permits automatic parliamentary control and criticism. These are conditions which render the corporation form the most logical one".[54]

The corporation form is also suitable where the whole industry is organised in the public sector and, therefore, involve questions of overall industrial policy, resource allocation in aggregate terms as well as between the units of the industry, pricing, consumer interest and control. It would be better if the corporation acts provide necessary machinery for dealing with these questions. In contrast, if the plant in the public sector is only a small part of the industry, the company form of organisation will be more suitable.

NOTES

1. R.K. Jain, *Management of State Enterprises in India* (Bombay, 1967), p. 44.
2. United Nations, *Some Problems in the Organisation and Administration of Public Enterprise in the Industrial Field* (New York, 1954), p. 6.
3. Earnest Benn, "Britain's Industrial Future: The Report of the Liberal Industrial Enquiry", Extracts Reprinted in A.H. Hanson (ed.), *Nationalisation* (London, 1963), p. 91.
4. Trade Union Congress, *Public Control and Regulation of Industry and Trade* (1932), cf. A.H. Hanson (ed.), *Nationalisation* (London, 1963), p. 94.
5. A.D. Gorwala, *Report on the Efficient Conduct of State Enterprises* (Delhi, 1951), pp. 13-14.
6. United Nations, n. 2, p. 6.
7. Florence, P. Sargent, *The Logic of British and American Industry* (London, 1953), p. 236.
8. M.E. Dimock, "Government Corporations, a Focus of Policy and Administration", *American Political Science Review*, Vol. XLIII, p. 1163.
9. H.K. Pranjape, "Organisation of State Enterprise in India", *Indian Economic Journal* (October 1954), p. 133.
10. *Ibid.*, p. 132.
11. A.H. Hanson, *Public Enterprise and Economic Development* (London, 1959), p. 342.
12. Shiro Okabe, "Public Corporation in Japan", *Indian Journal of Public Administration* (January-March 1950), p. 222.
13. Hanson, n. 11, p. 307.

14. Lord Herbert Morrison, *Socialism and Transport* (London, 1933), p. 149.
15. *House of Commons Debates*, May 6, 1946, 422, cols. 604-605.
16. Earnest Davies, *National Enterprise* (London, 1946), p. 24.
17. W.A. Robson (ed.), *Problems of Nationalised Industry* (London 1952), p. 16.
18. Message to Congress (U.S.A.) on the 10 April 1933 on the T.V.A.
19. *Report of the Commission on Government Commercial Undertakings*, p. 69.
20. Gyanchand in A.N. Aggarwal (ed.), *Public Corporations* (Allahabad, 1945), pp. 4-5.
21. Gorwala, n. 5, p. 33.
22. Chagla Commission Report, *Hindustan Times*, 14 February 1958, p. 11.
23. *Ibid.*
24. United Nations, n. 2, p. 11.
25. Economic Commission for Asia and Far East, *Seminar on Management of Public Industrial Enterprises*, Paper No. 25 (New Delhi, 1959), p. 22.
26. Appendix B, The Companies Act, 1956, Part XIII, Sections 617-29.
27. Economic Commission on Asia and Far East, *Report of the Seminar on Organisation and Administration of Public Enterprises in the Industrial Field* (Rangoon, 1954), p. 19.
28. Hanson, n. 11, p. 353.
29. *Ibid.*, p. 366.
30. Economic Commission for Asia and Far East, n. 25, p. 22.
31. Estimates Committee, *Report on Public Undertakings: Forms and Organisation* (New Delhi, 1960), para 15.
32. United Nations, n. 2, p. 12.
33. Estimates Committee, n. 31, p. 8.
34. Estimates Committee, *Report on Organization and Administration of Nationalized Industrial Undertakings* (New Delhi, 1955), p. 4.
35. *Ibid.*, p. 3.
36. A.K. Chanda, *Indian Administration* (London, 1958), pp. 203-04.
37. Dr. Lankasundaram, *Lok Sabha Debates*, 10 December 1953, col. 1918.
38. Economic Commission on Asia and Far East, *Seminar on Management of Public Industrial Enterprises*, Paper No. 26, p. 6.
39. Estimates Committee, n. 31, para 5.

40. Economic Commission on Asia and Far East, n. 27, p. 13.
41. Statement made by the Auditor General, Shri Narhari Rao, to the Sub-Committee of Public Accounts Committee on 13 December 1952 and quoted by Dr. Lankasundaram, *Lok Sabha Debates*, 10 December 1953, col. 1915.
42. Section 617.
43. Section 619(3).
44. Section 620(1).
45. Section 620(2).
46. V.V. Ramanadham, *The Structure of Public Enterprises in India* (Bombay, 1961), pp. 174-75.
47. *Lok Sabha Debates*, 15 December 1958.
48. *Ibid.*
49. Estimates Committee, n. 31, p. 5.
50. Cf. Administrative Reforms Commission, *Report of the Study Team on Public Sector Undertakings* (New Delhi, 1967), p. 24.
51. *Ibid.*, pp. 63-64.
52. Administrative Reforms Commission, *Report on Public Sector Undertakings* (New Delhi, 1967), pp. 39-41.
53. *Ibid.*, pp. 74-76.
54. Ramanadham, n. 46, p. 190.

3 Financing

The financial structure of an enterprise should be such as is adequate to meet the needs of fixed and working capital without putting unnecessary burden on the undertaking. It should be elastic so that it can be expanded and even contracted according to needs.

The financial structure considerably depends on the form or organisation adopted by the enterprise. If the enterprise is organised departmentally, for instance, all its expenditure will have to be shown under the demand for grants of the controlling ministry and will have to be voted upon by the Parliament. The field of discretion permitted to such enterprises is very much restricted and as a result they lack flexibility in planning and ability to take risks without elaborate procedures. They have to maintain their accounts on receipt and payment basis and are not required to prepare Balance Sheet and Profit and Loss Accounts which would give an idea of their operational efficiency. The accounts do not present a true picture of their operation. In view of these reasons and the need for putting them on commercial lines, the state undertakings have been entrusted to statutory corporations or to limited joint stock companies with varying degrees of financial autonomy and sufficient flexibility. Even though the Boards are appointed by the government with a number of restrictions and limitations and are subjected to government directives in regard to policy matters, the corporation as well as company form of organisation enjoys greater freedom in day-to-day financial administration. The Boards are required, of course, to seek approval of the Government, Central or State, as the case may be, for increasing their authorised capital, issuing unissued shares, raising loans, issuing debentures, incurring capital expenditure over the specified amount, entering into financial contracts or making purchases over and above the prescribed limits.

Sources of Finance

The major sources of finance for a public enterprise are: (a) funds from the government; (b) loans from banks and financial institutions; and (c) ploughed-back profits. The government is often the principal source of capital for a public enterprise. The government funds can be made available to public enterprises in the following major ways or in a combination of these ways: (a) as an outright grant; (b) as share-capital, giving government the right to receive the undistributed profits of the enterprise; (c) as an interest-bearing and repayable loan; (d) as an interest-bearing but non-repayable loan; (e) as a non-interest-bearing but repayable loan.

An out-right grant is not a very sound method of financing public enterprises. It may breed irresponsibility and inefficiency. "The fact that a rate of interest and/or amortisation payments are included among the charges that a public enterprise is required to meet stimulates efficiency more powerfully than the mere announcement that, eventually, it will be expected to yield a surplus of indefinite amount".[1] Further, if the entire profits of the enterprise are at the disposal of the government, it will not have the same urge to make profits as when its expansion and improvement depend, at least partially, upon its own accumulation of reinvestible funds. Loans carrying a rate of interest make the public enterprise recognise that capital is a scarce commodity which has a price and therefore is not to be wasted. Further, interest payments and repayments can provide funds for the government which can be used for development purposes.

In case of loans, the interest rates and terms of payment are suitably worked out. Particular care is taken in this respect in case of enterprises which are not expected to yield any return in the initial stages of their growth. Sometimes the government may grant a moratorium on interest payments and repayments. It may even exempt the enterprise from such obligations for a certain number of years without stipulating any subsequent higher payments. The enterprise may also be allowed to capitalise losses or it may be granted subsidise to cover losses.

Empirical evidence shows that public undertakings should prefer equity capital to loan capital. In case of loan capital, the interest obligation is fixed irrespective of the fact whether or not the undertaking is making any profit. Since the profits made by most of the public enterprises have been very low and many undertakings have been suffering losses, the fixed interest obligations of the loan capital have proved burdensome.

In India most of the manufacturing enterprises in the public sector are organised in the form of companies and as such are financed in the form of shares held by the government. Loans are another important source of finance. Often when funds are required for new construction or expansion, they are first made available in the form of loans and subsequently whole, or part, of them are converted into share capital.

Before the commencement of the Third Plan, broad principles for determining the loan-equity ratio in public enterprises in India had not been laid down. In 1961, the Government of India decided, vide letter of 13 June 1961 of the Ministry of Finance, that "while making provision for the projects in the public sector the working assumption will, unless there are exceptional reasons to the contrary, be that each project will be financed on the basis of approximately half its capital being in the shape of equity and the rest being in the shape of loans". Since then the attempt has been made to finance public undertakings in such a way as to reduce the imbalance that earlier investments had created between equity and loan. The balance between equity and loan, however, has not yet been attained in most of the undertakings. This is particularly true in case of new undertakings in which policy is to make initial investments in the form of equity. At the end of 2008-09, the share of paid-up capital in total financial investment stood at 26.25 per cent, while the share of long-term loans was 73.02 per cent. Total investment (equity plus long-term loans) in all 246 CPSEs stood at ₹ 528951 crore.[2]

It does not appear appropriate to prescribe a uniform loan-equity ratio of 1:1 for all public enterprises irrespective of their size and nature of production. Obviously different ratios would be required by capital intensive enterprises like the Hindustan Steel, Heavy Engineering Corporation, etc. and trading concerns like the State Trading Corporation of India and the Minerals and Metals Trading Corporation. In fact, the loan-equity ratio should not be treated as rigidly and unalterably fixed. There should be scope for flexibility and variations depending upon the generation of internal resources and the increase in the borrowing power of the undertaking.

In the initial years after Independence, loans from banks and financial institutions did not constitute an important portion of the total capital of public enterprises in India. More important was the assistance received from international agencies like the World Bank and foreign companies collaborating with new undertakings.

Working Capital Requirements

The needs of public enterprises for working capital are normally met through cash credit arrangements with the State Bank of India or its subsidiaries, or by temporary utilisation of internal resources. The government does not provide short-term loans to public undertakings unless there are exceptional reasons for that. This procedure, by and large, appears to be quite reasonable. But it needs to be recognised that in some cases the public enterprises might not be able to obtain funds in this manner, particularly in their initial stages. The projects of Bharat Heavy Electricals, for instance, experienced great difficulty in obtaining funds from the State Bank of India or its subsidiaries without a government guarantee. In such cases the government should agree to provide the required guarantee and also consider the request of public undertakings even for working capital requirements in case they are unable to obtain funds from the banks. This will ensure that the commissioning of projects or their operations do not suffer serious setbacks resulting in delayed production or loss of production.

The Central Government is the largest investment banker in the country. It holds equity portions in 240 enterprises in virtually all sectors of the economy. The problem is that the Central Government is not an efficient investment banker. With few exceptions, the dividends it earns on its investment in public enterprises are lower than the interest it pays on its debt. The reasons for this are well known and have to do with the fact that most managers of public enterprises do not have the mandate to function on profit-making basis.[3]

In the financial sector too, the public sector continues to be the major shareholder of India's largest banks, insurance companies, and contractual savings institutions. While barriers against the entry of private banks (domestic and foreign) have been released, public sector banks continue to hold around 90 per cent of the sector's assets and little progress has been achieved in reducing government equity holdings in the public banks or in improving their autonomy in key areas such as staffing and pay. As a result, financial intermediation costs remain excessive and the increased autonomy of financial sector institutions also remains in doubt.

Public Investment

It has been suggested that public may be invited to invest in government undertakings. This suggestion was first put forward by the Estimates Committee in its Sixteenth Report (First Lok Sabha).[4] It was suggested that at least 25 per cent of the total capital investment in public enterprises may be made available for subscription by the public. There should, of course, be a ceiling on individual holding of shares as well as on dividends. It was, however, pointed out by the government that for a variety of reasons the public may not be interested in participating in the capital structure of government enterprises. The hands of the private sector are full with their own undertakings. Normally the dividends declared by the public enterprises are too low to attract private funds. The Estimates Committee repeated the suggestion in its Nineteenth Report

(Second Lok Sabha). "The Committee would again like to point out that the implementation of this recommendation would evoke the enthusiasm of the public for participation in the national development and would also enable the undertakings to function effectively under the vigil of a body of shareholders, who would, in their own interests, keep a watchful eye on the working of the undertaking".[5]

As a result of this pressure, the government set up in early 1960 a Committee of officials (with the Secretary to the Department of Company Law Administration as Chairman) to go into this matter. The Committee was asked to recommend the proportion of a state undertaking's capital that may be subscribed by private individuals, devise safeguards against the concentration of such shares in a few hands, examine the voting rights of such shareholders as well as their right to be represented on the Board of Directors, and report on the desirability of the workers of an undertaking being given preferential rights to buy such shares.

The Committee submitted its report to the Planning Commission in October 1960 and made it clear that it was the general public and not the investing public, which it had in mind as the permissible candidate for participation in the capital of public enterprises. This was not because the Committee had any prejudice against the investing public as such but because it was anxious to see the participation of ordinary public in the capital structure of the state enterprises. The public participation would be meaningless if it resulted in a mere diversion of the present investment capital from private enterprises to state enterprises. It pointed to "dormant sources of surplus funds" existing in the organised as well as unorganised sectors of the economy and suggested that these should be tapped with the help of a "new class of operators in the capital market".

To enable participation of small investors, it has been suggested that the shares should be in denomination of not more than ₹ 100 each. There should be legal safeguards to prevent post-allotment transfer of shares to undesirable persons. Lastly, it has been suggested that the experiment may be initiated only in those enterprises which have started yielding profits because no small investor would like to invest his savings in an enterprise which is yet in an uncertain state.

While the Central Government has the majority equity holding in CPSEs (more than 80 per cent), investment in terms of both equity and long-term loans has been forthcoming from other parties as well such as the financial institutions, banks, private parties (both domestic and foreign), state governments and holding companies.

Borrowing Powers

Before the Second World War, a large number of state enterprises like railways, electricity projects and irrigation works were financed by the government through the floatation of public loans subscribed by domestic as well as foreign investors. To service these loans, sometimes the enterprises were allowed to maintain their assets, working capital and finance independently of the government. To attract private investors to such loans or to obtain funds through debentures, sometimes special terms were offered to investors in the form of guarantees or preferences on profits or revenues. Sometimes the enterprises were given independent borrowing powers. In the post-war years, however, the trend has been towards unified and centrally controlled financial policies and this has led to curtailment of the borrowing powers of the public enterprises. This applies in the case of India as well. If the public enterprises require additional funds for working or emergency purposes, they have either to obtain loans or grants from the treasury or to go to commercial banks, central banks or specialised financial institutions, for which permission of the government is required.

The borrowing powers of the state-owned private limited companies are seriously curtailed through the restrictive limits under the Articles of Association of the Company. Generally, for borrowing over and above a certain limit, sanction of the government has to be obtained.

The public corporations are not permitted to borrow from public through issue of debentures. Similarly, the companies are also not allowed to borrow from public. The argument in support of concentrating borrowing in the hands of the government is that in the absence of this government would lose centralised control over the financial markets and movement of capital. This would affect the channeling of funds in accordance with the development plans of the country.

In principle, when public enterprises are established outside the government as private limited companies, there is not much point in putting restrictions at every point. Such restrictions only mean that either the whole principle of autonomous body is wrong or the government has no faith in the Board of Directors appointed by itself. So far as the need for regulation is concerned, the objective can be achieved through a system based on the lines of Control of Capital Issue. Thus, the government can achieve the object of controlling the inner finance and regulating the capital market without impairing the flexibility and independence of the so-called autonomous bodies and, by adopting a liberal and systematic attitude, help the enterprises in coming over emergencies and meeting the need for expansion without putting an unnecessary burden on its own resources. There is not much point in making the undertaking completely dependent on government particularly when its own resources are scarce and when because of the financial procedure serious delays are involved in sanctioning funds.

Further, if the undertakings are allowed to borrow in the open market, their borrowing would indicate, in general, their creditworthiness, solvency and their overall productive efficiency. They will spur the management to be honest, competent and efficient so as to command the highest goodwill and credit in the financial circles. It would relieve the treasury of extra financial burden of providing working capital. The additional financial obligations and recurrent interest charges involved in the loans would compel the enterprise to work in an efficient and economical manner so as to earn a surplus.

The restrictions on borrowing powers hamper most the working of departmental organisations. The government is generally unable to give them adequate funds and they cannot go to the market for funds. The result is that they cannot expand their services and the public has to suffer for that. If certain undertakings are in a position to borrow from the open market at reasonable rates on their own credit, the purpose is productive and they are able to bear the burden, there is no reason for preventing them from going to the open market. In this category may be placed undertakings like the Railways, Posts and Telegraphs Department, etc. They have been unable to expand their services for want of change in methods of financing and the public have suffered from a denial of the use of services and facilities.

What should be the borrowing powers of the public enterprises? Should these be unlimited? This is a very delicate question. Borrowing by a public enterprise may affect the money market and credit control policies of the government. The public enterprises, therefore, cannot be permitted to exercise financial powers which are incompatible with the state monetary policy. Their borrowing powers should be suitably regulated and co-ordinated with the overall monetary policy of the country.

National Finance Corporation

If every public enterprise is permitted to borrow independently in the financial market, there is the risk that their financial programme may be subordinated to the market mechanism and behaviour of the investors. It has, therefore, been suggested that the finance for public enterprises should be raised in a planned and co-ordinated manner. This is possible if a single agency is set up to raise funds for all public enterprises. Such an agency can also negotiate foreign assistance for these enterprises at terms much more favourable than those at which different enterprises can obtain by acting in their independent capacity. The agency, which may be named as National Finance Corporation, would provide a liaison between the investors and the public corporations in constant association with the Treasury but not subservient to it. The National Finance Corporation may be authorised to accept deposits of different kinds from the public and investment institutions at reasonable rates of interest, to raise funds by issuing bonds and debentures bearing guarantee by the Treasury and to seek external assistance subject to the approval of the Central Government. Government guarantee of the securities of the Corporation is essential to enhance their marketability. The Reserve Bank should provide finance to the Corporation in a liberal manner to enable it to discharge its functions well.

Though the Corporation should possess an independent status, it should function in close co-operation with the government within its overall economic and financial policy. The initial capital to start the Corporation will have to be provided by the government. It will pay its way by its earning of interest on loans advanced to the public enterprises. Any deficiency during the initial stages should, of course, be met by the Treasury. The government assistance, however, should not compromise the autonomy of the Corporation. "It is essential that Government guarantees do not serve as a cloak for Treasury control of public corporation finance".[6]

A suitable procedure has to be evolved for the advancement of loans from the National Finance Corporation to the public undertakings. It would be better if every public undertaking prepares a budget at the beginning of the accounting year and submits to the Corporation for scrutiny so far as the requisite finance is concerned. Advance information about the funds required by different public undertakings during a year would enable the Corporation to decide its borrowing programme. The conflict is likely to arise if certain claims for funds of some undertakings are not met by the Corporation and it is very likely that the Corporation with its limited resources will have to reject some claims to maintain the priorities of the projects. The possibilities of the conflict can be minimised by the Corporation's having an Advisory Body, manned by experts, to scrutinize and advise on the financial assistance sought by different public undertakings.

Interest Rate

Another complicated problem relates to the interest rate to be charged from public enterprises. If the government advances funds to the public enterprises at a rate lower than the market rate of interest, there will be an element of subsidy. This not only impairs efficiency of public enterprises but also leads to accusation of discrimination against the private enterprise. The government should, therefore, by and large advance funds to public enterprises at the market rate of interest. If subsidization is considered necessary and justified in case of some public enterprises, it should better take the form of direct subsidies rather than being concealed in lower interest rates. The rates of interest to be charged by the National Finance Corporation should not be more than 1 to 1½ per cent higher than its own borrowing rates with a small rebate on payment by the due date.

It would certainly be desirable to have stable interest rates because this enables an enterprise to execute its investment programme without any fear of fluctuations in the money market. But "it would be perverse to hold interest-rates stable in the face of a major change in the attraction of capital development; that would be to invite a cumulatively excessive pressure or deficiency of demand and a wasteful allocation of the community's resources".[7] The policy, therefore, should be to remove only short-term violent fluctuations in the interest rates but the rates should be suitably adjusted in response to changes of a lasting nature in the demand for and supply of investible funds.

Expansion with Internal Savings

Expansion of business with the help of internal savings is a sign of strong financial base and proof of wise and efficient management. Savings presuppose (1) existence of profits and (2) retaining a part of them to meet future needs. As regards the first, in considering the surpluses generated by the public enterprises in India, it should be kept in view that a considerable portion of the public sector investment is still tied up in undertakings under construction or relates to promotional and development undertakings where accumulation of surpluses is only of secondary importance. At the end of second year of Eleventh Five Year Plan (31.3.2009), the total investment in 246 public enterprises stood at ₹ 528951 crore, out of which the investment in public undertakings under construction stood at ₹3,558.31 crore.[8]

In assessing the adequacy or otherwise of the profits yielded by the public enterprises, it is also essential to keep in mind the areas where large investments have been made. The industrywise investment pattern of investment in the Central Government undertakings, at the end of 2008-09, was as follows:[9]

Sector	(₹. in crores) Investment in terms of Gross Block	
	31.3.2009	31.3.2008
Agriculture	108.37	100.67
Mining	245,866.64	218,136.71
Manufacturing	262,647.06	230,230.94
Electricity	240,372.92	208,890.01
Services	225,249.66	202,770.55

A major portion of the capital invested in Central Government undertakings during the initial Plan periods was in the field of heavy industry having long gestation periods. Some of these industries have been set up in the country for the first time. Neither the trained manpower, nor the technical know-how required for these industries was available when the pioneering projects were launched.

There are some other factors also which need be kept in mind while comparing the profitability of public enterprises with that of private enterprises. The prices of commodities like steel, oil, coal and fertilisers, which substantially account for the total turnover of the industrial enterprises of the Central Government, are regulated or fixed by the government. Since most of these goods are considered to be essential commodities, the government is anxious to safeguard the interests of the consumers. As such the prices fixed are often on the low side and do not make sufficient allowance for the increased capital costs of setting up new plants in these sectors.

Despite the policy graded privatisation and disinvestment, the role of public enterprises and their contribution to the GDP has not diminished. During the Tenth Plan period, the number of profit-making enterprises has gone up from 120 to 157 and number of loss-making enterprises has decreased from 109 to 58.[10] The profits of profit-making enterprises increased from

₹ 36432 crore to ₹ 76240 crore and the losse of loss-making ones has come down from ₹ 10454 crore to ₹ 5752 crore during the same period.[11] The net profits made by the enterprises led to the accumulation of large reserves of ₹ 353641.62 crore at the end of the financial year 2006-07.[12] Thus, enterprises have accumulated large amounts of investible funds.

It cannot, however, be denied that still there is considerable scope for increasing the profitability of many public enterprises by reducing both the capital costs of projects and the running costs of operations. The portion of savings which the public enterprises can retain to meet their future requirements depends on the policy of the government directly or indirectly. It is painful to note that in this regard the policy of the government has not been sympathetic and helpful. The departmentally organised undertakings have particularly suffered for two reasons. In the first place, the government looks upon them as sources of revenue and tries to appropriate the maximum part of the profit, leaving little to be saved. Secondly, even when savings are there, since the funds form an integral part of the treasury finance and are merged in the general budget, their availability entirely depends on the budgetary position of the government.

If a part of the revenue earned by the enterprise is transferred to a reserve earmarked for development, with freedom for management to use it in the manner they think best, that would have healthy effect on the management. It would provide an incentive for the management to attain maximum financial success. The management would also gain in power and prestige when the enterprise grows. This would provide a still greater incentive for efficiency in production and economy in management.

NOTES

1. A.H. Hanson, *Public Enterprise and Economic Development* (London, 1959), p. 430.
2. *Public Enterprises Survey 2008-09*, Performance Overview, p. 2.
3. Zoubida Allaoua, *India: Five Years of Stabilization and Reform and the Challevges Ahead*, The World Bank, 1996, p. 60.
4. Estimates Committee, *Organisation and Administration of Nationalised Industrial Undertakings* (New Delhi, 1955), p. 36.

5. Estimates Committee, *Action Taken on the 16th Report (1st Lok Sabha) on the Organisation and Administration of Nationalised Industrial Undertakings* (New Delhi, 1958), p. 14.
6. Lincoln Gordon, *The Public Corporation in Great Britain* (London, 1938), p. 340.
7. *Report of the Committee on Working of the Monetary System*, H.M.S.O., August, para 495.
8. *Public Enterprises Survey 2008-09*, Vol. I, Chap. 2, pp. 21-24.
9. *Ibid.*, p. 24.
10. *Eleventh Five Year Plan, Vol. III: Agriculture, Rural Development, Industry, Services and Physical Infrastructure*, Planning Commission, Govt. of India, p. 153.
11. *Ibid.*
12. *Ibid.*

Price Policy

4

Distinctive Features of Pricing in the Public Enterprises

In a freely competitive market, the price of a commodity represents its utility to the buyers and average cost of production, including normal profits, to the producer. So far as the buyer is concerned, this principle holds true even in case of goods produced by public enterprises, particularly in countries where democratic freedom governs economic and social policy. The consumer is free not to accept the goods if he does not consider them worth the price. It is, of course, true that the consumer does not have much choice if the goods produced by the public enterprise are not produced by anybody else. But even in such cases, the demand for necessary goods may be inelastic only for small quantities; beyond a certain minimum, the demand may be highly elastic.

It is in the field of supply, however, that the position differs remarkably in public undertakings. In the long run, the private enterprises must obtain a price which covers total costs and provides an adequate return necessary to attract venture capital. In contrast, extra-commercial considerations may influence the determination of prices in public enterprises. Sometimes the public undertakings may conduct their operations, not with a view to recovering their costs, but to promote general welfare. In some cases, the public enterprises are obliged to incur losses in the public interest under explicit directives issued by the controlling government from time to time.[1] Indian Airlines suffered a loss of ₹ 7 lakhs in 1960-61 in stopping their service between Delhi and Bombay to provide a daily air connection to Bhopal, Gwalior and Indore en route under a directive issued by the Government of India. The State Bank of India was required by the Act of Parliament under which it was constituted to set up 400 new branches in areas not well served by banking facilities. The bank carried out this obligation within the period of five years permitted to it. At one stage 337 of these branches were operating at a loss, as was expected, because most of them were working in towns with populations less than 25,000. With a view to popularise the idea of insurance among low-income groups who had hardly any interest in this form of saving, the Life Insurance Corporation of India introduced at considerable risk its Janta Policy in 1958 which did not require medical examination and other formalities.

Where a public enterprise operates under competitive conditions, few special problems of pricing arise. The major problem in such situations is that of maintaining fair competition between public and private units. Most of the problems arise where public enterprises enjoy a monopoly. In fact, this is the position in most of the cases. The degree of monopoly, of course, varies in different cases. The monopolistic element has two implications. First, on the supply side, in the absence of competing units, it is difficult, if not impossible, to make cost comparisons. Secondly, on the demand side, there is scope for discrimination and exploitation.

The monopolistic element in Indian public enterprises varies in different industries. In a monopoly market, a public sector enterprise can fix the price that maximizes the mark-up as well as the gross profits. That may not happen, however, if the government intervenes to moderate the price and reduce the mark-up in the interest of consumers and user industries/sectors. In general, the governments fix/administer the price of goods (and services) produced by public sector entities based on the following principles:

a. true costs of goods and services plus a reasonable return on investment,
b. cross-subsidization between one group and another or between one sector and another,

c. differential price norm for peak and off-peak demand,
d. below cost to stimulate demand under conditions of excess/unutilized capacity,
e. lower price for providing an incentive to encourage consumption (e.g. fertilizer consumption) and higher price as a disincentive to discourage consumption (e.g. petroleum products) and
f. different prices/multi-tariffs to include discounts for purchases on larger volumes.

In the wake of post-1991 economic liberalization, industries in the 'core sector' are no more the exclusive preserve of the public sector. Consequently, a good many public enterprises have ceased to be monopolies and they face intense competition in the market. The government has gradually dismantled Administered Price Mechanism (APM) in most sectors/products and the public enterprises have been given the independence to fix the (competitive) prices on their own. The government, however, continues to be sensitive to the needs of the poor and the impact of rise in output prices (in the core sector) on the Wholesale Price Index (WPI). Any rise in price levels of these products that is not acceptable to the government is moderated through a combination of measures such as lowering of customs duties, excise and sales tax, administrative control on prices, grant of subsidies, etc.

Cost Conditions

The special features of the cost conditions of a public enterprise may be studied under three heads,[2] viz. (1) the cost behaviour, (2) the level of factor prices and (3) the anatomy of cost composition.

Cost Behaviour

The managers of the public enterprises have a tendency to extend production to the full capacity. The existence of underutilised capacity, therefore, may lead to such modification in price structure as expands consumption of the product. It is, of course, difficult to generalise on the question whether the investment planning of a public enterprise has a tendency to create heavy initial indivisibilities as against graduated additions to capital expendture. "Empirical evidence in some cases suggests that, on balance, there is bias for the setting up of large capacities at the very beginning".[3] One of the reasons for this is the economy in the subsequent stages of output expansion. The result is a tendency for the output to expand rapidly. The expansion in output is accompanied by a decline in the cost of production till the available capacity is fully utilised.

Factor Prices

There appears to be no reason why a public enterprise should be at a disadvantage in the purchase of its factors. In fact it may be in a more favourable position than the private enterprises. It will have the benefit of bulk purchases. It can avail of the expert services of the office of the Director General of Supplies and Disposals in making purchases, particularly from abroad. The most important economy in the purchase of factors lies in the availability of cheap capital either through government subscription or under government guarantee. A public enterprise may also obtain some of its inputs from other public enterprises or government departments at subsidised prices. The Mysore Iron and Steel Works, for instance, obtains firewood and charcoal from the Forest Department at considerably subsidised rates.[4]

Anatomy of Cost Composition

The special influences operating on the cost composition of a public enterprise may be examined under three major heads, viz. (1) social costs, (2) propriety costs, and (3) costs of public organisation.

1. Social Costs. The public enterprises incur social costs in at least four ways, viz. (i) by paying comparatively higher wages, (ii) by carrying more labour than required, (iii) by providing larger consumer amenities, and (iv) by bearing certain costs which in case of private enterprises are shifted to public enterprises.

(i) The public enterprises are expected to be model employers offering high wage rewards and other amenities. Political considerations may vitiate relating increases in wages to increases in productivity.

(ii) The government generally does not allow public enterprises to lay-off surplus workers. Also, strong employee unions in several public enterprises act as a barrier to mass lay-off of surplus labourers.

(iii) Sometimes, public enterprises tend to be magnanimous and provide undue consumer amenities, often, due to political pressures.

(iv) Another way in which public enterprises bear social costs is by providing some of its outputs to consumers and regions that do not pay the costs involved in full. Wherever subsidised outputs are offered on social grounds, the operations involve costs which are normally not borne by the private enterprises.

2. Propriety Costs. The public enterprises have to incur expenditures in facing external vigilance over their activities. These are unavoidable in a democratic society and may take the form of investigations by parliamentary committees, criticisms by the members of Parliament, audit by the Comptroller and Auditor General and public criticism in the press. "The public enterprises are impelled to conduct their operations, especially the expenditure operations, in such a way that all the relevant rules are satisfied and there is nothing 'irregular' about any transaction. The lowest tender system, the need to advertise the requirements of purchases, adherence to necessary hierarchical formalities in securing sanctions, and strict compliance with the original budget estimates are aspects of propriety on which the managers of public enterprises soon learn to place priority as against methods which may prove substantially better but, in the formal sense, irregular".[5] The complicated procedures evolved for the purpose of propriety lead to delays in the taking of decisions. This has two serious defects. In the first place, it may result into loss of some possible economies. Secondly, it in the long run discourages the managers from showing positive interest in prompt action. Speaking on "Public Administration and the Public Corporation" at the Indian Institute of Public

Administration, New Delhi, on 25 August 1961, Professor J.K. Galbraith even stressed "the importance of timeliness as compared with precision in industrial decisions". An interesting example of the loss from delayed decision-taking is provided by the statement of the Joint Secretary, Ministry of Steel, Mines and Fuel to the Estimates Committee on the Neyveli Lignite Corporation Ltd. "There were certain initial offers from the makers of the specialised equipment in Germany and certain dates were stipulated by them for acceptance of offers. Unfortunately it took some time for the Corporation to consider the tenders of the offer. By the time both the Corporation and the government could reach a decision, the equipment which the manufacturers had earmarked for supply to the Corporation had been sold to certain other parties. As a result of this slight upset in the time schedule and in order that the mining programme did not suffer, it became necessary for the Corporation to acquire some more conventional equipment. This accounted for increase of something like ₹ 60 lakhs over the original estimate."[6]

3. Cost of Public Organisation. The public enterprises are characterised by a tendency towards over-centralisation in administration which raises costs of organisation.

Theories of Pricing

A number of theories of pricing in public enterprises have been put forward. Most important of these are: (1) Marginal Cost of Production Theory, (2) No Profit, No Loss Theory, (3) Average Cost of Production Theory and (4) Theory of Making Profits. We briefly examine these theories below one by one.

Marginal Cost of Production Theory

The marginal cost pricing in public utilities in a mixed economy was first suggested by Prof. Hotelling in his article "The General Welfare in Relation to Problems of Taxation and of Railway and Utility Rates".[7] The marginal cost pricing in a socialist economy was advocated earlier, primarily by A.P. Lerner.[8] These contributions led to a heated discussion of the problem which continued for about a decade.

The theory holds that the prices should be fixed on the basis of the marginal cost of production which would ensure an optimum output and maximum utilisation of all factors of production.[9] The theory, however, suffers from a number of drawbacks.

In case of industries which are subject to the law of decreasing costs, and consequently where average costs are greater than marginal costs, the total sale proceeds from charging a price equal to marginal cost would be less than the total costs. The loss arising from fixing the price on the basis of marginal cost can be made good in a number of ways. One way would be to levy a tax on the product of the public enterprise equal to the difference between the average cost of production and the price. Such a tax would make the total price inclusive of tax equal to average cost and thus defeat the very purpose of marginal cost pricing.

An alternative will be that the tax, instead of being levied on the product of the concerned public enterprise, is levied *ad valorem* on the output in general. The loss can also be covered by other types of taxes, say income tax, capital tax, or death duty. No doubt, it will achieve the objective of the marginal cost pricing, that is, rectification of misdistribution of resources as between different industries resulting from inequality in the ratio of marginal cost to price in different industries, but it will have repercussions on income distribution, incentive to invest, propensity to consume, etc. whose net effect will have to be evaluated to reach a correct estimate of the net benefit or loss as a result of the marginal cost pricing. It is, however, not possible to quantify such effects and, therefore, it is very difficult to say anything definite about the merit or otherwise of the marginal cost pricing.

So long as there exists private sector in which imperfect competition is the rule rather than the exception, marginal cost pricing in the public sector will not lead to 'ideal' output. For attaining ideal output, the prices in the public enterprises would have to bear the same relation to marginal costs as exists on the average in the economy as a whole. But in a highly dynamic and complex industrial system, it is impossible to determine this ratio in actual practice.

In some cases where there are multiple products or services, the determination of detailed costs of each item may be a very costly and complicated affair. There may as a result be large economies of administration if services involving unequal costs are charged at a uniform rate. This is the reason why the post office charges the same price for carrying letters from one street to another or from one corner of the country to another.[10]

The marginal cost cannot be accurately assessed because the factors are indivisible and the various charges on new factor intakes are not the charges on factor-use needed for additional increments of output. Marginal costs would be high at points where capacity gets exhausted and for additional production new capacities have to be created. In such cases the costs incurred at such points are abnormally high and thus the marginal cost cannot be a basis for price fixation.

If the price is to equal marginal cost, fluctuations in demand and supply would lead to frequent fluctuations in prices which is not very desirable.[11] "Irregular and unforeseeable fluctuations are, however, a nuisance.... This is one of the reasons why uniform prices have been enforced by the law on railways and taxicabs, and by customs on department stores, hotels, professional men, and in many other fields".[12]

The fixation of prices at a level insufficient to cover costs may lead to inefficiency in management. It will also increase the need for widening the supervisory powers of the controlling authorities which would result in curtailing the freedom of management and thereby reducing flexibility of the policies of individual undertakings.[13]

The adoption of marginal cost pricing will make difficult the determination of the investment policy of the government. How far should each state enterprise be expanded and, because the demand for the product will increase if consumers can purchase state products at low prices, from where are the resources for expansion of enterprises to be obtained? If the limited factors are used too much to expand output in accordance with marginal cost pricing, there will be mal-allocation of resources because the factors which are retained in such enterprises would have earned more in alternative enterprises.

In several fields the marginal cost may be negligible or even zero. There would be hardly any marginal cost of an additional traveller on a road or a bridge. The unused capacity would be vast in case of museums, parks and broadcasting services and, therefore, there will not be any significant marginal cost if more persons avail of these services. The absence of marginal cost, however, should not mean that those who use the product or service should not pay.

The drawbacks of the marginal cost pricing mentioned above show that this principle is not very suitable for pricing the products or services of the public enterprises.

No Profit, No Loss Theory

The principle of 'no profit, no loss' was evolved by the Fabians in connection with the municipal trading and even now it has its supporters. It is argued that the government should not make profits and follow a policy of no profit, no loss. "The sort of price policy that a public corporation ought to follow can be stated simply in two rules: (1) it should make neither a loss nor a profit after meeting all capital charges; and (2) the prices it charges for different services should correspond to relative costs".[14] The traditional view is that the public enterprises are meant to serve the people and not to make profit. The public enterprises should distinguish themselves from private enterprises by promoting the public purpose rather than making profits. It is further held that the earning of profits is inconsistent with public purposes. Prof. Lewis states, "If the corporation makes a profit or loss it should be required so to adjust its prices as to eliminate the profit or loss".[15] He supports the principle on the grounds that it prevents over- or under-expansion of the industries concerned and avoids the inflationary or deflationary tendencies.[16] He is of the opinion that if in some circumstances, it is considered desirable to supply a product or service at a price below or above the average cost of production, it is better to use the method of subsidies and taxes than to cover loss in some parts of the undertaking by profits in its other parts.[17] "...the decision whether a profit or a loss is to be made is a decision not for the management of the public corporation, but ultimately for parliament.... These are public issues for ministers to decide. The instructions to the corporation should be to make neither a profit nor a loss, except to the extent specifically notified to it by a minister...where a loss is specifically ordered on the part of the service, it is usually better that a subsidy should be shown separately than the undertaking should merely be ordered to make it up by making surplus profits in other parts of the undertaking".[18]

Prof. Lewis goes even further and maintains that not only an undertaking should break even on its overall operations but also each part of the services should pay its own way, showing neither a profit nor a loss. "It would be a pity if naive demands for uniformity forced public corporations to adopt tariff which bore no relation to costs, for then, not only would it lead to wasteful choices by consumers, but it would also make the task of checking up on the efficiency of the corporations very difficult, since the profits and losses of different services would bear no relation to economic considerations.... Uniformity of charges where there is no uniformity of cost is the refuse of the lazy mind".[19] The INRICE Theory Committee in its Report on 'Price Setting in Public Undertakings' remarked, "As a general rule public undertakings—while complying with the rule of economic viability, which applies to them also—should refrain from seeking maximum profit and operate directly with a view to promoting the general interest".[20]

Many advocates of public enterprise have, in fact, argued that a great advantage of the public ownership would be the freeing of the industries from the tyranny of the profit and loss account.[21] The profit motive would be replaced by a spirit of public welfare. Some such Utopian sentiments are found in the Nationalization Bills. The National Coal Board, for instance, is required to make supplies of coal available "of such qualities and sizes, in such quantities and at such prices, as may seem to them best calculated to further the public interest in all respects". Similarly, the Gas Boards are required to "develop and maintain an efficient, co-ordinated and economical system of gas supply for their area and to satisfy, so far it is economical to do so, all reasonable demands for gas within their area". The duties of the Transport Commission in the 1947 Act are described in greater detail: "To provide, or secure or promote the provision of an efficient, adequate, economical and properly integrated system of public inland transport and port facilities within Great Britain for passengers and goods with due regard for safety of operation".

In the past, when state participation in economic activities was considered a necessary evil, the state undertook the provision of only such services as were considered absolutely essential for the public and were not attractive to the private enterprise. In case of such essential services, the principle of "no profit, no loss" was not very unsatisfactory. But now the entire concept of state participation in economic life has changed. It has been widely recognised that the state has to play an important role in accelerating the rate of development in the developing countries. This has necessitated a radical change in the desirable pricing policy of the public enterprise. The government is increasingly entering the highly profitable industries and trade to mop up profits for financing country's development, which were previously enriching a few capitalists. If the government operates on "no profit, no loss" principle in such industries, the possible investible surplus will be frittered away in consumption and the rate of capital formation would be slowed down because even the private capitalists invest a major portion of their profits.

The principle cannot work where public enterprises work in collaboration with local or foreign private capitalists because they cannot agree to invest their funds or to permit the use of their patent rights without adequate reward for the same.

Profits have played an important role in financing industrial development in private sector in advanced countries. Prof. Robson has calculated that public companies whose stocks of shares are quoted on the London Stock Exchange financed 75 per cent of their investment by retained profits and other internal sources during the quinquennium 1949-53. The comparative figure for the U.S.A. during the same period was 64 per cent.[22] To quote Shyam Nandan Sinha, "Besides financing private investment, profits of the private sector make a contribution towards financing government investment and expenditure. Profits are subject to corporation tax and income tax and the goods produced also are subject to indirect taxes. Thus private sector industries promote both private and public investment by raising the overall level of saving in the economy. If public undertakings are run on 'no profit, no loss basis' it will not only make no contribution towards the financing of public investment and expenditure but it will also throw the burden of its own development on the public exchequer".[23] The Taxation Enquiry Commission observes, "In considering pricing policies of State undertakings in a comparatively underdeveloped country like ours, regard must be had to the need for relating them to the economic and institutional context in which they operate rather than to the standards that are more appropriate to the conditions obtaining in the advanced economies such as those of some of the western countries".[24]

If a public enterprise does not earn profits, its expansion will have to be financed either by inflation, or by borrowing or by taxation. Prof. Lewis remarks, "It is a folly to keep prices down in the nationalised industries, thereby raise private sector profits and then to have to borrow these profits to finance investments in the nationalised industries".[25] Increase in taxation may be difficult and inflation dangerous.

It is now widely believed that public enterprises must make profits and "no profit, no loss" principle is inconsistent with a socialist economy. The supporters of "no profit" principle often confuse between profit motive and profit earning. The Taxation Enquiry Commission observes, "Public purpose rather than the profit should be the guiding factor in the operation of the public undertakings but the antithesis is more apparent than real. In the public sector, profit is not necessarily inconsistent with public purpose; on the other hand, it may itself constitute public purpose even if it remains secondary".[26] In fact, what is necessary is to emphasize that the public purpose and not the profit motive should be the guiding principle in framing the pricing policy for public enterprises. "In an underdeveloped economy, if the profit is utilised for capital formation and development of economic and social overheads which pave the way for the rapid development of the economy, leading to a rise in the national and per capita income and standard of living, no body can say that profit does not fulfill the highest social purpose."[27] The desirability of making a profit by the public enterprises has been further discussed while examining the fourth theory, viz. Theory of Making Profits. Now we turn to the second part of this theory, that is, 'No loss' principle.

A public enterprise operating on loss may well be contributing to the welfare of the community through cheap gas, cheap electricity, cheap transport or cheap postage far in excess of its loss. In some cases, it may not be uneconomic to operate an enterprise on planned losses. Philip E. Taylor brilliantly points out that "The interests of Government are inevitably broader than those of private enterprise. The consequence to cost calculation or broader public interest is that almost every government-produced good is more than one good—it is a good providing individual utility to the buyer, while at the same time providing utility to the community in terms of more general welfare. The second is normally regarded as a by-product of the first, and although there can be no exact science of allocating joint costs among multiple products it is logical that the by-product should bear some share. It is upon this type of analysis that operation of some public industries at less than cost (the balance to be made up from the general fund) can be justified".[28]

The principle that public enterprises should not be run at a loss is based on a number of considerations. In the first place, a policy of losses would contribute towards inflation. A public enterprise puts money into circulation by paying for services, materials, etc. and takes money out of circulation by charging for its products and services. Thus any loss by a public enterprise would be inflationary unless it is deliberately offset in some other manner. Secondly, if a public corporation has to consistently operate at a loss, additional taxation would be necessary to recover this loss, the adverse effects of which may far outweigh the benefits likely to flow from operating at a loss. Thirdly, if costs are not covered and the product is sold at a loss, there might be an over-expansion of the industry concerned. This would particularly be the case if the demand for the product concerned is fairly elastic. Fourthly, there is no justification to subsidise consumers as a class.

The above analysis shows that even this theory is not satisfactory for pricing the products or services of the public enterprises.

Average Cost of Production Theory

The average cost principle is considered to be fair and just because of the following reasons:[29]

1. The public undertakings are expected primarily to meet needs, that is, to provide an optimum volume of supplies cheaply without seeking any profit.
2. Every purchaser pays the entire cost of the unit or units consumed by him instead of paying only the additional cost of producing these units.
3. Since nobody is required to pay more for the goods he purchases than the amount it actually costs to produce those goods, there is no exploitation.
4. The average cost price is a reliable criterion for investment in many cases.
5. The average cost principle ensures that the entire expenditure of the undertaking is covered and thereby secures the viability and the autonomy of the undertaking.

The theory, however, suffers from a number of drawbacks. From the macro-economic point of view, the determination of average costs is not as easy as it appears from the purely accounting point of view. "...the recommendation...that prices should be fixed in terms of average unit costs is in practice inapplicable. To take one example, in transport sector...no satisfactory method of allocating costs according to their origin has yet been found. The problem is at present insoluble on account of practical considerations; moreover, the task of correctly allocating cost elements is fraught with theoretical difficulties of principle, which cannot be overcome by any degree of improvement of the accounting systems of individual economic units and the economy as a whole".[30]

The problem of appropriate distribution of depreciation allowances over different periods has been a matter of considerable controversy. Similarly, there has been considerable discussion over whether depreciation should be calculated at original or present-day replacement costs, and even on whether depreciation allowances should be calculated not only to replace existing equipment but to cover investment in technically improved equipment.

The problem of social costs has also given rise to much controversy. The term 'social costs' covers all the disadvantages and all the production losses—both tangible and intangible—which do not appear in the cost accounts of the public undertakings, e.g. cost of industrial concentration, of damage to health caused by smoke, fumes and noise, of the degradation of land, or river pollution, of the social disadvantages resulting from the growth of big towns. It is widely recognised that social costs should be taken into account in determining the prices in public enterprises. But it is very difficult to accurately measure social costs.

In the controversy over social costs, sufficient attention has not so far been paid to their opposite, that is, social benefits. If such benefits are taken into consideration, the operation of some undertakings may be in the public interest even if the prices charged for their products do not cover their entire costs.

The average cost pricing may result in hiding excess capacity or undue restriction of investment where potentialities exist. It is not sufficiently flexible to accommodate price adjustments. It does not provide incentives for the managers of the public enterprises to reduce costs.

Theory of Making Profits

In centrally planned economies a predominant part of the revenue is derived from the profits of the public enterprises or from taxes on the products of public enterprises. Public undertakings even in predominantly private enterprise economies appreciably contribute to the revenues of the state. Some of the Latin American and Middle Eastern countries obtain substantial revenues from non-tax sources. In some countries of South-East Asia and the Far East, state ownership covers not only some basic industries but also trading in certain major articles of export which offer scope for substantial profits. "In Cuba, Philippines, and Puerto Rico profits made in the Govt. or Govt. sponsored projects are deliberately used as a source of finance for further development. State trading and state monopoly in rice and timber in the economy of Myanmar has been responsible for sizeable revenues to the exchequer. Similarly monopoly of export trade in rice and fiscal monopoly in opium and tobacco have made remarkable contribution in the case of Thailand's economy".[31]

The fundamental guiding principle in private enterprises is to maximise profits. Though this principle is not very relevant to the pricing in public enterprises, in underdeveloped countries, in view of the increasing requirements for funds for executing development plans, the public enterprise fostered on public revenues are expected to yield surpluses which can be used either for their own expansion or for financing other public enterprises. Pleading in favour of public enterprises making profits, Dr. Rao states that the pricing policy "should be such as to promote the growth of national income and the rate of this growth...public enterprises must make profits and the larger the share of public enterprises in all enterprises, the greater is the need for their making profits. Profits constitute the surplus available for savings and investment on the one hand and contribution to national social welfare programme on the other; and if public enterprises do not make profits the national surplus available for stepping up the rate of investment and the increase of social welfare will suffer a corresponding reduction;... Hence the need for giving up the irrational belief that public enterprise should, by definition, be run on a no-profit basis".[32] S.S. Khera is also of the view that the "Public enterprises have to play a more positive role in the economic development of a country like India, which is suffering from an acute shortage in capital for investment and where, therefore, much of the development activities have, of necessity, to fall on the state".[33] The Taxation Enquiry Commission observes, "...in certain cases where the State has made substantial investment, a policy of regulating prices so as to secure an adequate return on the capital invested is not only unobjectionable but may, indeed, be desirable. This is particularly so in the conditions of economically underdeveloped countries, where public enterprise itself, fostered at State expense, may in turn play a role in financing the country's development."[34] Prof. Galbraith remarks, "If I had to lay down a measure for performance of the publicly owned corporations in the developing country, it would be the earnings that it is able to put into its own expansion.... The most successful firm would be the one which by its efficiency and drive finds the earnings that allow it the greatest growth".[35] The Menon Committee on Parliamentary Supervision over State Undertakings also holds the view that "Government Companies should not only pay their way but make legitimate profits".[36] The public enterprises should not lag behind the rest of the economy in capital formation. To achieve a rapid rate of economic development, it is very essential to ensure that the capital is accumulated at every convenient point of activity and there is no leakage of investible funds into current consumption.

Profits are necessary if the enterprises are to self-finance their growth following the path of successful private enterprises which quite often meet a major portion of the expansion costs from their profits. The Hindustan Machine Tools provided an excellent example of this policy. It built a second machine tools plant out of its profits at Bangalore and a third at Pinjore near Chandigarh in Punjab. The Second Plant has rightly been called Hindustan Machine Tool's "gift to the nation". A policy of profits is necessary also to build up adequate reserves which are essential to meet unforeseen contingencies.[37]

A policy of profits will be necessary to provide funds for improvement and modernisation.[38] Public enterprises usually perform essential public services and in such cases, the quality is no less important than the cost. It would, therefore, be desirable that the public enterprises create a surplus for improving the quality of service or that of products.

Every economic activity must prove its eligibility to the share of national productive factors it seeks to employ in the performance of its work. The justification for the use of economic resources in an economic activity depends primarily on the profits which it can earn under its conditions of demand and cost of production. Shifts in resource allocation must take place in response to changes in the relative profitability of different industries or industrial units. Unless the public enterprises make profits comparable to those made by the private sector, there tends to develop a disparity in the criteria of resource allocations as between the two sectors.[39] There is the risk of an excessive allocation to, and development of, industries in the public sector. Excepting industries whose development is considered socially necessary irrespective of the financial return (e.g. food production), the public sector should not be exempted from the normal criteria of expansion or investment. The industries in the public sector should be guided, like the private enterprises, by the prices that consumers are ready to pay for their products. If they lead to high profits, additional investment would be justified by consumer preference. The low profits, in contrast, would indicate that the consumers do not desire an expansion of the industries.

Upholding the test of profit in public enterprises lessens the possibilities of the investment decisions being subject to political pressures. It also safeguards against inefficiency in management. "To set a positive target of profit and indicate bias in favour of the maximal principle in working towards it, is not only a guarantee of efficiency but a contribution to the sense of pride on the part of the managers of public enterprises who have no personal gain to seek out of their operations. The maxim of 'no profit, no loss' is, therefore, inadequate because, apart from other economic reasons, it falls short of the dictum of efficient administrative organisation".[40]

Unless the public enterprises follow a deliberate policy of profits, it is feared that they may disturb the pattern of government revenues.[41] In the first place, nationalisation by the State Governments reduces the income tax receipts of the Central Government, e.g. departmental organisation of nationalised road transport. Secondly, in case of some public enterprises, there may be pressure from the State or Central Legislators for subsidized or non-profit prices. For them this may be the very purpose of state's replacing private enterprise. This would lead to a decline in receipts of the government from taxation. Thirdly, many public enterprises have suffered losses which eat into government resources collected from other sources. Fourthly, if it is assumed that private enterprise is more effectively inspired than public enterprise towards profit maximisation, the tax receipts based on profits, probably also those based on sales, would be lower under public enterprises. If the decline in government revenue is to be avoided, it is necessary either to devise an appropriate system of taxes on public enterprises or to direct them to earn profits.

Because of the increasing participation of state in economic activities and the adoption of welfare state principles in many developing countries, there has been a steep increase in government expenditure. This has necessitated a substantial increase in government revenues. All this increased revenue cannot come from direct taxes and an increasing proportion has to come from taxes on the products of or profits from public enterprises. While advocating a policy of profits, care should, however, be taken that "public enterprises do not indulge in profiteering or use their power to follow a price policy based on a narrow criterion of maximisation of profits on the model of private enterprise".[42]

The Rangoon Seminar on "Organisation and Administration of Public Enterprises in the Industrial Field" held under the auspices of ECAFE came to the conclusion that public enterprises should make a profit. Since the underdeveloped countries suffer from a shortage of capital resources, a portion of this surplus should be made available for industrial development in the country as a whole while the other portion should be ploughed back into the industry itself for its further expansion.

Some states have before them the goal of building a socialist society. Socialism basically implies equal opportunity for all. The responsibility for providing equal opportunity for advancement for the children of the poor classes, who cannot meet the cost of bringing up and education of their children at a level enjoyed by the children of the richer classes, will have to be taken by the state which requires huge funds. There is, however, a strict limit to which funds can be collected by levying taxes without adversely affecting incentives to work and to save and invest. The profits of public enterprises will have to be an important source of funds required for the building of a socialist society. To quote Dr. V.K.R.V. Rao, "The theory of 'no profit, no loss' in public enterprises is particularly inconsistent with a socialist economy, and if pursued in a mixed economy it will hamper the evolution of the mixed economy into a socialist society. The sooner, therefore, this theory of 'no profit, no loss' in public enterprises is given up and the policy accepted of having a price and profit policy for public enterprises such as will make the state increasingly reliant on its own resources (as distinguished from taxing the personal incomes of its citizens), the quicker will be the evolution of a socialist society".[43] Similarly, Om Prakash remarks, "...socialist industrialisation rests on the profitability of public enterprises. They provide a less cumbersome source of public finance".[44]

Profits and Taxation

The pricing of public enterprises and taxation are closely related to each other. The two can be used either as complementary or alternative methods of raising revenue for the government. One of the objections against using price policy as a source of revenue is that if profits earned by a particular industry are used for general purposes, it will amount to benefiting the general tax payers at the cost of the consumers of a particular product. A.D. Gorwala states, "Public enterprises should not as a rule be expected to assist Government finances. To tax the consumer of a particular product in order to have the revenue and help the general tax payer is in most circumstances wrong."[45] This objection would be valid only on the assumptions that the consumers of the commodity concerned belong to the low income class and the general tax system is highly progressive. As both of these assumptions are unrealistic there does not appear to be much force in this objection.[46] The Taxation Enquiry Commission observes, "Where revenue requirements necessitate the levy of taxes on commodities or services which are as 'basic' or as 'essential' as those which are the products of public enterprises, we consider that the state should not regard itself as being precluded from using its monopolistic or semi-monopolistic power to secure larger revenues by an appropriate price policy."[47] It further states, "The argument that it is wrong to tax the consumer of a particular product or service in order to help the general tax-payer, often underlies the objection to running public enterprises at a profit. This may, perhaps, be relevant where substantial profits are made out of a limited and specialised clientele for the benefit of the wider community of tax-payers; even here, there would be a case for making profit, provided its incidence falls on the well-to-do classes and the benefits its finances accrue to the larger community of the not-so-well-to-do. In any case, the argument has much less relevance to public enterprises which involve huge investment and cater to a vast circle of beneficiaries, and the returns from which contribute to the widening of the range of their operations so as progressively to extend their benefits to more and more people."[48] Dr. Lakdawala remarks, "The tax element in pricing of public utilities, however objectionable it may seem, has to be weighed against the expansion of public investment or increase in public expenditure that it makes possible and generally the latter has the balance of advantages to its favour.[49] .... Our great needs for increased revenues have made us considerably modify our earlier ideas on the subject of commodity taxation. Time was when we considered it as only justifiable when imposed on comfort and luxuries; a tax on essential commodities was ruled out. Now, almost all the State Governments look upon general sales taxation covering almost all items of expenditure as the mainstay of their finances."

The transfer of profits from one enterprise to another gives rise to the question whether the consumers of one industry should be made to pay for the building of another industry. This problem can be resolved by devising a suitable tax on the products of the former enterprise so that funds invested in the latter enterprise do not come from profits of the former enterprise but from tax receipts of the government realised in one or the other way.

No doubt, this is merely a technical escape from the problem and the effects on the consumers of the profit-making enterprises are the same; yet, there are some healthy differences between the tax method and profit method.[50] The imposition of tax is subject to parliamentary approval and is reviewed every year. This means that the imposition of tax and its quantum are the result of due deliberation and discussion. In contrast, the profit method lacks parliamentary attention. In case of autonomous enterprises, the decisions as regards the quantum of profits may be taken by the internal management without receiving effective attention from the Parliament.

The management prefers the tax method to the profit method because of several reasons. It gives them a clear idea of what they are required to earn over and above the costs. They are relieved of the uncertainty faced under the profit method as to what quantum of profits would satisfy the government on the one hand and be free from the public criticism on the other hand. They are free from any grudge from the consumers' side because the consumers know that the higher prices are owing to the tax element and not due to the management's decision. They do not have to face labour's demand for sharing profits because the profits take the form of a tax by the government. This would give a more accurate idea to the consumer organisations and price tribunals, if any, of the transfer of profits to other purposes and thus better enable them to evaluate the desirability of such transfers. The possibility of government's informal pricing pressure on managers can be minimised if it is formally decided that the prices would be fixed by the managers and tax elements would be separately determined at the government's instance.[51]

Howsoever superior the tax method on analytical grounds may be, its use is limited because it does not fulfill the canon of convenience, which is quite important from the government's point of view, particularly when it is not sufficiently strong and popular among masses. The Finance Minister has a tendency to be tempted by whatever profits are possible from whichever public enterprise.

Arguments Against Policy of Profits Examined

If high prices are charged for intermediate and capital goods supplied by the public undertakings, it would raise the cost of production of those commodities for which they constitute inputs. The rise in the prices of finished goods will have inflationary tendencies. It is suggested by some that the "surplus price" policy should be followed in the consumer goods industry and "break even" principle should be applied to intermediate and capital goods."[52] This type of sweeping distinction does not appear to be very scientific. High prices of consumer goods can also lead to a wage-price spiral by raising the cost of living. Further, the Tariff Commission has allowed high profit rates even in basic industries in the private sector, e.g. cement and steel industries. There is, therefore, no reason to deny profits to public enterprises producing capital or intermediate goods. In fact, as pointed out by Prof. Arthur Lewis, a surplus price policy will be deflationary because this means a public enterprise absorbs more money than it has paid out and also because a higher price reduces demand.[53]

It is feared that such a policy may be a constant source of temptation for the government to raise prices of the products of public enterprises to meet its fast increasing needs for revenue. The danger of misuse of this policy is particularly great in India. Since most of the undertakings are run as companies, the government can raise the prices of goods without consulting Parliament. In public enterprises operating under monopolistic conditions, the managers, knowing that the consumers have no alternative, may adopt an attitude of "take it or leave it". In contrast, the prices in the private sector are determined by competition among different suppliers. Such fears, however, are often exaggerated. In a democratic set-up, the hostile criticism from press, parliament and public platforms provides an important check to the despotic policies of the managers of the public enterprises. The public enterprises have also to face scrutiny of the Minister concerned, the Estimates and Public Accounts Committees and the Consumers' Councils.

This type of taxation is likely to be regressive, particularly in India where there is a tendency to levy taxes where they can be easily collected. It cannot be denied that on social grounds progressive taxes are more commendable than taxes of a regressive nature but there are strict limits to the amounts which can be raised by progressive taxes without adversely affecting the incentive to work and the incentive to save and invest. To quote Taxation Enquiry Commission, "We agree that as a form of taxation, profit from public enterprise has less to commend it than direct taxation, but we must also affirm that it is not less suitable as a means of raising revenue than many of the indirect taxes to which resort is necessary in the alternative. We would, therefore, emphasise that in considering pricing policies of state undertakings in a comparatively underdeveloped country like ours, regard must be had to the need for relating them to the economic and institutional context in which they operate rather than to the standards that are more appropriate to the conditions obtaining in the advanced economies such as those of some of the Western countries".[54]

There may be a tendency to cover inefficiency and consequent higher costs by raising prices. There is a considerable force in this argument and suitable measures must be taken to safeguard against this danger. A rise in price should not be permitted without a thorough scrutiny of the relevant data by some independent and competent agency.

Extensive financing of the enterprise through ploughing back of profits arbitrarily compels the immediate consumers to pay for installations whose cost ought to be spread over the entire duration of their productive utility. The Herbert Committee on British Electricity Supply Industry remarked, "To make present consumers subsidise in this way the capital requirements of future consumers would in our judgment be quite inequitable".[55] Unless the profit element in the price is absorbitant, there is not much weight in this argument. The present generation is enjoying the fruits of the sacrifices made by our forefathers in the form of saving and investment and there is nothing unique in our making some sacrifice for the benefit of the coming generations.

Profit Making by Public Enterprises in India

Before Independence, excepting a few public utility undertakings like railways, posts and telegraphs, etc. the whole economy was in the hands of the private enterprise. As a result, though a small contribution to national exchequer was made by railways and posts and telegraphs, non-tax revenue from public enterprises was not significant. During the First Plan the state did not embark on public enterprises in a significant way and therefore much importance was not attached to the surpluses from public enterprises. Before the Second Five-Year Plan, state participation in public enterprises was not so much regarded with a view to earn revenue as for other non-fiscal purposes like the undertaking of utilitarian activities like railways, the setting up of basic industries of national importance as steel and fertilizers, the establishment of capital goods industries which are not very attractive to private enterprise and the initiation of pioneering enterprises to induce private enterprises in new fields.

The Second Plan envisaged an expanding public sector. The Industrial Policy Resolution of 1956 stated, "it is to be expected that public enterprises will augment the revenues of the state and provide resources for further development in fresh fields. But such enterprises may sometimes incur losses. Public enterprises should be judged by their total results." The Planning Commission stated in the Second Five-Year Plan: "It must be recognised, of course, that taxation has its limits, and this means in turn that it has to be supplemented by institutional arrangements which bring directly into the public exchequer the surpluses which accrue from the sale of goods and services to the public. It is through devices of this type, that is, through appropriate pricing policies in respect of the products of public enterprises and through state trading or fiscal monopolies in selected lines that some of the underdeveloped countries with levels of living not much higher than those in India are raising the resources required for their developmental effort".[56] Referring to Railways, it stated, "It is understandable—and indeed inevitable—that the Railways should draw upon the general exchequer to a significant extent at a time when the new developments envisaged in the economy require them to shoulder large additional responsibilities in a short space of time.... Nevertheless, a contribution of ₹ 150 crores by the Railways for their Plan can only be regarded as the minimum they must achieve. We would like to reiterate the point that the Railways, like all developing enterprises, public or private, should endeavour to provide a sizable part of their needs for expansion from their own resources".[57]

The Plan did not say much about other public enterprises as it was realised that most of them would be in their infancy during the Plan period. Speaking of the gap in the resources for the Plan, it stated, "It is recognised that the gap has ultimately to be filled by raising additional domestic resources, and...the only possible source that can be drawn upon for meeting this gap is taxation and, to the extent possible, profits of public enterprises".[58] No specific amount, however, was envisaged from public enterprises other than Railways.

The question whether the public enterprises should follow a policy of yielding profits for investments either within the profit-yielding enterprises themselves or in other parts of the public sector was widely discussed at the time of the formulation of the Third Five-Year Plan. There was a fairly large consensus of opinion that the public enterprises should generate surpluses or profits. The Planning Commission stated, "When public enterprises run efficiently and follow a proper price policy for their goods and services, the results of their operations must be reflected in larger earnings and surpluses. In a developing economy, these constitute a ready and increasingly important source for financing investment either for the expansion of the enterprises which yield these surpluses or elsewhere in the economy. It is, therefore, incumbent on public enterprises to produce efficiently and to accumulate surpluses which should be earmarked for further development".[59] It wanted "the management of a public enterprise...to be largely responsible for preparing the Plans for further development and for securing the requisite resources".[60] It pointed out that "increases in prices of products of public enterprises, will, it must be recognised, tend to raise prices and costs but this is part of the calculated sacrifices that have to be made".[61]

The Third Plan expected the Railways to show a surplus of ₹ 100 crores over their working expenses;[62] this was to be exclusive of any additional resources which the Railways might raise during the Plan period by way of adjustments in fares and freights. The Plan envisaged a surplus of ₹ 450 crores from other public enterprises, of which ₹ 300 crores was to come from Central Government enterprises and ₹ 150 crores from State Government enterprises.[63]

The Fourth Plan envisaged a crucial role for public enterprises and stated, "A matter of crucial significance will be the emergence of the public sector as a whole as the dominant and effective area of the economy. This will enable it to take charge more and more of the commanding heights in the production and distribution of basic and consumer goods."[64]

The Fifth Plan stated that "Public enterprises should be so managed as to yield a reasonable return on investments made. There is still considerable scope for improvement in the working of Electricity Boards. These are not charitable institutions or welfare organisations. Beneficiaries should pay a fair price for the benefits they receive."[65]

The Sixth Five-Year Plan was formulated taking into account the achievements and failures of the past three decades of planning, as well as economic developments at that time. The removal of poverty was the foremost objective of the Sixth Plan even though it recognised that given the magnitude of the task, it cannot be accomplished in a short period of five years. The Plan stated, "As the public sector invests a major part of its available resources in irrigation, basic industries and infrastructure development which have extensive forward and backward linkages, the growth of the rest of the economy gets closely linked to the growth of the public sector. Thus the exploration of alternative development scenarios boils down largely to a choice among alternative investment allocations in the public sector."[66]

The Seventh Plan reiterated that "the public sector will continue to play an important role in the core sector of the economy. It will also be a pace-setter and encourage emerging new high technology industries. Besides, contributing in no small measure to industrial growth, it will generate sizeable resources for investment. A major employer of the country's engineering manpower, the public sector will play a leading role in stimulating development of efficient ancillary manufacturing; and will strengthen the sinews of industry."[67]

In view of the resource constraint, while allocating investible funds in the public sector, the Seventh Plan gave preference to "areas where the rates of return are higher or the needs of additional capacity are more immediate...over new projects which will yield output only after the Seventh Plan."[68]

The Eighth Five-Year Plan went into the details examining the alternatives and identifying the specific projects in various sectors. It credited the public sector for developing India's crucial infrastructure sector and many other vital segments of the industrial sector. The Plan stated that "the public sector has contributed richly to the widening and diversification of our industrial structure" and "will continue to perform a key role in the coming years." However, the plan defined and limited the role of public enterprises and laid down the objective principles of its operations due to "its increasing ineffectiveness in achieving the targets and depletion of its resources crippling its ability to carry on its activities without high-cost borrowing."[69]

However, during the Eighth Plan period, public enterprises could not mobilize funds from the market through bonds to the expected level due to adverse money/capital market conditions and some inherent weaknesses of public enterprises. The failure to undertake necessary price revision to meet the rising input costs resulted in poor financial performance of most of the undertakings. Hence, they could not compete successfully with the private corporate sector for funds in the market.

The Ninth Plan stated that the financial sector reforms have enabled the corporate sector including public enterprises to raise resources from the market both at home and abroad. It added that the public sector enterprises "have to compete with their private sector counterparts for raising resources."[70] This, in turn, necessitates more autonomy for public enterprises to enable them to improve their financial performance and thus, maximise generation of revenue.

The Ninth Plan experienced a phenomenal increase in the Government Debt to GDP ratio, despite a decline in the public sector share in aggregate investment. The initiatives to curtail government expenditure led to a shortfall in public sectors' contribution to gross domestic capital formation, since the compulsion to maintain the publicly provided services in the social sector made the government consumption expenditure rigid downward.

By the end of the Ninth Plan, the private sector became strong and vibrant. The public sector became much less dominant than it used to be in many critical sectors. Its relative position is likely to decline further as government ownership in many existing public sector organisations is expected to decline substantially.

The Tenth Plan stated that the "financial and managerial problems" in the public enterprises "have prevented adequate investment in balancing and/or upgradation, leading to inadequate utilisation of the capital assets or to the lack of market competitiveness."[71] As a measure to reduce idle capital stock, the Tenth Plan suggested rapid privatization of public enterprises, particularly those, which are working well below capacity.

The Tenth Plan envisaged that the relative role of the public sector as a distinct entity will decline due to the process of disinvestment. It called for "increasing government savings and internal resources of the public sector"[72] by compression of the consumption expenditure of government, and mobilisation of additional revenue resources.

The public enterprises registered a strong performance during the Tenth Plan. The number of profit-making public enterprises went up and the number of loss-making ones reduced. However, granting of full autonomy to public enterprises remains an unfinished agenda before the government. The

Eleventh Plan stated that "a great deal of progress has been made in the revival of sick CPSEs, but close monitoring would be needed to implement their restructuring plans. Another issue of importance is the development of a mechanism to ensure optimum investment decisions by large profit-making enterprises."[73]

The Eleventh Plan outlines the new priorities for the public sector. These relate to reviving dynamism in agriculture and building the necessary supportive infrastructure in rural areas, expanding access to health and education, especially in rural areas, undertaking programmes for improving living conditions for the weaker sections and for improving their access to economic opportunity.

An important aspect of the Eleventh Plan is that most of the public sector programmes are in areas that are normally in the domain of State governments and where implementation depends upon the active involvement of local level bodies including the Panchayati Raj Institutions. This is especially true of elementary education, health, rural drinking water, rural sanitation, child nutrition, housing for the poor, the national employment guarantee, and schemes for watershed management.

The public enterprises in an underdeveloped country like India should not ape the price policy adopted by the public enterprises in advanced countries where cost-price relativity is a dominant factor. The price policy of public enterprises in developing countries should be conducive to economic development. "In the advanced and self-generating Western economies where public undertakings (mostly public utilities) are like tiny islands in the ocean of privately owned enterprises, it would not matter if public enterprises are run on 'no profit, no loss' basis or even if they make planned losses".[74] The Indian economy envisages an expanding public sector. This is evident from the Industrial Policy Resolution of 1956, the Directive Principles of State Policy, the Parliament's resolution declaring the establishment of a socialistic pattern of society as the ultimate objective of the social and economic policy of the government and the pattern of investment envisaged in the Five-

Year Plans. In an economy where public sector is fairly large and expanding fast, unless the public enterprises yield surpluses, it will be difficult to attain a reasonably high rate of capital formation.

Statutory Position in Britain

Before we examine the statutory position in regard to profit policy of public enterprises in India, it would be of interest to briefly study the same in Britain.

The British public enterprise Acts by and large lean towards the principle of average costs. The government's general policy is to be found in Section 36(1) of the Electricity Act, 1947, which states, "It shall be the duty of [the British Electricity Authority] so as to exercise and perform their functions...as to ensure that the combined revenues...are not less than sufficient to meet their combined outgoings properly chargeable to revenue account taking one year with another". Other Acts provide more or less the same thing in somewhat different words. Though the Acts usually use the phrase "taking one year with another", the Coal Act uses the phrase "on an average of good and bad years". The general purpose, of course, is the same, that is, the total costs need not necessarily be covered every year but that must be done over some not very well-defined period. Though none of the Acts specify the period over which total costs must be covered, the general impression that a person forms after reading the discussions is that some short period is intended. Discussing this matter, Hugh Gaitskell remarked, "We say that over a period of years the accounts must balance.... There may be circumstances which may involve them for a time in loss.... Private companies make losses and recoup them later. There might even be occasions when the Government might feel, if there was a heavy slump and a lot of unemployment, that it might be desirable on the whole not to insist on costs being covered. I agree that may be a rather remote contingency, but it is the kind of thing referred to in the Coalition White Paper on Employment Policy, and we have, therefore, provided for it here. I would emphasize that I attach a great deal of importance to the principle that normally we should expect area boards to cover their costs each year".[75]

An important point worth noting is that the wording applies to each board's operations as a whole, whether considered geographically or functionally. The board can, for instance, make a loss year after year in some areas provided it covers its total costs over a period by making profits in other areas. Similarly, where a board supplies several products, it can regularly sell some of the products at a price below the average cost provided it covers total costs over a period by making profits on other items. The National Coal Board, for instance, produces and sells, in addition to coal, bricks, coke, motor benzol, and some other products. The Act governing the National Coal Board does not contain anything which prevents it from selling any of these products below their average cost provided the losses are covered by profits on other items.

The accounts to be published by the various boards, however, must show the financial results of different activities.[76] The general rule is found in the Coal Industry Rationalization Act. The Accounts of the National Coal Board "shall conform with the best commercial standards and...shall distinguish the colliery activities and each of the main ancillary activities of the Board". For electricity the accounts of the central authority and of each area board must be shown separately and separate information must be given for generation, distribution and for other major activities, e.g. selling appliances.

Public interest is the guiding force in all the Acts. The National Coal Board, for instance, has among its duties "making supplies of coal available, of such qualities and sizes, in such quantities and at such prices, as may seem to them best calculated to further the public interest in all respects, including the avoidance of any undue or unreasonable preference or advantage". Similarly, one of the duties of the Gas Boards is to "develop and maintain an efficient, coordinated and economical system of gas supply for their area and to satisfy, so far as it economical to do so, all reasonable demands for gas within their area". The duties of the Transport Commission in the 1947 Act are enunciated in greater details: "To provide, or secure or promote the provision of, an efficient, adequate, economic and properly integrated system of public inland transport and port facilities within Great Britain for passengers and goods with due regard for safety of operation". But the Acts nowhere state that revenues should be adequate to provide funds for new investments. The White Paper on Financial and Economic Obligations of the Nationalised Industries in U.K., however, indicates a new approach to the pricing in public enterprises. It states, "There are powerful grounds in the national interest for requiring these undertakings to make a substantial contribution towards the cost of their capital development out of their own earnings—and so to reduce their claims upon the nation's savings and burden on the Exchequer; this is particularly so for those undertakings which are expanding fast and which have relatively higher capital needs".[77]

Statutory Position in India

The statutes governing the public corporations do not unequivocally call for commercial bias in their operations. Only a few Acts clearly require it. For instance, Section 24 of the State Financial Corporations Act, 1951, requires that "the Board in discharging its functions under this Act shall act on business principles". Strangely, there is no similar provision in the Industrial Finance Corporation Act, 1948, though this Corporation has been making more profits. Section 9 of the Air Corporations Act, 1953 requires the Air Corporations to "act so far as may be possible on business principles". Section 22 of the Road Transport Corporations Act lays down that "it shall be the general principle of a Corporation that in carrying its undertaking it shall act on business principles". Section 29 of the Delhi Transport Authority Act, 1950, contains a similar provision, though the wording is qualified: "The Authority shall Act as far as possible on, business principles". The Electricity Supply Act, 1948, is another one which contains a clear bias in favour of commercial performance.

None of the Acts governing the public corporations lay down the upper limit to the profits to be earned. This lacuna may prove serious in case of monopoly public enterprises. To safeguard the interests of the consumers, it is essential that the

Acts should prescribe the maximum rate of profit to be earned by the enterprise. It may, however, be mentioned that the possible threat to the consumer interests from the absence of such a provision has not materialised so far in most of the cases.

Though it may be assumed that the statutes expect the enterprises to recover not only their costs but also interest or dividend on capital, specified provisions to this effect are available in only two Acts. Section 59 of the Electricity Supply Act lays down: "the Board shall not...carry on its operations under this Act at a loss". Section 28 of the Road Transport Corporations Act stipulates not only interest on capital but dividend on capital raised by the issue of shares as "a part of the expenditure of the Corporation".

Most of the public corporation Acts require that profits remaining after transfers to reserves should be passed on to the government. Under Section 37 of the Damodar Valley Corporation Act, 1948, "the net profit, if any, attributable to each of the main objects, namely, irrigation, power and flood control, shall be credited to the participating governments in proportion to their respective shares in the total capital cost attributed to that object". Section 32 of the Industrial Finance Corporation Act, 1948, provides for the transfer of final surplus to the Central Government. Section 35 of the State Financial Corporations Act, 1951, stipulated that "if...there is a surplus in the net profits after declaring a dividend...such surplus shall be paid to the state government".

Turning to the government companies, there are fewer clear financial stipulations. In most of the cases, the matters are left to be decided by, or under the approval of, the President. Since the equity capital constitutes the major segment of government company capitalisation, the extent of profits liable to transfer to the government is proportionate to the rates of dividend which the government, through the board of directors, may determine.

Some of the corporations are authorised to declare dividends as against the payment of interest charges. The rates of dividends are flexible, of course, within limits. There is no parallel provision in the British corporation acts. The dividend provisions are probably the result of a mixed capital structure in some enterprises. To the extent the objective of the mixed structure is to attract private capital, the flexible dividend mechanism is a welcome feature. But the ceiling on the declarable dividend is too low for this purpose, e.g. five per cent for the I.F.C.

Most of the acts provide that the amounts to be credited to the reserves and the purposes for which the funds may be utilised are to be determined by the government or in accordance with its directions. This provision opens way for the government to subordinate the corporation's need for reserves to its own expectation of profit-receipts from time to time.

An important difference between the Indian and the British Corporation acts is that while Indian acts do not define the profit targets, the British acts include more or less uniform provision that the receipts shall not be less than the expenses. This provision does not prevent a corporation in Britain to make any amount of profit it chooses or can make. At the same time, it cannot be criticised for not having aimed at more than self-sufficiency. The provision in many Indian acts that the net profits shall be passed on to the government, however, appears to suggest as desirable the earning of surpluses. But both the Indian and British acts are inadequate to the extent they do not enunciate even approximately the desirable size of surpluses or accumulation in reserve funds. This gives rise to the possibility of the corporation following their own diverse policies of capital formation.

Another important difference between the Indian and the British Corporation acts is that while the profits of the corporations in Britain remain with them for their own purposes, most of the Indian corporations have to hand over their net profits to the government or have to use them in the manner directed by the government. There is, of course, no specific provision for passing on the profits to the government in case of a few corporations like the Air Corporations, the Warehousing Corporations, and the State Bank of India.

Disposal of Profits

The problem of utilising the profits of the public enterprises in the best possible manner is of crucial importance. The crux of the problem is to achieve a synthesis between the needs of the undertaking, sound principles of finance and meeting the demands on profits of the various claimants, viz. the state, the workers and the consumers.

According to sound principles of financing, the first charge on profits should be various reserves, particularly (a) depreciation reserves, (b) the renewals and repairs reserves, (c) the development reserve, (d) the revenue reserve and (e) staff welfare fund, etc. The main purpose of such funds is to strengthen the financial position in general, meet the future requirements, provide stable returns and also amenities to staff and to consumers. As regards the remaining profits, if the arrangement is such that the entire profits are passed on to the government, the management may not have an urge to make profits. "It is bad for the morale of an enterprise to be regarded as a milch cow, yielding the whole or most of its profits to people who appear to have contributed little or nothing to their accumulation".[78] The argument that it would further development of the country may not be sufficiently stimulating to the management.

At the same time, it should be recognised that the public enterprises financed by the government have an obligation towards the country. Further, complete freedom to the enterprise in regard to disposal of its profits is not in keeping with sound economic planning. The financial relationship between a public enterprise and the government have to be established into a given developmental perspective. In view of this, in most countries, the disposal of profits is left to the discretion of the government and not to that of the Board. The public enterprise, however, must have adequate reserves to meet unforeseen exigencies and business fluctuations. It also must have funds for the expansion of its business if that is envisaged in the overall plan of the country.

Discriminating Prices

The principle of discriminating prices, if used judiciously, can be an important instrument of promoting economic welfare. In some cases, it makes possible the provision of a service where it would not be possible otherwise. This is particularly true in case of industries with large escapable indivisible expenses. The demand of those who are ready to pay a higher price for the service may not be adequate to justify the incurring of indivisible expense while the poor class offering large demand may not be in a position to pay the full cost of production. In such a situation if the richer class agrees to bear a comparatively higher proportion of the indivisible expenses, the combined demand of, the rich and the poor classes may be adequate to cover the full cost of production and thus the provision of service may become possible. Discriminatory prices may benefit all. The richer class may gain to the extent they have to pay a lower price because a part of the indivisible expenses is borne by the poor class. The poor class gains because they have to pay a low price. The economy as a whole gains from the setting up of an additional enterprise. In the words of Arthur Lewis, "It secures an output nearer the optimum, and levies the indivisible cost on those who get the greatest benefit (measured by their consumer's surplus) from retaining the indivisible resource in this line of production. Moreover, it is possible in some cases that the net result may be that everyone pays a lower price for the commodity than he would if there were no discrimination. This is certain if the undertaking is trying to maximise its net revenue and (but not otherwise) if marginal divisible cost is falling".[79] The discriminatory prices are quite equitable because the richer classes are made to pay higher prices.

Stimulation of the rate of growth requires an encouragement of investment and discouragement of consumption. Since several goods like coal, mineral oil and electricity are used for production as well as consumption purposes, investment can be stimulated by so fixing the prices as to charge more for consumption and less for production.

Discriminatory prices may be used to charge a higher price from those who have the capacity and are willing to pay more for the same commodity. This type of discrimination is practised, for instance, by railways and is popularly known as what the traffic will bear. This has proved an important instrument of earning substantial surpluses from public enterprises which can be used for executing development programmes of the country.

Price discrimination may take several forms such as discriminating between different types of consumers, discriminating between different areas served, and discriminating between services of different nature. Price discrimination is more pronounced in case of public utilities like transportation, electricity, gas, etc. The difference between the first and third class railway fares, for instance, is much more than that justified by the difference in costs of running the first class and the third class bogies.

The public's attitude to price discrimination is not capable of rational exposition.[80] Broadly speaking, it disapproves discrimination but tolerates it in special cases. Discrimination on the basis of income practised by doctors, for instance, is not resented, but would probably be unacceptable if practised by the baker or the bus conductor. In railways, it is accepted between different commodities but will not be approved between different parcels of the same commodity. Normally, it is not called in question when attributed to different standards of service and different marginal costs. Though in favour of discrimination, Prof. Lewis recognises that in some cases it may lead to unfair results. "The man who has to cross Dupuit's bridge to see his dying father is mulcted thoroughly; the man who wishes only to see the scenery on the other side gets off lightly".[81]

Necessary Conditions for Price Discrimination

Three conditions are necessary for success in price discrimination:

1. There should be a monopoly on the supply side of the market.
2. The total demand should be capable of sub-division into separate markets, each having a different elasticity of demand.

3. It should be possible to insulate one market from the other so that those who are supplied at lower prices cannot resell to those who would have to pay higher prices.

Two-part Tariff

It is, now, widely accepted that the price should cover not only the marginal but also the overhead costs. A price equal to marginal cost will not cover total costs unless the marginal cost and the average cost are equal. Two-part tariff is one of the methods of covering total costs. The concept means a charge to be paid to get access to the benefit of the service and a price per unit of supply or service. In telephone system, for instance, a fixed rent is charged and thereafter a certain price per call. Water and electricity systems provide other similar important examples. It involves discrimination against different types of consumers.

This principle has the benefit that it assures a stable return undisturbed by any variations in inputs or outputs and periodical fluctuations in demand. The two-part is usually applied in cases where technical conditions require setting up of plants and lines at a distance from the operating spot and the maintenance of line is essential for the service. The initial cost and the maintenance costs are ultimately necessary for the extension of the service and as such have got to be recovered from the consumers and the two-part tariff appears to be one of the best methods for this purpose.

Most of the industries are characterised by regular fluctuations in the demand for their products. Demand is big at some times and small at other times. Every day the demand for gas, water, electricity, transport, etc. is at peak during some hours and very low during some other hours. The marginal costs are higher at the peak hours than at other times. Consequently, in many cases the prices are higher at peak hours than at slack hours. The transport undertakings frequently offer cheap tickets on Sundays and other holidays. The telephone system offers cheap rates at night. Shipping rates and hotel charges fluctuate seasonally. Such price differentiation is not price discrimination because price discrimination, correctly speaking, refers to differentiation based on differences in the elasticity of demand while the differentiation here is the result of differences in marginal costs. Though the common method of allocating the standing charges where there are peaks is simply to charge different prices at the peak and in slack periods, the same results can be achieved by the two-part tariff also.

Responsibility for Pricing

In the private sector, subject to broad policies laid down by the shareholders and government regulation, the decisions on pricing are taken by the managers. In contrast, in the public sector, the responsibility for pricing is diffused over the minister, the department, and managers. The difference is not without a purpose. It is essential because of several factors",[82] viz. (a) the monopoly element in public enterprises involving the possibility of a damage to consumer interests, (b) the desirability of proper inter-sectoral and inter-enterprise conventions under conditions of a mixed economy, (c) the need to prevent the managers of public enterprises from unreasonably encroaching upon tax powers, and (d) the national need to realise socio-economic ends through appropriate pricing and profit policies.

The pricing function has two aspects, viz. (1) optimum pricing policy and (2) optimum price structure. The public enterprise board cannot be given a completely free hand in deciding the price policy.

Optimum Pricing Policy: The decision in regard to the overall level of profits of a public enterprise has to be taken not by its board but by the government because this appreciably influences the level of prices. Similarly, the decision regarding the extent of profits to be transferred from public enterprise to other purposes has to be taken by the government. Broad lines for determining the claim of employees to the profits of the public enterprise have also to be indicated by the government or some public agency.

Optimum Price Structure: The public enterprise board should have the autonomy to determine the price structure as well as the price level within the externally set overall targets of profit and self-financing by adopting the most economical and pro-consumer principles of output determination and price discrimination.

In actual practice, it is very difficult to maintain an accurate dichotomy between the price policy and the price structure. As the two appreciably affect each other, it is difficult to take decisions on pricing policy in complete isolation of those on price structure. Secondly, the government may not strictly limit its interest to the price level. It may be genuinely interested in the distributional implications of the price structure. Even in this respect, though in theory the government may be satisfied with the enunciation of policies, in practice, most governments are anxious to go further. To the extent this happens, the autonomy of the management in determining the price structure is impaired. Thirdly, the management of the public enterprise has a tendency to interpret the public interest in their own way, wherever the need for this arises in their view. Thus, the price structure, whose autonomous determination should essentially depend on objective criteria, tends to be characterised by non-commercial considerations whose enunciation is logically within the jurisdiction of the parliament and government.

The purpose of formal division of responsibility between the government and the management would be realised in practice only if the government desists from informal interference with the price structure. But the experience in Britain as well as in India shows that "while the government has been reluctant to own its dominant share in a pricing decision going in the name of the enterprise, governmental insistence, behind the screens, has been the real genesis of many a decision".[83] In India the government intervention may occur in two ways. In the first place, the government may take advantage of the opportunity of examining the budget estimates of a public enterprise for influencing its price structure. Secondly, the boards, in which the government officials have usually a majority, can, and normally do, carry out the government's wishes in the field of pricing. "...the pricing decisions apparently originate in the board room and bear the board's stamp, whereas their unnoticed parentage is traceable to the government department or the minister".[84]

The pricing of some public enterprises like Indian Telephone Industries Ltd. and Hindustan Aircraft Ltd. has been particularly under great government influence. A possible justification for government intervention to this extent is that the government happens to be the major consumer for these industries. There, however, does not appear to be much weight in this argument because the government enterprises or departments which purchase these products ultimately employ them commercially and the cost implications are borne by the ultimate consumers. The prices of even such products, therefore, should be determined on their merit and if the government desires to subsidise the eventual consumers of these products, it is more reasonable that it asks for a subsidy for this purpose while presenting its budget demands.

Price Control

The need for price control over public sector is no less than that over private sector. There often prevails a misconception that the elimination of the private capitalist, whose objective is to maximise profits, removes the need for price control over public sector and that the public enterprises work in the interest of the consumer. In fact, the statutes of public enterprises hardly give any consideration to the interests of the consumers. Nor is there any provision for statutory control over public enterprises.

Since many public enterprises operate under monopolistic conditions, in fact, there is greater need for price control to ensure that they do not exploit the consumers by their attitude of "take it or leave it" when the consumers have no alternative source of supply. In private enterprise economy, in contrast, competition, where it is effective, safeguards the interests of the consumers. "Although the primary aim [of private enterprises][85] is to maximise profits and service is rendered to the consumers only as an incidental consequence, the forces of competition help to bring the prices to the level of actual costs".[86]

Price control is also essential to ensure that the target of profit fixed for a public enterprise is realised through prices that are the lowest possible "and outputs that are the largest possible". From consumer's point of view, mere regulation of profits is not adequate. It has to be ensured that the prices, apparently oriented to a given target of profit, are derived from conditions of maximum possible efficiency. Further, it should be ensured that the price structure adopted by the enterprise is the best possible, consistent with its price level and profit target.

The Acts of the public corporations should clearly enunciate the price policy to be followed by any public enterprise, giving full reasons in support of the particular price policy suggested.

All public enterprises should be brought under a well-conceived overall structure of price control. There should be a price tribunal for every major public enterprise, particularly where it operates under monopolistic conditions. For other public enterprises there may be a common price tribunal for enterprises falling in a broad category. The Railway Rates Tribunal functioning in the Indian Railways since 1921 has proved of great value to the consumers. It was able to secure justice in many cases and the relief cases amounted to 60 per cent of the total, excluding those withdrawn.[87] The very existence of the price tribunals would check arbitrary actions of the public enterprises because they would be afraid that such actions might be resented by the consumers and become a subject of decision by the tribunal. The tribunals should also be empowered to scrutinise the structure and to advise on the pricing policy of the public enterprises.

Same principles of price control should be applied to state and central enterprises because it does not make any material difference to consumer whether the product he consumes is produced by the State Government or the Central Government. The establishment of common principles of an inter-State and State-Central character has the additional advantage of giving equal treatment to all consumers irrespective of the State to which they belong.

It has often been suggested that a Public Enterprise Commission should be set up under the Ministry of Finance, enjoying the status of an expert semi-independent tribunal.[88] Such a Commission would provide a converging point for the price tribunals' activities. The Commission should play an important role in deciding the profit targets and the price policies of the public enterprises. The Public Enterprise Commission at the apex of the price control mechanism would ensure uniform approach to pricing in public enterprises, whether owned by Central or one or the other State governments. The tribunals may operate as the specialised and federated wings of the Commission, relieving it of the detailed expert work on pricing matters of individual enterprises while working under the principles set by it.

Such a Commission can also be of great use for settling problems involving inter-undertaking disputes on prices which are coming up increasingly. At present such disputes are being settled, to some extent, through lengthy correspondence and discussion between the different Ministries.

The Public Enterprise Commission will not interfere with the autonomy of the enterprises. It will, on the other hand, help the managers by enabling them to operate towards clearly laid down financial targets. The Commission will not compromise the rights of the Parliament. It will rather strengthen the Parliamentary Committee on Public Undertakings and any special committee on public enterprises with its objective assessment of the working of the public enterprises.

The Commission may consist of an economist, an accountant, a financial expert and a person with established reputation in public affairs.

A similar suggestion has been made by Dr. Rao. He has suggested the setting up of a central authority for determining the price policy of public enterprises which is different from the authority that operates individual enterprises. In the absence of such an authority, he maintains, "there is a great deal of possibility of waste and inefficiency and the bringing of non-economic considerations into economics, which is not the business of the manager and which gives him the most tremendous loophole in the public enterprise to cloak inefficiency and incapacity under the theory of all sorts of considerations in the name of public interest. Any loss or profit made should be the deliberate responsibility of the central authority and not of the individual enterprise".[89]

The managements of most of the public undertakings, however, are not in favour of any such proposal on the ground that it would further erode their autonomy in the fixation of prices. It is further argued that such a Commission would require a huge mass of information and data for according its approval to the price structure proposed by the management which would considerably increase the work of the enterprise.

To protect the interests of the consumers, many countries have adopted the device of consumers' councils. Some of the British nationalisation Acts make special provision for such councils. In France, the Boards of management themselves include representatives of consumers. In practice, however, these councils or consultative committees have not been able to function effectively partly because they have been excluded from really important matters which affect production and prices.[90] "At no stage is the consumer placed in a position to influence policy, at no point is he given an opportunity to get at the facts from the inside, to see the various alternatives which were available to the board, or to obtain an insight into the forces which determined the issue. Instead, he is left outside the ring fence which encircles the happy fraternity of producers, fluttering his wings in a vain attempt to discover grounds for complaint without any right of access to books, statistics or other relevant information".[91]

PRICING IN PUBLIC UNDERTAKINGS IN INDIA

Before we examine the principles and problems of pricing in public enterprises in India, it would be of interest to briefly study the pricing policies being followed by the important public enterprises.

Integral Coach Factory

The Ministry of Railways have stated that since the entire output of the Factory is used by the Indian Railways, there is no pricing or profits in the ordinary sense of the term.[92] The costing, however, is done in a very comprehensive manner covering all indirect charges including proportionate dividend payable by the Railways to the General Revenues on the relevant portion of the capital. The sales price is revised from time to time according to changes in the cost of production. The difference between sales price and the cost of production goes to a Development Suspense Account. The sales price is also varied to adjust any credit or debit balance in this Account.

Hindustan Aeronautics Ltd.

No definite principles are followed in fixing the prices charged by the Hindustan Aeronautics Ltd. The price policy is approved by the Board of Directors. During the first three years after the Second World War (From 1940 till 1963, the name was Hindustan Aircraft Ltd.), the work was mainly done on a cost plus basis, the objective being to make a profit of 12½ per cent both on labour and material. Again, following the view expressed by the Air Transport Enquiry Committee that the prices charged were excessive, "all-in-prices" were introduced which resulted in a considerable reduction in prices.

The margin of profit on I.A.F. manufacturing projects is fixed on an ad hoc basis keeping in view the overall cost of the aircraft engines, the volume of work involved, the number of man-hours put in by the Hindustan Aeronautics Ltd., and the cost of the materials utilised.[93] Generally, the government has allowed five to six per cent profit on manufacturing projects and 10 per cent on overhaul projects. The difference between the two margins is because of the fact that, while in the case of overhaul the entire capital employed was of the Company, in the case of manufacturing projects the cost of materials, jigs, tools, etc., was often paid from the I.A.F. funds.

Hindustan Shipyard Limited

The prices of ships built by the Hindustan Shipyard Ltd. are fixed by the Pricing Committee on the basis of the "U.K. Parity" formula. The Hindustan Shipyard Ltd. has described the working of this formula as follows:[94] "Prices of vessels are fixed by negotiation between the shipyard and the owner concerned. In these negotiations the cost of construction of a similar type of ship in U.K. shipyard is constantly kept in view. This is done by obtaining an estimate from a firm of consultants in U.K. of the price likely to be quoted by shipyards of average capacity and reputation in U.K. for a similar ship. Since it is not a practicable proposition to ascertain an inconvertible figure of U.K. parity price, the price fixed as a result of negotiations varies not infrequently from the estimates obtained by the shipyard. In any case, the agreement about the price of a ship can be concluded by the owners only when the price quoted by the Yard is also acceptable by them. Then again the owners even contend that the 'U.K. Parity Price' may also not be the representative ruling world price of a vessel and in a very competitive international market of shipping, it may not be fair to expect them to subsidize the indigenous shipbuilding. Therefore, the arrangement concerning subsidy and pricing is in practice worked with a certain amount of flexibility. The subsidy that is eventually paid by Government represents the difference between the price fixed by negotiation between the shipyard and the owner concerned and the actual cost incurred by the shipyard in the normal course".

Thus the procedure of working of the U.K. Parity Price is far from being mechanical and simple. It involves reconciliation of prices obtained independently from the buyer and the supplier probably from different U.K. firms for the supply of same type of ship. The fact that ships are available from other countries at lower prices is also taken into account.

The "U.K. Parity" price is not scientific and the shipowners have been urging for its replacement by the international parity price. "It is being urged by the shipowners that the U.K. prices are no longer the lowest prices quoted in shipbuilding. Japan and some of the continental countries have been quoting prices which are lower than those quoted by shipyards in the U.K."[95]

This formula of pricing suffers from several other defects also. It is difficult to select a country which would continue to represent the most reasonable standard prices over a fairly long period. Further, there are differences in construction and design. As the ships are built on the basis of particular orders and specification, different ships may not be quite comparable. The entire difference between the actual cost of production and the Parity Price is met out of subsidy, and there may not be much incentive to reduce the cost of production by improving the level of efficiency.

The Estimates Committee was not in favour of this method of pricing and suggested an alternative method.[96] The Committee noted that the demand of the shipowners that ships be supplied at the lowest world prices would involve the same difficulties as faced in the operation of the U.K. Parity Price Formula. It would not be possible for the shipyard to ascertain the price which would not be challenged by the buyers. This method does not provide any incentive for the shipyard to make efforts to reduce the costs of production. Shipbuilding is subsidized in all countries except in the U.K. which has a century old tradition in ship-construction. It may not be possible for the Hindustan Shipyard to function without a subsidy in one or the other form, at least, for some time to come. The method of subsidization and pricing suggested by the Estimates Committee is like this: "The Committee have elsewhere recommended the necessity of standardisation of ships built in the Hindustan Shipyard. The cost of such standardised ships should be capable of standardisation to a large extent. Based on such standardised costs, the Government may periodically determine the subsidy to be paid for each unit of construction related either to the Tonnage or the Cost. With this margin, the Shipyard should be able to quote competitive prices, if not the lowest world prices to the buyer. To the extent the actual cost of construction of a ship could be brought down, the profits of the Shipyard would go up. Failure to construct a ship within the permissible subisdy would indicate lack of efficiency on their part".[97]

The 2009-10 Annual Report of Hindustan Shipyard said, for the purpose of recognition of profit, weightage shall be given to three factors—the proportion that cost incurred to date bears to the estimated total cost of the contract, stage completion, and revenue received—which shall reach a minimum of 20 per cent individually.

The Hindustan Antibiotics

The agreement entered into between the Government of India, and the W.H.O. and the UNICEF in 1951 for the setting up of a plant for the manufacture of penicillin and other antibiotics made no specific mention of the price at which penicillin was to be sold. It only provided that the plant would operate on "a sound business basis but entirely on a non-profit basis".[98]

In the beginning, the Board of Directors of the Hindustan Antibiotics approved sales of a limited quantity of bulk penicillin to the trade at ₹ 31.02 per mega unit (m.u.). This price was based on the international price of penicillin and was a little less than the estimated cost of production. Such a price had to be fixed because of "excessive world-wide competition and the dumping of the foreign made penicillin at drastically cut rates in India".[99]

The Estimates Committee which examined the working of the Unit recommended that the selling price of penicillin should not be below the cost of production and that "at any rate, it includes a certain amount of return on capital, etc."[100] With a view to reduce competition from penicillin dumped by foreign countries, the import quota was drastically reduced, and, in consultation with the trade, it was decided that before additional imports are licensed, the bottling plants would be required to take the surplus of the bulk penicillin of the Unit "at such prices as the Government might fix".[101]

The bulk penicillin was being sold at 69 paisa per m.u. up to 1st October 1959 and thereafter the price was reduced to 50 paisa per m.u. A special discount is given to government, semi-government and charitable institutions using penicillin. This discount was 5 per cent up to 1 April 1959 and thereafter 10 per cent up to 1 May 1960 when it was raised to 15 per cent.

The annual report of the company gave the following reasons for the bulk prices being higher than the C & F cost of imported penicillin:[102] (1) Most of the exporting countries started production of penicillin nearly 10 years before the Hindustan Antibiotics and the value of their plants had been written off several times. (2) The companies exporting to India maintained indigenous prices at a relatively higher level and their low export prices were unrelated to cost of production. (3) The policy of the Hindustan Antibiotics was to provide reasonable surpluses for further expansion instead of approaching government for additional funds which mean additional burden on the plan resources.

The Public Accounts Committee did not approve of the price policy of the Unit and was of the view that in a welfare state the undertakings manufacturing drugs and medicines of common use should not be run for profit motive.[103] The objective should be to render service to the common man by selling the products at the cheapest price. The Committee suggested that the question of the sale price of penicillin be referred to the Tariff Commission.

The Unit is responsible for developing the science and production of antibiotics in India. The original agreement between the Government of India, W.H.O. and UNICEF states that the Hindustan Antibiotics is "to render the country eventually self-sufficient in this science without dependence on foreign help".[104] The pricing policy of the Unit has to be examined in this light. The Annual Report of the Unit for the year 1962-63 states, "Surpluses made are being utilised or proposed to be utilised on the committee expansion programme of the Company, viz. ₹ 215 lakhs for Streptomycin project, ₹ 60 lakhs for Streptomycin plant doubling, ₹ 10 lakhs for Tetracycline plant, ₹ 40.5 lakhs for penicillin substantial expansion, ₹ 30 lakhs for Hamycin project and ₹ 10 lakhs for pilot plant, ₹ 37.5 lakhs for subsidising Streptomycin production in the early stages and ₹ 8.5 lakhs on exports of the Company's product".[105]

After reporting an operating loss in 1997 the company was reported to the Bureau of Industrial and Financial Restructuring (BIFR). On 17 January 2009 the company was taken off the books of the BIFR after reporting a record turnover of ₹ 120 cr.

Railways

The Ministry of Railways has formulated the general basis of regulation of railway fares and rates as follows: "Railways are no doubt a commercial concern but they are hardly a commercial concern in the conventional sense. As a state undertaking they owe it to the public, to provide transport at the cheapest rates, consistent with the maintenance of their financial solvency and providing means for their development. Unlike ordinary commercial concerns, they must not aim at maximising their profits, all the more so because they are a semi-monopolistic concern. Consequently, they must aim at charging not necessarily what the traffic can bear but what is justified in relation to their costs of operation and essential development".[106] In fixing their rates, the railways have to take into account potentialities of traffic, reasonableness of rates and competition from other modes of transport. The principles governing railway fares and freights keep in view the need for ensuring solvency of railways and the need for expanding trade and commerce and helping the growth of industries in general.

The Railway Ministry, in their note to the Taxation Enquiry Commission, 1953-54, did not approve of the imposition of taxes on railway fares and freights. The Ministry considered a tax on freight as a multi-point tax which would considerably raise the cost of production and increase inflationary pressures. Further, such indirect taxes on commodities were not considered the best form of taxation.

The Taxation Enquiry Commission made a distinction between fares and freights in principle. The freights, according to the Commission, should be so regulated as "not to leave a profit over and above meeting the costs of operation and essential development". It suggested the setting up of a committee "to consider the formulation of an adequate freight rate policy, having regard to the interests of industrial and economic development, on the one hand, and the resources required for railway development, on the other".[107]

With regard to fares, the Commission did not advise the exploitation of monopoly power with a view to maximise profits but saw no objection in principle to using travel as a basis of taxation like other services or commodities of general consumption. Such taxes are an important source of revenue in many countries. They are imposed in Japan, Turkey, Spain and some States in U.S.A. A tax on travel is not more regressive than many other taxes.

As of 2009, freight tariff on Indian Railways was among the highest in the world. On the other hand, passenger fares were low compared to most foreign railways. The high freight rates and low passenger fares make the fare-freight ratio of Indian Railways one of the larests in the world.[108]

Air Transport

In the case of Air India, the fare structure is quite arbitrary and there is no standard basis to fix the fares. Previously, the Indian Airlines Corporation used to compute the fares on the basis of instructions given by the Air Transport Licensing Board which allowed the Airlines freedom to fix fares up to a specified limit. The companies, therefore, fixed the fares according to what the traffic would bear on each line. On the other hand, the fares and freights of the Air India International, as in the case of other International Airlines, were determined by the International Air Transport Association (IATA) and were enforced after they were approved by the Government of India.

The merger of erstwhile Air India and Indian Airlines had witnessed a significant re-structuring of operations between the networks of the two erstwhile airlines—since August 2007.

Road Transport

In regard to road transport services, the accepted policy in most States is to fix fares and freight charges so as to cover the costs of operation, depreciation and interest charges, leaving a small margin of profit for the government.

Postal Services

In the case of postal system, service rather than revenue is considered to be the test of success. Countries with a high density of population, e.g. England and France, earn substantial profits from their postal systems. In contrast, there are countries with great expanse of territory, like the United States, which have often shown losses. But countries with a low density of population charge rates which cover the costs of operation or which yield moderate profits. This policy governs the operation of Indian postal system and is considered to be quite appropriate for this elementary service.

D.V.C.

The D.V.C. (Damodar Valley Corporation) provides an interesting case study in the field of pricing of its services—water for irrigation, water for industrial purposes, and electricity. The price policy is fully embodied in the following speech of N.V. Gadgil, the then Minister for Works, Mines and Power, delivered by him before the Corporation actually started operating: "The test by which the whole thing would be judged would be whether the supply of the power would be cheap. Purely revenue considerations are now universally regarded as inadequate in determining the rates to be charged by public utilities. The tendency everywhere, including India, is to strike a proper balance between considerations of revenue and those of social well-being. The rate policy especially of a state-owned public utility is, therefore, increasingly based not on what the traffic will bear, but on, if one may say so, what the service will bear. That is to say, the rate should be fixed at or near the lowest level compatible with the overall financial soundness of the utility concern so as to leave the customers a relatively high benefit or consumer's surplus. This social consideration is often reinforced by an economic one. Lower rates stimulate consumption so that the total revenue may increase in spite of a lower margin of profit. That is what is known as Henry Ford's principle, 'the lowest margin of profit and the largest possible turn-over'. And I have no doubt that the Corporation, when it starts working, will certainly take all these factors into consideration before finalising the rates".[109]

The price policy for water for irrigation purposes has been based on the policy that the Corporation should charge a price that would be an equitable price, without taking other factors into account. For purposes of irrigation, it has been decided to fix the price on the principle of no profit, no loss. The price covers interest liabilities, operation cost and depreciation and there exists no provision for profit. Certain peculiar problems have dictated the adoption of this policy. Since the river passes through mountainous regions of Bihar which are not fit for the construction of irrigational channels, these channels have been constructed only in the lower regions. Irrigation facilities, therefore, exist only in the lower regions lying in West Bengal. Since the cultivators in the lower region produce only one crop, they depend entirely on the monsoon which are fairly regular in the region. The cultivators, therefore, have to be taught to use irrigation facilities provided for them and keeping this in view, a decision has been taken to fix the price on the principle of no profit, no loss.

Though there exists an acute demand for electricity in the D.V.C. area, it has been decided not to fix prices on the basis of what the traffic would bear because that would adversely affect the development of that area for which the D.V.C. is responsible.

Electricity

Though the electricity rates in India vary from state to state, the general policy is that the prices should cover costs of generation, transmission and distribution and operational, maintenance and depreciation charges. The rates also vary for different uses of electricity. The rates for industrial use are lower than those for domestic use. In regard to power sold at Bhakra Nangal, the special Tariff Advisory Committee laid down certain considerations which should determine the rates of power supplied. They are (a) a reasonable return on the capital invested, (b) a comparison of the rates prevailing in other states and (c) the principle of what the traffic will bear.

Bharat Electronics

The prices charged by Bharat Electronics are based on the actual cost of inputs, plus certain overhead charges and a ten per cent profit.

Hindustan Machine Tools

The prices of various items produced by the Hindustan Machine Tools are fixed by the board of directors taking into consideration "all relevant factors including the cost of production and the prevailing price of comparable machines imported into the country".[110] The policy of the company has been to keep prices close to the landed cost of imported items instead of charging higher prices which it could have done because of a lack of competition and also to maintain the selling price for the machines below the landed cost with a view to help the customers. Further, a part of the benefit of reduction in the cost of production is also passed on to the customers by way of reduced prices. However, the policy of the company was not approved by the Estimates Committee of the Parliament.

Indian Telephone Industries

The prices of the equipment produced by the Indian Telephone Industries are based on costs plus a certain margin of profit, of course, the margin varies in the case of products sold to the government departments other than Posts and Telegraphs Department and to private parties.

Sindri Fertilizers

The price of ammonium sulphate is determined after taking into consideration the costs of production, price trends in foreign markets and the purchasing power of consumers. In fixing prices, the emphasis is laid not on commercial considerations but on non-commercial aspects. The pricing policy is governed by the need to make fertilizers available to cultivators at low rates.

The Sindri fertilizer plant operated consistently in profit till 1967-68 and again in 1969-70. But in spite of modernisation, the factory could not maintain profit thereafter even after exceeding rated (attainable) capacity, mainly because of higher production cost and comparatively lower sale price of fertilizers. The Government of India eventually decided to close the factory operation in September 2002.

Coal

The prices of coal produced by the state collieries are fixed under the Colliery Control Order, 1945 on the basis of cost of production plus a reasonable margin of profit.

Export Risks Insurance Corporation (Now Export Credit and Guarantee Corporation)

The government set up the Corporation with the intention of running it on a 'no-profit, no-loss' basis. The guiding principle in fixing the premium rates, therefore, has been the obtaining of such an income as would be just sufficient to pay for the management expenses after paying and building enough reserves to meet any unforeseen heavy losses.[111] At the same time, the rates should be such as the trade can bear. The actual premium rates are fixed taking into consideration a number of factors like countries involved, terms of payment, commodities, spread of risks, claims experience, etc. A higher rate of premium is charged if the market is riskier and the period of credit is longer.

For premium purposes, the commodities have been classified into three categories on the basis of their nature and saleability. Group 'a' comprises raw materials and traditional commodities like jute, cotton, textiles, tea, coir goods, etc. and standard rates are charged for such commodities. Semi-manufactured and manufactured goods have been classified in groups 'b' and 'c' and an additional 10 per cent and 20 per cent respectively is charged on the standard rate.

As regards the basis for grouping, the standard commodities are those which are readily saleable while the non-standard commodities are those which do not have a ready market. In case of non-acceptance of non-standard commodities, the risk of losses is greater. The premium rate for such commodities, therefore, is somewhat higher.

Normally the Corporation covers up to 85 per cent of the loss. The premium rates depend on the country to which exports are made and the period of repayment. At least 20 per cent of the total amount of the premium for the cover for Buyers Credit and Line of Credit is taken in advance. The balance amount is collected on a quarterly basis in proportion to the amount of credit disbusred.

Life Insurance Corporation

The system of premium rates of the Life Insurance Corporation has been more or less inherited or continued from the days when the constituent companies, which now form Life Insurance Corporation, were private companies. These insurance premia are based upon actuarial calculations of life expectation. A life insurance company never fails because there is built-in-profitability which is due to actuarial basis upon which premia are calculated, being in favour of the concern.

CHARACTERISTICS OF PRICING IN PUBLIC SECTOR IN INDIA

A study of the techniques of pricing in public enterprises in India shows that[112] (a) the pricing policies have been evolving haphazardly and without due deliberation of principle in several cases, (b) the monopoly power enjoyed by some public enterprises has been exploited indeterminately, and (c) the consistent principle of pricing has not been applied in many enterprises because the government is their major customer.

The results obtained in case of most of the public enterprises are not the result of conscious policy. The public corporation Acts make hardly any references to pricing principles. Section 7(1) of the Air Corporation Act 1953, speaks of "reasonable charges"; Section 59 of the Electricity (Supply) Act 1948, appears to disapprove of the charges that lead to losses and Section 46 lays down certain details of the "grid tariff". Barring these exceptional references, the Acts provide no positive indication of pricing criteria. Such inadequacies are more prominent in the case of government companies.

The price policies of public enterprises in India are neither uniform nor based on any definite commercial principles. Sometimes the prices are fixed on the cost plus basis while in other cases, they are determined on "no-profit no-loss" basis or on "below-cost" basis or "what the traffic can bear" or "more than it basis".

A notable characteristic of pricing policy of the public enterprises in India is that the prices are biased in favour of government departments and other public enterprises. "Public Corporations and Government Companies, as sons and daughters of the State, cannot be completely shorn of maternal affection." The State Trading Corporation of India, for instance, supplies imported cars acquired by it to the government departments and other public undertakings at prices that are much lower than those realised from sale to private buyers through the system of tenders.

We examine below the main principles on which are based the prices in Indian public enterprises.

Prices Subject to Fixation by Government

The prices of some products like steel and fertilizers are fixed by the government. The prices are fixed on the recommendations of the Tariff Commission or specialised agencies like the Fertiliser Pool. The reason for such price fixation is not that all the production units are in public sector but that the government considers it desirable to regulate the prices of some essential commodities, produced in either sector. The fixation of prices, therefore, does not have much relation to the principles of public enterprise pricing. The prices are fixed keeping in view the overall national policies without attaching much importance to the profits of individual public enterprises.

"No Profit, No Loss"

In the absence of an adequate description of the pricing policies in the annual reports or other documents of public enteprises, it is difficult to say in how many cases the breakeven principle is adopted. The working of some enterprises like the State Electricity Boards of Bihar and Madhya Pradesh, however, shows that they work on the principle of "no profit, no loss".

Under Article V(7) of the Joint Plan of Operations dated July 19, 1952, drawn by the Government of India, the World Health Organisation and the United Nations Children's Emergency Fund, the Hindustan Insecticides is required to operate on a no profit, no loss basis. Similarly, for Hindustan Antibiotics, a

Joint Plan of Operations was signed in July 1951, by the Government of India, WHO and the UNICEF. The objectives, as stated in Part I of the Agreement, *inter alia*, are:

1. to produce penicillin most economically as a national enterprise on a sound basis but entirely on a non-profit making basis;
2. to maintain supply of penicillin and other antibiotics for purchase by state and municipal hospitals for free treatment of patients, particularly women and children; and
3. to provide for free distribution to children in India under arrangements mutually satisfactory to the Government and the UNICEF.

"Cost-plus" Prices

The Indian Telephone Industries Ltd. and the Hindustan Aeronautics Ltd. operate on this principle. The main reason appears to be that the government is the major consumer of their products and is interested in paying prices bearing a definite and low relationship to the costs. The cost-plus criterion is of value in the early years of an enterprise, when it has not reached its full height of efficiency. But in the long run, it may encourage lethargy and inefficiency because the enterprise is sure to recover its full costs whatever it may be. If this principle is to be adopted permanently, therefore, it should be followed by a thorough assessment of the cost efficiency of the enterprise at regular intervals.

Profit-oriented Prices

There are yet hardly any examples of public enterprises which have worked towards a set percentage of profit on capital. From the fact that some enterprises have earned profits, it may be construed that they have followed a profit-oriented price policy; it is difficult to assert the level of profit actually aimed at.

Undefined-profit Prices

Most of the profit-earning public enterprises fall in this category in the sense that they make whatever profits they make.

The case of railways is different to the extent that by the "convention" they have a specific dividend obligation to the government, though the level of profits that may be earned by the railways is not the subject of any parliamentary decision.

Subsidy Prices

All the enterprises operating on loss fall in this category. Some enterprises have been clearly considered as eligible to the subsidy while others are not. The Hindustan Shipyard belongs to the former category, the government offering subsidy on each ship sold to the extent of the difference between its cost of production and the price fixed by the Pricing Committee on the basis of the "U.K. Parity" price.

Competitive Prices

Many State Government enterprises and some Central Government enterprises, operating in competitive markets have to accept whatever prices are offered by the market. The competition, however, is nominal in most cases either because the public enterprise accounts for a substantial portion of the industry or because it operates in a seller's market. Real competition is faced by such enterprises as the Shipping Corporation Ltd.

Guiding Principles for Pricing in India

Because of the diverse objectives sought in the setting up of public enterprises, the degree of essentiality of their product, the nature of the service provided by them, the size of their market, the class of their consumer and their paying capacity and the conditions of market under which they operate, their role in stimulating growth, whether or not their products will be taken unless sold at a low price, the social benefits conferred by them, it is not possible to lay down any principles of pricing which will be uniformly applicable to all public enterprises. Further in a dynamic economy the pricing policy has to undergo changes along with changes that are constantly occurring in such an economy. The maximum that we can do is to lay down the important guidelines and considerations which should be taken into account in formulating the pricing policy in different enterprises. This is what is briefly attempted below.

Transport and communications being key factors in economic development, recovery of full costs may not be insisted upon. But keeping in view the vast sums invested in this industry, subsidization should not be permitted beyond narrow limits. In case of a world competitive industry like shipping, the government should not charge the Indian shipping companies a price higher than the world price. In the interest of the nation's health, items like penicillin (manufactured by the Hindustan Antibiotics) and D.D.T. (manufactured by Hindustan Insecticides Ltd.) should be sold on "no profit, no loss" basis. To achieve our food and other essential agricultural products targets, the supply of fertilizers may be subsidized temporarily. Once the farmers realise the increase in production that is possible with the help of fertilizers, they would be prepared to buy these at a price which yields a reasonable rate of return.

Profits may not be expected from enterprises which are not in full operation because in their case overheads are spread over a small quantity of production. In some public enterprises, the early years are the years of experimentation through trial and error method and the attainment of reasonable efficiency takes time. "...long periods of unprofitability or relatively low profitability have been unknown in the history of many reputable business houses".[113] But the later profits in such cases must be adequate to compensate the earlier losses.

There are some public enterprises whose products are almost entirely bought by the Central or State governments or public corporations. The entire production of the Hindustan Cables Ltd., for instance, is bought by the Posts and Telegraphs Department. The Indian Security Press works for the government. The Bharat Electronics Ltd. is intended to meet the requirements of equipment of the Armed Services and the government. The Chittaranjan Locomotive Works caters to the needs of railways. Some people are of the view that much emphasis need not be laid on commercial pricing in case of such enterprises. This, however, does not appear to be a correct attitude. Commercial pricing is necessary even in such enterprises to safeguard against inefficiency and also to correctly know the cost of production of the enterprises using their products.

The enterprises which operate under competitive conditions generally produce consumer goods. Such undertakings should fix prices of their products with the objective of maximising profits. They should also be subjected to all taxes which the private enterprises have to pay.

In the initial stages, in case of some industries, the prices may have to be fixed at a low level with a view to encourage demand and to widen market in the long run. In such cases subsidies may be necessary; but they should be allowed for a specified period and the conditions to be fulfilled by such enterprises should also be laid down so that the burden of subsidies on the general tax-payer is not unnecessarily prolonged.

The Administrative Reforms Commission has recommended[114] that the following principles should be kept in view in formulating the pricing policies of public enterprises.

1. Public enterprises in the industrial and manufacturing field should aim at earning surpluses to make a substantial contribution to capital development out of their earnings besides making a contribution to the Exchequer.
2. Public enterprises should in any event pay their way and should not run into losses except in pursuance of express directives issued by the Government in public interest.
3. In the case of public utilities and services, greater stress should be laid on output than on return on investment, the former being extended up to a level at which marginal cost is equal to price.
4. While determining the price structure commensurate with the surpluses expected from them, public enterprises should keep the level of output as near the rated capacity as possible subject, of course, to the volume of demand for the product.

NOTES

1. Dilip Mukerjee, "Prices and Efficiency in the Public Sector", *Indian Management* (January-February 1963), p. 17.
2. V.V. Ramanadham, *The Finances of Public Enterprises* (Bombay, 1963), pp. 59-77.
3. *Ibid.*, p. 60.
4. Public Accounts Committee, *Report on the Appropriation and Finance Accounts of the Government of Mysore for 1958-59 and the Audit Reports thereon.*
5. Ramanadham n, 2, p. 67.
6. Estimates Committee, *Minutes of Evidence on the Neyveli Lignite Corporation Ltd.* (New Delhi, 1961).
7. *Econometrica* (July 1938).
8. A.P. Lerner, "Statics and Dynamics in Socialist Economies", *The Economic Journal* (June 1937).
9. J.E. Meade, "Price and Output of State Enterprises", *Economic Journal* (1944), pp. 321-28.
10. W.A. Robson, *Nationalised Industry and Public Ownership* (London, 1960), pp. 291-94.
11. W. Arthur Lewis, *Overhead Costs* (London, 1951), p. 18.
12. *Ibid.*, p. 19.
13. Theodor Thiemeyer, "Theories concerning the Problem of Price Setting in Public Undertakings", *Annals of Collective Economy* (July-September 1962), pp. 257-58.
14. W. Arthur Lewis, "The Policy of Public Corporations" in William A. Robson (ed.), *Problems of Nationalised Industry* (London, 1952), p. 181.
15. *Ibid.*, p. 189.
16. *Ibid.*, pp. 181-82.
17. *Ibid.*, pp. 188-90.
18. *Ibid.*, pp. 188-89.
19. *Ibid.*, pp. 192-93.
20. INRICE Theory Committee, "Price Setting in Public Undertakings", *Annals of Collective Economy* (July-September 1962), p. 272.
21. Francis Cassell, "The Pricing Policies of the Nationalized Industries", *Lloyds Bank Review,* October 1956, Reprinted in A.H. Hanson (ed.), *Nationalization* (London, 1963), p. 217.
22. Robson, n. 10, pp. 306-07.
23. Shyam Nandan Sinha, "Price Policy in Public Undertakings and Developmental Planning", *A.I.C.C. Economic Review* (January 4, 1962), p. 17.

24. Government of India, *Report of the Taxation Enquiry Commission, 1953-54*, Vol. I (Delhi, 1955), p. 203.
25. Cf. A.H. Hanson, *Public Enterprise and Economic Development* (London, 1955), p. 436.
26. Government of India, n. 24, p. 202.
27. Sinha, n. 23, p. 18.
28. Philip E. Taylor, *The Economics of Public Finance* (New York, 1952), p. 213.
29. Thiemeyer, n. 13, p. 263.
30. INRICE Theory Committee, n. 21, p. 273.
31. K. Shamanna, "Price and Profit Policy in Indian Public Enterprises", *A.I.C.C. Economic Review* (22 March 1961), p. 36.
32. V.K.R.V. Rao, "The Public Sector in India" in V.V. Ramanadham (ed.), *Pricing, Labour and Efficiency in the Public Sector* (Hyderabad, 1962), p. 3.
33. S.S. Khera, *Government in Business* (Bombay, 1963), p. 235.
34. Government of India, n. 24, p. 200.
35. Prof. J.K. Galbraith's address on "Public Administration and the Public Corporation" at the Indian Institute of Public Administration at New Delhi on 25 August 1961.
36. All India Congress Committee, *Report of the Sub-Committee on Parliamentary Supervision over State Undertakings* (New Delhi, 1959), p. 33.
37. R.L. Varshney, "Price Policy in Public Enterprises", *A.I.C.C. Economic Review* (15 September 1959), p. 17.
38. R.L. Varshney, "Pricing Policy Under Public Enterprises", *The Indian Journal of Commerce* (March 1958), p. 43.
39. V.V. Ramanadham, *The Structure of Public Enterprise in India* (Bombay, 1961), pp. 92-94.
40. V.V. "Ramanadham, "Pricing in the Public Sector" in V.V. Ramanadham (ed.), *Pricing, Labour and Efficiency in the Public Sector* (Hyderabad, 1961), p. 15.
41. Ramanadham, n. 39, pp. 89-91.
42. Rao, n. 32, p. 4.
43. V.K.R.V. Rao, " Prices, Income, Wages and Profits in a Socialist Society", in All India Congress Committee, *Ooty Seminar Papers* (Delhi, 1959), p. 176.
44. Om Prakash, *The Theory and Working of State Corporation* (London, 1962), p. 182.
45. A.D. Gorwala, *Report on the Efficient Conduct of Public Enterprises* (New Delhi, 1951), p. 28.

46. M.S. Shukla, *Administrative Problems of Public Enterprises in India* (Delhi, 1959), pp. 205-26.
47. Government of India, n. 34, p. 200.
48. *Ibid.*, pp. 202-03.
49. D.T. Lakdawala, "Contribution of Public Enterprises", *Indian Economic Journal* (April 1960), pp. 396-97.
50. Ramanadham, n. 39, pp. 108-10.
51. Ramanadham, n. 2, p. 90.
52. N.K. Rohatgi, "The Surplus Principle of Price Fixation", *The Economic Weekly* (28 October 1961) and by the same author, "A note on Price and Profit Policy in Indian Public Enterprises", *A.I.C.C. Economic Review* (7 February 1961).
53. Lewis, n. 14, p. 181.
54. Government of India, n. 34, p. 203.
55. *Report of the Committee on the Electricity Supply Industry* (London, 1956), p. 90.
56. Government of India, *Second Five-Year Plan* (New Delhi, 1956), p. 91.
57. *Ibid.*, pp. 80-81.
58. *Ibid.*, p. 78.
59. Government of India, *Third Five-Year Plan* (New Delhi, 1961), p. 273.
60. *Ibid.*, p. 264.
61. Planning Commission, *Third Five-Year Plan—A Draft Outline* (New Delhi, 1960), p. 50.
62. Government of India, n. 59, p. 97.
63. *Ibid.*
64. Government of India, *Fourth Five-Year Plan Document*, New Delhi.
65. Address of the Prime Minister to the meeting of the National Development Council on September 24, 1976, reproduced as Foreword to the Fifth Five-Year Plan. *Fifth Five-Year Plan Document*, Govt. of India, New Delhi.
66. *Sixth Five-Year Plan Document*, Chapter 2, Govt. of India.
67. "Development Perspective: Towards the Year 2000", *Seventh Five-Year Plan Document*, Vol. I, Govt. of India.
68. "Objectives, Strategies and Pattern of Growth in Seventh Plan", *Seventh Five-Year Plan Document*, Vol. I, Govt. of India.
69. "Objectives and Orientation", *Eighth Five-Year Plan Document*, Vol. I, Planning Commission, Govt. of India.

70. "Public Sector Plan: Resources and Allocation", *Ninth Five-Year Plan Document*, Vol. I, Chapter 3, Planning Commission, Govt. of India.
71. http://planningcommission.gov.in/plans/planrel/fiveyr/10th/volume1/10th_vol1.pdf
72. *Ibid.*
73. http://planningcommission.gov.in/plans/planrel/fiveyr/11th/11_v1/11th_vol1.pdf. p. 36
74. Sinha, n. 23, p. 17.
75. Gas Bill: Standing Committee Official Report: Session 1947-48: Volume 2, column 1145.
76. D.N. Chester, "Note on Price Policy Indicated by the Nationalization Act", *Oxford Economic Papers,* January 1950, Extract reprinted in A.H. Hanson, *Nationalization* (London, 1963), p. 211.
77. *White Paper on Financial and Economic Obligations of Nationalized Industries* (London, 1962), para 22.
78. Nabagopal Das, *The Public Sector in India* (Bombay, 1961), p. 105.
79. W. Arthur Lewis, *Overhead Costs* (London, 1951), p. 21.
80. *Ibid.*, p. 21.
81. *Ibid.*
82. Ramanadham, n. 40, p. 20.
83. Ramanadham, n. 2, p. 78.
84. *Ibid.*
85. Words within parenthesis added.
86. Das, n. 69, p. 43.
87. Amba Prasad, "The Railway Rates Tribunal", *Indian Journal of Public Administration* (January-March 1955), p. 92.
88. Ramanadham, n. 2, pp. 96-97.
89. "Price Policy in Public Enterprises", a lecture delivered by Dr. V.K.R.V. Rao at the Indian Institute of Public Administration on 9 March 1961.
90. Das, n. 69, p. 44.
91. "Public Enterprise", ed. by W.A. Robson.
92. Estimates Committee, *Report on Integral Coach Factory* (New Delhi, 1964), p. 7.
93. Estimates Committee, *Report on Hindustan Aircraft Limited* (New Delhi, 1961), p. 11.
94. Estimates Committee, *Report on Hindustan Shipyard Ltd.* (New Delhi, 1961), pp. 11-12.
95. Hindustan Shipyard, *Seventh Annual Report,* 1958-59, p. 6.

96. Estimates Committee, n. 94, pp. 12-13.
97. *Ibid.*, p. 13.
98. Subsequently 'no profit' clause was dropped from the original agreement in 1961-62.
99. Estimates Committee, *Report on Hindustan Antibiotics and Hindustan Insecticides* (New Delhi, 1956), p. 11.
100. *Ibid.*, p. 36.
101. Estimates Committee, *Action Taken on the 27th Report (1st Lok Sabha) on Hindustan Antibiotics and Hindustan Insecticides* (New Delhi, 1958), p. 6.
102. *Annual Report,* 1960-61, p. 11, para 7.
103. Public Accounts Committee, *7th Report,* 1962-63, pp. 33-34.
104. Estimates Committee, n. 99, p. 26.
105. *Ibid.*, p. 11.
106. Government of India, n. 24, p. 194.
107. *Ibid.*, p. 198.
108. White Paper on Indian Railways, Govt. of India, Ministry of Railways (Railway Board), December 2009, p. 74.
109. Constituent Assembly of India (Legislative), 16 February 1948.
110. Estimates Committee, *Report on Hindustan Machine Tools Ltd.*, (New Delhi, 1960).
111. Estimates Committee, *Report on Export Risks Insurance Corporation Ltd.* (New Delhi, 1964), p. 29.
112. Ramanadham, n. 40, p. 15.
113. Lakdawala, n. 49, p. 400.
114. Administrative Reforms Commission, *Report on Public Sector Undertakings* (New Delhi, 1967) (Mimeographed), pp. 102-03.

Appendix to Chapter 4

Railway Rates and Fares

The determination of railway rates and fares is a very complicated problem. It requires a high degree of skill, foresight, courage and alertness on the part of the Railway authorities. In this context, the remarks of Sir William Acworth are worth quoting: "Fixing of railway rates is, in one word, an art and not a science, and it is an art which, in Bagehot's phrase, must be exercised 'in a sort of twilight', in an atmosphere of probabilities and doubt where nothing is clear, where there are some chances for many events, where there is much to be said for several courses, where nevertheless, one course must be determinedly chosen and fixedly adhered to".[1] The railway charges must be correlated with the general economic conditions of the area served. The demand for railways is 'derived' and not fundamental. The railways serve trade and industry and are in turn fed by it. Jackman remarks, "In order to be prosperous themselves the railways must serve prosperous communities. The rates which are established are tentative, and the ultimate test of each rate is the degree of prosperity which it brings to the producer, the carrier and the consumer of the products transported. No matter how thoroughly conditions are studied before a new rate is made, the results of the application of former rate must be gathered promptly and in detail; and if the outcome as shown by experience has not been satisfactory, the rate must be changed in the light of facts".[2]

The two main principles on which railway rates are fixed are the "cost of service" and "value of service". The former principle means that the charges are based on the cost incurred in rendering the service. A few years ago, even the Inter-State Commerce Commission of the U.S.A. regarded the basis of the cost of service as logical and sound.[3] *Prima facie*, this principle seems to be very simple. But a deeper analysis of cost will show that it is well-nigh impossible to base rates and fares on costs actually incurred. Under the "value of service" principle an attempt is made to extract the maximum possible out of the value added by conveyance of an article from one place to another.

Difficulties in Ascertaining Cost of Service

There are peculiar difficulties in determining the cost of transport services. In case of factories producing bicycles, sewing machines, shoes, etc., one unit of output is more or less similar to the other units. In contrast, in railway services, it is difficult to determine a unit of output. It may be said that a unit like 'ton miles or passenger miles' may serve the purpose because transport charges are generally based on the unit (in case of passengers) or weight (in case of goods) conveyed multiplied by the distance travelled. But the cost of constructing different miles of railway track differs. The cost of constructing a mile of railway which has to pass through a tunnel would be several times of that of a mile of railway laid across the level ground. 'Tons' of commodities would also differ considerably according to bulk, mode of packing and accommodation required. Passengers also differ in regard to their bulk and weight. In the words of Bonavia, "But a ton-mile can represent carrying a ton of eggs at sixty miles an hour through a tunnel that costs £500,000 a mile to build—or carrying a ton of coal at twelve miles an hour along a branch line laid across level fields. 'Tons' differ enormously in bulk, fragility, method of packing and accommodation required; 'miles' have a wide range of possible expansiveness".[4]

The fixed costs and most of the operating costs are not capable of allocation to various services, except in an arbitrary manner. Further even the approximate cost can be determined only after the service has been rendered; but the rates have to be fixed in advance. The charges are calculated on certain assumptions and if those assumptions prove wrong, the calculations will also be upset. Sir William Acworth states, "Even if it were, which it is not, possible to say what it would cost to carry X units of traffic, no one could so fix a rate as to obtain precisely that cost plus a determined percentage of profit, because the percentage of profit varies enormously according as the actual volume of traffic carried recedes on the one side or the other from the assumed volume X".[5]

Joint Products

The difficulty in ascertaining the cost of service is enhanced because the railway services are joint in nature. The various railway services are very similar to the production of a number of commodities by a single plant simultaneously at joint and indistinguishable costs. A railway train, for example, carries a heterogeneous merchandise and differently graded passengers and the cost of moving a single commodity or passenger is indeterminable. Some railway services may be joint products in the strict sense of one service being the necessary complement of another. "A service of trains in one direction implies a corresponding service in the opposite direction; the two services are joint products and the expenses arising out of the provision of the particular services have to be shared between them in the manner which proves more expedient. If the demand for accommodation is much smaller in one direction than in the other, the bulk of the expenses will have to be borne by traffic moving one way. When it is a question of filling wagons which must otherwise be returned empty, any rate which more than covers the difference in expense between running them full or running them empty is better than no rate, provided there is not much delay in securing the freight and it may pay to quote specially low rates to obtain return traffic".[6]

The cost of transport is the result of manifold conditions under which the transport business is done and hence it is variable. The rate charged itself affects the cost of transport service. To base rates entirely on cost would, therefore, be tantamount to trying to find one unknown quantity by using another.

The mode of packing affects the cost of carriage. Sir William Acworth points out that, "hay as cut from the stack and hand-trussed loads so badly that an ordinary wagon is generally full with little over 30 cwts.... When hay is compressed with a hand machine, 80 cwts. can be loaded in a wagon, whilst when the hay has been hydraulic press packed a wagon will hold at least 3 tons".[7] Thus the charges will differ even in case of a single commodity, say hay, if they are based on the cost of service principle.

The cost of carriage depends on whether the traffic is conveyed by express or by slow train and the distance over which it is carried. No doubt, the working expenses increase with an increase in the distance covered but they do not increase proportionately. A longer haul utilises the rolling stock more effectively than a shorter haul. Acworth states, "Long hauls get more mileage out of engines, wagons, train staff, etc., than a number of short hauls, necessarily with waits between; engines and wagons are better loaded and the lines are more continuously utilised".[8]

The cost of service differs even in case of physically similar services if they are rendered at different times and seasons of the year. A certain amount of equipment is required to meet the normal demand of traffic and thus would be fully utilised because that amount of traffic will be available at all times. But if there is rush of traffic during certain hours of the day, additional equipment will be required to handle it and this additional equipment will not be fully utilised during normal hours. Special suburban trains are run, for instance, at the time of the opening and closing of factories and these trains are not used for the rest of the day. The cost of service principle would suggest that the expenditure incurred in running such trains should be borne by the traffic for which the provision is made. According to this principle, the fares for travel during busy seasons and at busy hours of the day should be higher than the fares charged at normal times. The phrase 'cost of service' is itself not unambiguous. It may refer to marginal cost or the average cost.

The cost of service principle pays attention only to one side of the problem, that is, the supply side. It does not take into consideration the factors that influence the demand side. Thus the rates based on purely the cost of service have no relation to the capacity of the article to bear it. Cheap articles, which constitute the bulk of commodities seeking transport, will not be able to bear such rates. The 'cost of service' principle will also discourage long distance traffic. Thus it will adversely affect the total tonnage available to railways and thereby the development.

If the charges are based on the cost of service principle, these would vary from place to place, from railway to railway and from year to year. A changing railway rate structure is not congenial to the growth of industry. It creates uncertainty and the traders are not able to ascertain beforehand the transportation expenses. A system, however justified it may be on theoretical grounds, cannot be approved if it adversely affects the economy.

The above analysis shows that it is impossible to fix railway charges entirely on the basis of the cost of service. In the words of Sir William Acworth, "The nature of railway business being what it is, rate fixing cannot be an exact science; to claim that rates shall automatically be fixed on the cost of carriage, is to claim what is impossible".[9] The U.S. Inter-State Commerce Commission observed, "The rates and charges of a railroad cannot be based entirely on the cost for each particular character of service rendered".[10]

In spite of its limitations, the cost of service principle cannot be ignored completely. Since the railways operate under partially monopolistic conditions, the cost of service principle must be kept in view to safeguard the public from the vagaries of the railway authorities who may justify unduly high rates on the principle of value of service. Similarly, it is very useful in providing the lower limit below which the rates should not be fixed because every service must pay at least its out-of-pocket expenses. It checks the uneconomic use of transport service. Railways are a commercial undertaking and the capital invested in it must be remunerated at the normal rate of interest. "All the rates must among them cover all the expenses and leave, if possible, sufficient margin to pay interest on capital at the normal rate. *Inter se*, the rate must be so adjusted that each item of traffic bears its fair share of the total cost of the entire railway service".[11]

Value of Service Principle

The value of service is represented by the difference between the value of a particular commodity before transportation and after transportation. "While the producer will not sell his product below his cost of production, the buyer will not pay more than the utility he derives from the product. The utility determines one's ability to pay. In case of goods, the ability to pay depends mainly on their value while that of the passengers depends largely on their income. Goods of small value and passengers with low incomes cannot afford to pay high charges. The value of service may be very high for a particular businessman but he may not be willing to pay full for it if alternative means of transport are available to him. In such cases the railways cannot charge what a person can bear but only what he is willing to bear.

If the demand for railway service is adequate, the rate or fare, according to this principle, would touch the maximum limit. "Measured objectively, the value of service is equivalent to the maximum demand price or the highest rate can be charged without destroying traffic".[12] The principle of value of service gives rise to differential charging. According to Prof. Pigou, it is a discriminating monopoly of the third order.[13]

We saw that the cost of service principle over-emphasizes the supply side of the railway services and errs by completely ignoring the demand side. In contrast, the value of service principle lays undue emphasis on the demand aspect and errs on the other side by ignoring the supply aspect.

In fact both the principles are necessary for determining the railway fares and freights. The cost of service principle prescribes the lower limit of the charges while the value of service principle lays down the upper limit. A via media between the cost of service principle and the value of service principle is the principle of "charging what the traffic will bear". Sir William

Acworth explains this principle as follows: "The total railway revenue is made up of rates which, in the case of traffic unable to bear a high rate, are so low as to cover hardly more than out of pocket expenses; which in the case of medium class traffic, cover both out of pocket-expenses and a proportionate part of the unapportioned cost; and which finally in the case of high class traffic, after covering that traffic's own out of pocket expenses, leaves a large and disproportionate surplus available as a contribution towards the unapportioned expenses of the low class traffic, which such traffic itself could not afford to bear".[14] All rates, however, must cover all costs, if possible, including interest charges on capital at the normal rate. *Inter se*, the rates should be so adjusted that each item of traffic bears its fair share of the total cost of the entire railway service.[15]

The principle of what the traffic will bear has important benefits and has, therefore, been adopted in almost all countries of the world. In some cases, it makes possible the construction and operation of railways on a self-supporting basis where it would not be possible otherwise. In all cases, it enables the railways to carry far more traffic than would be possible otherwise. It enables the commodity to move freely with the least burden on the producer and the consumer and thus promotes a free flow of traffic. In the words of Sir William Acworth, "It is a principle not of extortion but of equitable concession to the weaker members of the community".[16]

The fixing of reasonable rates is a very difficult and complicated task. The varying conditions requiring a constant adjustment in the charges in a dynamic economy makes the task still more difficult and complicated. Dr. Johnson states, "The task of fixing a reasonable rate is at once most delicate and difficult, and those entrusted with the task of rate making can do no better than make tentative experiments, each step being a milestone in the progressive realization of maximum satisfaction. Rate making in a dynamic society presents new problems of ever increasing complexity. Categorical generalisations are impracticable. Indeed, there cannot be any one rate said to be fair in all cases and at all times; it varies in different cases and at different times".[17]

Differential Rates

The value of service is not uniform to different passengers and traders. Differential rates have, therefore, been applied all over the world. The broad principle underlying the system of 'differential charging' is that since the railways operate under conditions of increasing returns and every increase in traffic tends to reduce costs, it is in the interest of railways to carry all types of traffic.

The differential rates are in everybody's interest. It "leads to the achievement of the Hedonistic ideal of the greatest good for the largest number".[18] The low traffic gains, because without discriminations it will probably not be carried. It is in public interest because new traffic is created. High class traffic gains, because in the absence of low class traffic it would have to bear a greater share of the standing charges. The railway industry is also benefited because discrimination increases traffic which facilitates the operation of the law of decreasing costs. In the words of Tiwari, "It has been rightly said that the cost of carriage is a function of the rates, not the rates of costs".[19] The principle of 'differential charging' is very equitable insofar as the rich passengers, valuable freight traffic with the advantage of geographical situation close to the markets and the like contribute of their abundance while poor third class passengers, bulky articles of small value, traffic which has to move a long distance to find its market and so forth have to pay less on account of their poverty. According to Ripley, "where, for example, articles representing different stages of manufacture have to be graded, it is but fair that the raw material or partly made product should be graded lower than the finished article. Similarly, articles which may fairly be substituted for one another ought to be classified with reference to their common market value. The relative value of commodities, as controlling classification, clearly governs the treatment of hard and soft coal".[20] In the words of Tiwari, "A well thought out pattern of discrimination based on a detailed and careful statistical analysis of traffic should be an integral part of the modern rate structure".[21] He further remarks, "Discrimination is essential in rate making to promote fuller and effective utilisation of the railroad plant and a more rapid economic development of the country. The practice of local discrimination is, therefore, desirable, so long as the rate quoted is sufficient to meet the marginal cost of transport and leaves a surplus to defray the fixed costs".[22] In the words of Bigham and Roberts, "An equalisation of rates on all articles would discourage the movement of basic commodities and stimulate the transport of so-called luxuries. The raw materials of industry could move only short distances, despite the circumstances that these materials are frequently far removed from the centres of manufacturing. If the present rates on the products of mines were raised to the average level of all rates, the long distance transportation of mineral products would be practically destroyed."[23] Professor Edgeworth observes, "I am therefore confirmed in the deduction that discrimination accompanied with a moderate control is likely to be better, both for the customers and the monopolist, than monopoly forbidden to discriminate".[24] This method has been found as a result of empirical working for years. It is a practical solution of an otherwise insoluble problem.

Conditions Facilitating Discrimination

Discriminatory prices are charged successfully for the products whose production is subject to decreasing costs. Railways satisfy this condition up to the saturation point. With the increase in railway traffic, the cost per unit of traffic declines. The railways, therefore, try to increase traffic by adopting discriminating rates.

Secondly, discrimination is possible where the demand for the product or service is elastic. In railways, a small reduction in charges leads to a considerable increase in traffic not only of those commodities that are carried by some other agency but also of those commodities which would, otherwise, not have been moved at all.

Factors Determining Classification

It is not possible to have a separate charge for each commodity and, therefore, with a view to facilitate railway charging, a large variety of commodities are grouped into classes. Proper classification of goods is very important for determining suitable freight charges. In the words of Acworth, "the classification of goods is the foundation on which the edifice of railway rates is built up, it is the framework to which the tariffs or schedules of the rates are attached".[25] A wrong classification will not only do injustice to the public but would also be inimical to the growth of the undertaking itself.

The intention in grouping various goods is to charge a different rate for goods falling in each class. The conditions which govern the railway rates, therefore, must be taken into consideration in determining the classification of goods. On the demand side, the ability to pay, roughly indicated by the value of the article concerned, is the most important factor. The higher the value of the article, the higher would be the rate applicable to it. Thus cheap articles like cattle fodder, waste material, bricks, cement, iron, agricultural commodities, etc. are put into categories bearing low rates while costly articles like fine cloth, luxury goods, motor cars, petrol, furniture, etc. are made to bear high freights. Different rates are charged for hard coal and soft coal. Similar is the case with paper bags, gunny bags, canvas bags, cloth bags and leather bags. In the same way different rates are charged for lac bangles, wood bangles and ivory bangles. In case of cheap articles like bricks, freight forms an important part of the total cost and, therefore, a higher freight rate would tend to check consumption by raising the price. In the words of Douglas Knoop, "The lower the value of goods, the larger the proportion of their cost which will be represented by some particular charge for transportation; and the more easily the freight will check their sales, the smaller a passenger's income, the less the sum he can afford to pay for conveyance".[26]

Another basis of classification on the demand side is the elasticity of demand for the commodity. The demand for necessaries of life like sugar, foodstuffs and coal is comparatively inelastic and, therefore, a limited increase in freight rate for them will not much affect demand for them. In contrast, a rise in freight rate for raw materials required by industry would inhibit the movement of raw materials and manufactures and thereby the industrialisation of the country.

On the supply side, the classification is influenced by a number of factors. It is influenced by the conditions that affect the cost of handling such as bulk, fragility, liquidity, explosiveness, structure, etc. Extra care is needed to carry perishable and dangerous goods. Higher rates would be necessary for services which require special equipment. If this equipment is not used regularly, a higher rate would have to be charged for each act of service.

Articles large in bulk but light in weight cost more to carry. Consequently, light and bulky articles are placed in a class bearing a higher rate. In the words of Locklin, "The cost of transporting the light and bulky commodity is greater per unit of weight than the cost of transporting the heavier ones. More equipment is needed to carry a given weight of the lighter commodity; more switching may be necessary and more yard space required to take care of it. More dead weight must be transported, furthermore, since the weight of the car is greater in proportion to the weight of the contents".[27]

Consideration is given to the liability to damage. With certain exceptions, the railways are responsible for the loss or damage of goods entrusted to their care. Goods which are more easily liable to damage require more careful handling which costs more. Because of this consideration and the actual compensation claims which are likely to arise in spite of all cares and precautions, such goods are placed in a class bearing a higher rate. The liability to damage may arise due to a number of factors. The commodity may be liable to breakage. It may deteriorate in quality in the course of the transit because of its perishable nature. Inflammable or explosive goods are also placed in a higher class. Such articles are not only easily liable to damage but also a source of danger to other goods carried in the same train. A reduced rate is granted if the commodity is carried at owner's risk.

Good packing not only reduces the risk of damage but also facilitates handling and enables better loads to be obtained. The method of packing determines the maximum load that can be carried by a wagon. Commodities are normally charged a higher rate if they are transported in crates than in boxes. The better the packing, the lower the class in which the article is placed. But in some cases better packing may be because of the high value of the article. In such cases the better packed article will be placed in a higher class.

The cost of carriage differs according to the size of the consignment. Other things remaining the same, the cost of carrying small consignments would be more than that of large consignments. Handling of small consignments involves additional expenditure by way of separate collection, delivery, invoicing and accounting, etc., at the terminal stations. In the words of Acworth, "Small consignments mean to a railway several distinct sources of serious additional expense; separate collection and delivery, separate handling, invoicing, accounting, etc., at the terminal stations; bad loading in the railway wagons, probably one or more transhipments enroute and extra liability for loss or damage".[28] In contrast, if the size of the consignment is large and such consignments are moved in wagon-loads, the railway has nothing to bother about their handling which becomes the responsibility of the consignor and the consignee. A good wagon load reduces the amount of tare weight to be hauled in proportion to paying load. This is particularly important in case of commodities which cannot be loaded in the same wagon.

The classification is influenced by the time within which the traffic is to be conveyed. The longer the time for which the traffic can be held up after it has been delivered for conveyance, the better the load that can be obtained and the more economically the service can be rendered.

In case of commodities which are dispatched more or less regularly, there is tendency to place them in classes bearing comparatively lower rates than those charged for commodities which are moved only occasionally because the former traffic enables a better utilisation of the capacity than the latter.

The articles which compete with, or are substitutes for, each other have a tendency to be placed in the same class. For instance, various types of raw materials for paper—esparto grass, wood pulp and rags—are placed in the same class provided they conform to certain conditions of packing, etc.

The classification is influenced by the type of wagon required for conveying the traffic because it affects the investment required for rendering the service. Some commodities are sent in closed wagons, others in open trucks, still others in especially constructed wagons. Open wagons are used for the movement of timber, wood, coal, girders, stones, etc. Foodgrains, sugar, cotton, cloth, machines, books, etc., are sent in closed wagons requiring a comparatively larger investment. Such commoditities are, therefore, placed in a higher class. Commodities requiring special services like refrigeration, icing, ventilation, etc., are placed in a still higher class because they are moved in specially constructed freight cars.

Competition between carriers also influences the class in which an article is placed. In case of some commodities, particularly for short distances, there exists competition between railways, waterways and road transport. Articles which can be attracted by alternative means of transport are normally placed in a lower class than those commodities which do not enjoy the benefit of altenative means of transport.

To decide the classification of an article, in the words of the Inter-State Commerce Commission, the railway authorities must consider, "Whether commodities are crude, rough or finished; liquid or dry; knocked down or set up; loose or in bulk; nested or in boxes; or otherwise packed; if vegetables, whether green or dry; desiccated or evaporated; the market value and shipper's representation as to their character; the cost of service, length and direction of haul; the season and manner of shipment; space occupied and weight; whether in car-load or less than car-load lots; the volume of annual shipments to be calculated on; the sort of car required, whether flat, gondola, box, tank or special; whether ice or heat must be furnished; the speed of trains necessary for perishable or otherwise rush goods; the risk of handling, either to the goods themselves or other property; the weights, actual and estimated; the carrier's risk or owner's release from damage or loss".[29]

The classification of goods is a very delicate and complicated problem and cannot be done by a mechanical application of a few general principles of the nature discussed above. It grows as a result of experience and is always in a process of evolution in the light of further experience.

There are a number of systems of charging rates, viz. zone system, the postal principle, the flat or horizontal or equal mileage rate, the tapering or the telescopic system. We briefly examine below the relative merits and demerits of these systems.

Zone System

Under the system, the entire railway area is divided into certain zones. There is only one charge within a single zone irrespective of the distance travelled by the traffic. The rate changes only when the traffic enters a different zone. At the time of the centenary of Indian Railways, the zone system of fares was introduced in India for passenger traffic for a few months. The whole country was divided into six zones and the fare for each zone for 15 days was fixed at ₹ 30. Within the prescribed time, a zone ticket-holder was entitled to travel anywhere within the zone. This facility was much appreciated by the tourists.

In fact, every railway undertaking adopts the zone system of charging to some extent. Generally, the zone is of one mile but in some countries, particularly for long distance traffic, the zone ranges from 3 to 5 miles for passenger as well as for goods traffic. The zone is of one mile in India; for any fraction of a mile, the traffic has to pay the charge for full one mile.

The zone system has the advantage of simplicity. It is easy to remember the charges when there is only one charge for traffic within a zone. There is no need to maintain an elaborate rate book. It simplifies checking of tickets and economises printing and account-keeping.

The charge within the zone is based roughly on its average distance. As a result, the short-distance traffic has to pay more than its due share while the long-distance traffic pays less. The zone system assumes that the long-distance as well as short-distance traffic would be forthcoming so that the losses on the long-distance traffic are offset by profits on the short-distance traffic. In practice, however, the system discourages short-distance traffic and encourages long-distance traffic. The result is that the traffic which brings profits to the railways decreases while that which brings losses increases. This may necessitate a revision of the charges which would further discourage profit-yielding traffic and encourage traffic involving losses. The continuous repetition of this process may ultimately lead to a giving up of the zone system of charging.

Postal Principle

This system treats the entire country as a single zone and a single rate is charged within the whole country irrespective of the distance travelled by the traffic. It is commonly used by the postal department for carrying letters, parcels and packets. This system also encourages long-distance and discourages short-distance traffic. It favours travellers of long-distance at the cost of the travellers of short-distance. People would prefer to use rail transport for long distance and alternative modes of transport for short distance and consequently the traffic which brings losses would decrease and that which brings profits would increase.

This system of charging rates is more suitable for postal services than for railways. In the case of a letter, the cost of transit is a very small part of the total cost. The major part of the cost is incurred in collection, sorting and delivery which is invariant of the distance. In contrast, the major cost of passenger and goods traffic is that of conveyance. This system of charging rates, therefore, has been abandoned all over the world.

Equal Mileage Rates

Under this system, the charge is directly proportional to the distance. The principle is very simple to understand. Even a layman can calculate the charges that he would have to pay for his traffic. To that extent it promotes trade and business. It eliminates scope for discrimination. Discrimination, though an important instrument of betterment, is often misused and thus leads to distrust. To a common man this system appears to be quite fair. In fact, it is not very fair because the cost of conveying traffic does not increase in direct proportion to the distance. The longer haul obtains a better utilization of rolling stock and spreads the terminal expenses over a greater mileage and, therefore, is less costly as compared with the shorter haul. It is thus quite reasonable that declining rates should be charged for every increase in distance. Equal mileage rates would discourage long distance traffic, particularly in case of cheap articles where the freight charges constitute an important portion of the total cost.

This system does not take into consideration the physical conditions of railway operation. The cost of operation, for instance, is higher in hilly areas than in plains. It would cost much more to haul a ton of goods a mile on a steep ascent than to haul the same on level ground. Under such conditions equal mileage rates will not be just.

The biggest defect of this principle is that it does not take into consideration "the ability of commodities to pay". It penalises movement of goods of low value. Commodities like coal which have low value and large bulk will not be able to bear large expenses involved in long haul and would thus not reach distant markets. According to S.R.N. Badri Rao, the system is "harsh, inflexible and untrue to actual conditions; it claims to be stabilising agent, but this very merit is its chief drawback; it penalises the movement of some commodities and tends to prevent the utilisation of the most economical means of transport. Above all, it is a restricting influence and tends to crib, cabin and confine transportation within a small area".[30]

Tapering System

Under this system, the charge per mile slightly decreases with every increase in distance. This system attempts to adjust long and short distance traffic rates on a fair basis. It encourages long distance traffic. Of all the systems discussed above, it is considered to be the best method of determining the railway rates. The Indian railways adopted this principle in 1955.

The Best Principle

The best principle of railway rate making is that which is evolved out of past experience. If a particular rate applied earlier does not suit the conditions and does not bring economic prosperity to the community, it must be changed. In the words of Jackman, "No matter how thoroughly conditions are studied before a new rate is made, the results of the application of the former rate must be gathered promptly and in detail, and if the outcome as shown by experience has not been satisfactory, the rate must be changed in the light of facts".[31] Similarly Professor Douglas Knoop observes, "Railway charges have been fixed by practical men feeling their way step by step with little or no reference to theoretical considerations, the system of charging so built up undoubtedly conforms to certain principles, just as a boy who learns to ride a bicycle without any lessons and in ignorance of all physical laws will, by experience, come to maintain his balance in accordance with sound principles".[32] In the words of Acworth, "In truth, though we have personified the management and imagined a man fixing the system of railway rates, no one man and indeed no combination of men, could erect such a system off hand from the foundations. It can only grow gradually, developing here and changing there, as the country itself develops and its industry and trade are modified by time and circumstances".[33]

NOTES

1. William Acworth, *Elements of Railway Economics* (1932), p. 73.
2. Jackman, *Economic Principles of Transportation* (1935), p. 102.
3. E.R. Johnson, *The Railroads and Public Welfare,* p. 157.
4. Michael E. Bonavia, *The Economics of Transport* (London, 1936).
5. Acworth, n. 1, p. 59.
6. J. Johnson, *The Economics of Indian Rail Transport* (Bombay, 1963), p. 139.
7. Acworth, n. 1, p. 122.
8. *Ibid.,* p. 54.
9. *Ibid.,* p. 58.
10. *Annual Report of the Inter-State Commerce Commission* (U.S.A.), 1927.
11. Acworth, n. 1, p. 74.
12. Bigham and Roberts, *Transportation* (1952), p. 351.
13. Pigou, *The Economics of Welfare,* p. 256.
14. Acworth, n. 1, p. 85.
15. *Ibid.,* p. 74.
16. *Ibid.,* p. 84.

17. Johnson, n. 6, pp. 142-43.
18. S.R.N. Badri Rao, *Road-Rail Transport* (1956), p. 56.
19. R.D. Tiwari, *Railway Rates in Relation to Trade and Industry in India* (Bombay, 1937), p. 23.
20. W.Z. Ripley, *Railroads—Rates and Regulations,* pp. 317-18.
21. R.D. Tiwari, *Railways in Modern India,* p. 197.
22. *Ibid.,* p. 203.
23. Bigham and Roberts, n. 12, p. 351.
24. *The Economic Journal,* 1913, p. 225.
25. Acworth, n. 1, p. 125.
26. Douglas Knoop, *Outline of Railway Economics* (1923), p. 177.
27. D.P. Locklin, *Economics of Transportation,* p. 45.
28. Acworth, n. 1, pp. 128-29.
29. Cf. Pigou, n. 13, p. 293.
30. Badri Rao, n. 18, p. 60.
31. Jackman, n. 2, p. 102.
32. Knoop, n. 26, pp. 182-83.
33. Acworth, n. 1, pp. 73-74.

5

Governing Boards

In view of the existence of the ministerial and parliamentary control over public enterprises working in pursuance of the policy already laid down by the government for the public sector, there arises the question as to what is the necessity of a Governing Board at all. Could not the policy of the government be executed through a Managing Director, or a General Manager or at best a committee of Management? The opinions in this regard differ. The opinion prevalent in the United States is that, "Congress is the overall Board of Directors; it determines the major objectives, policies and controls. Congress is analogous to the stockholders' committee of a private corporation. The Government Corporation's own Board of Directors, in contradistinction, is the operating Board of Directors, determining the minor matters of policy, organisation and control. It is analogous to the Executive Committee of a corporation".[1] The Hoover Commission on 'Federal Business Enterprise' accordingly discarded any corporate Board between Congress and the corporation's executive management and held that "where Boards or part-time Boards are established, they should be wholly advisory and be appointed by the President".[2]

But the Board has a definite role to play and cannot be dispensed with. It is neither feasible nor desirable to have all supervision from the Ministry. A public undertaking is set up with an avowed objective to carry on the project within the broad framework of the Government policy and "once that objective is given to the corporation, then how it is to be done is a matter primarily for the policy making functions of the Board of Directors".[3] The Board is needed to formulate policies for running the enterprise with a view to attain the given objectives. "As every practical observer of Government knows", observes Prof. Dimock, "there is an important area of sub-policy and decision making midway between the overall action of Congress and the point where the administration takes. It is this area that a representative and resourceful Board of Directors must occupy if Government corporations are to operate with efficiency and accountability".[4] The Board of Directors, therefore, is not a superfluous body.

The success or failure of a public enterprise depends to a considerable extent on the quality of Boards which are responsible for their direction and governance. "For, from this flow all the decisions on policy and administration which together make up good or bad management".[5] "Whatever the form", states A.D. Gorwala, "without suitable men at the highest level of management, the Governing Board or the Board of Directors, the likelihood of success is very little".[6]

It is very important to distinguish between the board of a public corporation or company and that of a private company. The directors of the latter are true representatives of shareholders while the board of a public undertaking has got much wider responsibility than the board of a private undertaking. The board of a public enterprise has to keep in view the interest of the consumers, of employers, of the government and the nation at large. The managers of a public enterprise, particularly one operating under monopolistic conditions, are in a different position from those of a private concern. "They are not solely concerned with maximising profits or even with lowering costs, but have a certain responsibility to the community at large and to the employees within the industry in their role as citizens and human beings".[7] Since such a board has to look to the interests of various parties, the nature of its composition is of paramount importance.

Functions of Boards

The important matters with which the Board of a public corporation has to deal include:[8] the appointment of the chief executive and the principal officers; the programmes of current and future output; plans for development and reorganization; major projects for new equipment; relations with Ministers on matters of policy; the consideration of serious criticism by Parliament, consumers or the public and the action to be taken; the result of negotiations with, or demands by, trade unions on important matters; general policy concerning finance, capital expenditure, prices, surpluses and deficits; the policy of the undertaking in staff matters, including questions of wages, incentives, morale, and consultation with employees; the promotion of further legislation (whether private or public Bills) and the attitude to be taken towards other Bills; the methods by which the corporation is to comply with ministerial directions and the attitude of the corporation to requests or proposals by Ministers; serious conflicts of interest or policy with other public corporations or with private interests; the allocation of sums to reserves, and the management of reserve funds; the action to be taken by the corporation to reduce operating deficits; the adoption of important new inventions, processes or improvements; policy on research and development, training and education. The Advisory Committee on Organization of National Coal Board in the U.K. stated that, "It is the Board's task to secure uniformly good management for various units for which they have become responsible. They must secure efficient capital development and the replacement capacity. They must see that the benefits of large-scale organization are rapid throughout the whole undertaking.... The Board must also establish for management new standards of performance since in a big undertaking, however, financial profits and losses are not by themselves a sufficient delicate instrument for measuring the success of particular units. Last, but perhaps most important of all, the Board must establish confidence, loyalty and discipline among the management team".[9]

Types of Board

A very important question is whether the Board should be a functional or policy-making one. The functional Board consists of full-time Members in charge of particular branches of the work, say, marketing or purchase of raw materials, while the policy Board consists of men, full-time or part-time, none of whom is responsible for specialised functions as an executive head. The functioning of a policy Board is of supervisory nature and the Board concerns itself merely with matters of general policy and not with operational details. As such, the Members of a policy Board are not supposed to be experts or specialists in a particular branch or line of operation in the undertaking. The Members of the functional Board are selected on the basis of their specialized knowledge and experience in a particular branch of industrial activity, e.g. production, distribution, planning and research, finance, industrial relations. In selecting Members consideration is paid not only to their ability to carry out the function assigned to them but also their ability to work as a team taking joint responsibility for operations as a whole. The Members of a Functional Board are generally full-time members and have more influence and knowledge of the enterprise's operations.

It is generally agreed that a functional Board consisting entirely of full-time Members in charge of particular branches of work is less effective as a directing organ than a policy Board which is composed both of part-time and full-time Members, none of whom are responsible for specialized functions as executive heads. In a functional Board, the Directors being too much engrossed in departmental details are apt "to see only the trees and not the forests".[10] In contrast, the policy Board watches the affairs of the enterprise from outside with a more comprehensive outlook and larger vision and then advocates the policy. In the words of A.D. Gorwala, "the members of a policy board not immersed in detail are perhaps better able to see the picture as a whole and to take broad decisions".[11] In a functional Board the instructions flowing down "a series of parallel vertical pipes from each functional member would not only sometimes be difficult of co-ordination but may tend to split up the undertaking into a number of specialised 'empires' and the replacement of one clear line of command by a series of parallel and unrelated ones".[12] The functional Board involves the danger that the decisions may be arrived at by a process of rather unprincipled compromise along the lines of "I will support what you want if you will support what I want".[13]

The current thinking almost all over the world has a tendency to prefer 'policy Boards' to 'functional Boards'. In Canada, Prof. Hodgetts observes, "the tendency seems in favour of which Prof. Robson calls the 'policy' Boards rather than the 'functional' Board".[14] In Japan, the Board of Directors is a "policy determining body".[15] In France, "the governing Board is supposed to decide all major questions of policy".[16] In Asia and Far East region, the general view is against the 'functional' type Boards which have been held "as a rule, undesirable".[17] In India, the opinion is overwhelmingly in favour of policy Board.[18]

The National Coal Board (NCB) in the United Kingdom provides a conspicuous example of gradual transformation of functional Board into a policy Board. The NCB was set up in 1946 with all Members serving on a full-time basis. Each Member was incharge of an executive department such as production, marketing, finance, manpower and welfare, labour relations and scientific research with the exception of the Secretariat and the Legal Departments which were not headed by Board Members. The transformation resulted from the recommendations of the "Burrows" Committee. The Amendment Act of 1949 incorporating the recommendations of the Committee provided for an increase in the Members of the Board from nine to twelve and for appointment of two Members as Deputy Chairmen. The Act also provided for appointment of part-time Members and laid emphasis on the policy Board. Subsequently, the NCB introduced "a blend of departmental and non-departmental functions such as are found in latter-day cabinets".[19] Finally, the process was completed by the reorganisation of the Board following the recommendations of the Fleck Committee in 1955. The Committee stated, "It is essential that all Members of the Board should be capable of taking a wide view on all the issues which the Board have to decide. This quality must not only be present, it must be exercised all the time. Nevertheless, a full-time Board Member can and should be given a field of responsibility and interest, of which he should have a greater and more detailed knowledge than the Board as a whole can have. With a Board organised in the way we propose there would always be at least one Member of the Board who, when a particular question arose at the Board table, had a sphere within which that question obviously and naturally lay".[20] The reorganisation somewhat restored the functional principle to predominance but essentially maintained the character of a policy-making Board as under the revised arrangement each full-time Member was given a special field of responsibility without, however, being the head of the department. This position of a Member is similar to that of the Executive Director of the modern type of Boards in commercial organisations. This is the emerging pattern of the organisation of Board in nationalised industries in Britain. There is a blend of full-time and part-time Members, the former having specific fields of responsibility without being the heads of the departments and the latter being men of wide experience to bring fresh air into the organisation with "a more detached view".[21]

The policy Board, however, is not free from defects. It has its own shortcomings. In a policy Board, those who are responsible for the formulation of policy are not responsible for carrying it out. If the Board itself have to carry out the policy formulated by it, it would probably be more careful and realistic than when execution is the responsibility of someone else. There may also arise some hostility between the Board and the executive management. "The Board may tend to regard the executive management as a rather naughty boy and the management to regard the Board as an ignorant nuisance. That sort of situation can arise, and has arisen".[22]

The policy Board has been criticized on the ground that "if its members consist only of non-specialist administrators, there is a danger that technical advice may be rejected by men who do not understand its nature. If, on the other hand, they do have specialized knowledge, they must either take a day-to-day interest in the work of specialist department in which case the

Board would be 'functional' in fact, if not in name, or there would be nothing for them to do except get in each other's way".[23] In a policy Board composed of only non-specialist administrators, "there is always the feeling that technicians are being over-ruled by people who do not understand technical matters".[24] There is also the danger of political appointments of persons who do not possess requisite qualifications. In a policy Board, it is difficult to fix responsibility for any adverse results. In a functional Board, each Member is in charge of a particular field of activity and any credit or discredit directly goes to him unless the result is a consequence of any direction from the top.

In the present scheme of things where policy is laid down by the government and important powers of financial control are either reserved to the government or in reality come to be exercised by the controlling Ministry, the role of the policy-making Board becomes somewhat ambiguous and atrophied. It cannot deal with high policy matters because these are a prerogative of the government. It cannot deal with day-to-day matters which lie within the jurisdiction of the Chief Executive. It is because of this that the policy-making Boards have invited the criticism of being ineffective and even redundant.

In fact, the type of Board that would be more suitable differs from enterprise to enterprise, depending primarily on the nature of its functions and its size. In case of a finance institution like the State Bank of India, for instance, a policy Board may be more advantageous but a functional Board may be preferable in case of industrial or commercial undertakings where technicality of operation is involved requiring responsible handling of policy matters and execution thereof. For major public undertakings, be it a multipurpose project or railway, a functional Board with a few full-time Members would be preferable while in case of small sized enterprises, the management may be carried on by a managing director and a policy Board may be set up to advise him on various issues of policy and procedural aspects.

In most of the cases, a combined type of Board would be more effective than either an exclusively policy Board or functional Board. In such a Board there should be a few full-time Members holding executive charge of some departments and a large number of part-time Members having no departmental responsibility. This type of Board would have to a considerable extent the benefits of both the policy and functional Boards.

A study of the composition of governing Boards of public enterprises in India shows that, by and large, the policy-making type of Board has been preferred to the functional type. There are also a few cases of mixed type of Boards having both full-time and part-time Directors. Generally, these Boards have a full-time Chairman who is also the Managing Director, as in the case of Bharat Heavy Electricals Ltd., Bhopal and the Neyveli Lignite Corporation, and, in a few cases, a part-time chairman with a full-time Managing Director as in the case of the Bharat Electronics, Hindustan Aeronautics Ltd., etc. Barring a few exceptions, all Directors except the Chief Executive on the Board serve part-time and are representatives of the Central Ministries, and, in a few cases, of the State Governments. There are also a few non-officials who serve as part-time members of the Board. The controlling Ministry and the Ministry of Finance are almost invariably represented on the Board.

Size of Boards

No hard and fast rules can be laid down as to the size of the Board for public enterprises. The Board should neither be too small to be dominated by a single man nor too large so that its Members can "become a genuine team".[25] In the words of a business executive, "a board should not have so many directors as to make free discussions impossible, nor so few that the necessary breadth of viewpoint is not obtainable".[26] The Estimates Committee has advocated for a Board of three or four Members, one being the Chairman.[27] The Krishna Menon Committee has recommended a small Board consisting of five to nine Members depending upon the size and nature of the enterprise.[28] According to Gordon, "the most satisfactory Board is small, containing from five to nine members".[29] Prof. Robson is in favour of "flexibility of members" for "Ministers to have a certain latitude in determining the size of the Board".[30] The functional Board with full-time members, would, however, obviously have a smaller number of Members than the policy making Board consisting of both full-time and part-time Members.

Public corporations of a financial nature generally have large boards.[31] The Central Board of the Reserve Bank consists of one governor, three deputy governors, eight directors nominated by the Central Government, four nominated from four local boards and one Central Government official.[32] In the State Bank, in addition to a Chairman, vice-chairman and two managing directors, six directors are appointed by the shareholders, eight by the Central Government, one by the Reserve Bank and one is a Central Government official.[33]

In England, the various Acts simply indicate the lower and upper limits of the number of Members that the Board can have and the Minister is free to appoint any number of Members within these limits. Such flexibility is advantageous to the Minister who can, if need arises, add more Members to the Board to get his policies adopted. This way of getting the thing done is easier than the dismissal of a Board or a Member, or even giving a directive to the Board.

The Acts of various public enterprises in India do not allow such flexibility. Normally, a specific number is laid down in case of statutory corporations while no such number is provided for enterprises set up under the Joint Stock Companies Act. In government companies, the most usual provision is, as in Sindri Fertilizers, that "the President shall from time to time determine in writing the number of the directors of the company".[34] The Articles of Association of the Hindustan Steel (brought under Steel Authority of India Ltd. in January 1973), however, provide that the board shall consist of not less than six and not more than twelve directors.[35] In case of Bharat Electronics Ltd.[36] and the National Research Development Corporation,[37] there is no minimum limit but the maximum is of nine.

Thus, no uniform pattern exists in the Indian system of Board of Directors in public enterprises. Some Boards are very compact consisting of full-time Executive Directors, with a few nominees of the government. Generally, where consumer interests are required to be protected, Boards are made large with representation of non-official, political and consumer interests.

Appointment of Civil Servants on Boards

A proper composition of the Board is very important for the success of a public enterprise. An undertaking which calls for "energy, drive, enterprise and specialised management" must have a competent Board for conducting it successfully.[38] Herbert Morrison remarked that the Board should be composed of "the best brains that we can secure" and for this "we must insist upon all the members being persons of business ability and capacity".[39]

There has been a lot of controversy as to whether the Directors should be selected from civil servants or from private sector or from specialists in professions. In fact, the criterion should be, on the one hand, to have a team of able and honest persons who could work in a co-operative manner and, on the other hand, to have only such persons and from such ranks that the autonomy of the Board is not impaired. A.D. Gorwala made two broad statements in regard to the composition of Boards. Negatively, the composition should not be such as to obscure the essential condition of autonomy. It should not give rise to overlapping of responsibility or lead to introduction of control and interference by the back door. Positively, the composition of the Board should be such as to subserve only one purpose, that is, good and efficient direction in the public interest. Three things follow from the first principle. In the first place, to avoid overlapping of responsibility and to maintain integrity of political life, membership of the Board should be closed to certain categories of persons, e.g. M.Ps., M.L.As., V.I.Ps., etc. Secondly, the Ministers should be excluded from the membership. Thirdly, departmental representatives and display directors should have no place on the Board because their presence often leads to control and interference by the back door which impairs the autonomy of the enterprise.

These principles, unfortunately, have not been implemented in India. The membership of the Board is open to M.Ps. and M.L.As. The Ministers, Secretaries and departmental representatives are appointed as Chairmen and Members of the

Board in their ex-officio capacities. In all boards, the government is directly represented by a Director nominated by the administrative ministry concerned and a Director nominated by the Ministry of Finance. These government nominees undoubtedly carry prestige and prerogative which makes their role extremely critical and sensitive. However, a great deal depends on the personality of such directors and the equations they are able to make with their other colleagues on the boards.

A number of reasons have been advanced in support of appointing secretariat officials on the boards. The major reason usually put forward is that the entire or major part of the capital is provided by the Government and, therefore, it is natural for the enterprise to be run by a Board consisting all or mostly of officials. It is argued that "the presence of some officials on the Board of Directors is necessary as the majority of the matters which come up before the Board have financial implications and an impact on Government policies regarding equipment. The association of Secretariat officials, therefore, helps in taking decisions and in accelerating matters."[40] During the early phases of their development most public enterprises were not self-sufficient financially or otherwise, so it was considered convenient to associate officials who had a hand in negotiation with foreign collaborators. Some of the enterprises were set up primarily to supply goods to government departments and not for sale to the public; for this reason, the user departments were represented on the Boards. The presence of the Secretary on the Board was considered desirable particularly in the early stages of nationalisation to ensure proper planning, unity of purpose and co-ordination between the Ministry concerned and the nationalized undertaking. Non-officials, on the other hand, might not have either the necessary time or the necessary enthusiasm to attend to the affairs of the concern because they have hardly any financial stake in it. In some concerns, like defence industries, the production is of secret nature and association of non-officials in such concerns may not be in the national interest.

The arguments mentioned above from government side for appointing the officials on Boards may be helpful in some respects but in no way override the formidable disadvantages inherent in such an arrangement. The official element increases ministerial interference. The official Chairman and the Members of the Board cannot devote adequate time to the enterprise. Experience shows that the civil servants in the performance of their dual role have more allegiance to the department than to the public enterprise. In such cases in Board meetings generally "the agenda is run through, each officer giving his department's point of view and then hurrying back to his post of duty"[41]

A Board consisting of government officials may not be successful in operating an enterprise on business principles. The appointment of government officials on the Board has tended to blur the Secretariat functions of laying down policies and the executive functions of implementing them, "...the association of Secretariat officials with the Board of Directors had blurred the responsibilities of the Company and the Government inter se and had thereby vitiated the very purpose of forming a company. It had also, to a large extent, come in the way of an objective examination of the proposals of the Board by Government, especially in cases where the secretary of the Ministry and the joint secretary (Finance) were members of the delegation of the company which negotiated a number of agreements and contracts for the projects, some of which had to be approved by Government, i.e., generally by the same persons in their capacity as advisers to Government. This would mean that Government would have to share directly a good measure of responsibility for the working of the projects."[42] To quote the Estimates Committee again, "the presence of the secretary of Government on the Board of a corporation or a public utility undertaking, particularly which runs at a loss, would only result in his becoming a party to its state of affairs and management and consequently he will find it difficult to retain an objective outlook on major issues such as the regulation and management of economic policies which a secretary to Government should possess".[43] An overwhelming majority of officials on the Board tends to develop an official outlook, characteristic of the departmental administration, and bureaucratic approach to the organizational and functional problems of a public undertaking and to that extent defeats the very purpose of constituting a company or corporation. The Estimates Committee observed with particular reference to the Bharat Electronics Ltd., "The Board of Directors should not have an overwhelming majority of officials as the presence of a large number of officials invariably tends to bring to the organisation and its functioning, an official approach of a type which is generally found in most Government Departments".[44]

The civil servants are generally characterised by excessive caution, lack of administrative vitality, negative will, desire to shirk responsibility, tendency to delay decisions, absence of adaptability and lack of drive which result in a super-structure of hierarchy, multiplication of committees and lengthening of 'red-tape'. Jawaharlal Nehru rightly remarked, "I do hope that it (state enterprise) is not going to be run by people who have worked in the ruts of the departments, but by persons of vision, push and drive; not by people who write on the files but who do the work".[45]

The civil servants cannot be expected to have the necessary technical background, neither practical experience, nor can they afford enough time to study the problems of the enterprise concerned. The frequent transfers of civil servants lead to frequent changes in the composition of the Board which impairs its efficiency.

Even in matters of safeguarding the special interests of the user departments while formulating production programme and of facilitating co-ordination between them and the company or corporation in matters of common interest, the purpose intended to be served by having their representatives on the Board can be attained by laying down specific duties and responsibilities on the Members of the Board. As regards the argument that the presence of the Secretary is necessary to deal with bilateral agreements, it may be pointed out that the execution of bilateral agreements between different countries does not necessarily involve government participation in the organisational and managerial affairs of a particular enterprise. The Estimates Committee observes, "Every international airline requires bilateral agreements to operate in foreign countries, but it does not necessarily have high Government officials on its Board of Management. Even in India, prior to nationalization, Air India International Ltd., did not have the Secretary of Communications Ministry on the Board of Directors."[46]

If a Secretary is appointed as the Chairman of a particular Board of Management, he may render both the Board and the Managing Director useless functionaries because the junior officials who are in charge of various public undertakings often find it difficult to exercise independent judgment in various matters on account of their loyalty to their senior holding posts in the Secretariat. Further, he may not be an effective Chairman of a large number of Boards of undertakings sponsored by his Ministry since it depends, among other things, "on his ability to wear two or more hats, his ability to think and act one way for a Corporation and another way for the Ministry".[47]

The Estimates Committee in its sixteenth report remarks, "The Board of Directors who have been appointed to the various public undertakings have not been fulfilling any useful role, inasmuch as they are all nominated by Government, mostly from the Government officials of the various Ministries, their powers being limited. They meet after long intervals and except for being modelled on the pattern of organization usually adopted in a Private Joint Stock Company, nothing of importance either from the point of Government or from that of the undertaking has been done by them."[48] The propriety of appointing civil servants on the Boards of public undertakings was examined at length by the Krishna Menon Committee which disapproved appointments of "Secretaries or Senior Officers of Government while they are still functioning in Government".[49] But the government did not agree with this view and the matter was referred to a committee of Central Secretaries headed by the Cabinet Secretary (Vishnu Sahay). This committee was of the view that "there should not be any objection to the appointment of officials as the Chairmen or Managing Directors of the public undertakings". In case of part-time appointment as a Director, however, the committee held that it must not go to the Secretary of the Executive Ministry. This view of the committee was endorsed by the Central Government.[50]

Appointment of civil servants on the Board is to a considerable extent a necessary evil and there is no escape from this in developing countries. It was especially so, during the Cold War years because in most developing countries there were so few other sources of people who possessed even the most elementary qualifications for membership.[51] The evil effect of this arrangement can, however, be lessened by ensuring that the persons selected have requisite qualifications and aptitude for the work entrusted to them and also that they sever their connections from the administration. Simultaneously efforts should be made to gradually replace officials by non-officials. The Estimates Committee recommended, "Keeping in view the tasks to be performed and the requirements, therefore, members of the Board of Directors might be drawn from a wide sphere than at present and more technical experts, experienced men from public life and from various non-official sources be appointed to the Board, though care would have to be taken that no one with a direct interest in the same industry in the private sector is appointed."[52]

Over several years, it has become the practice in Indian state industrial enterprises to appoint a few non-officials on the board of directors.

Appointment of Legislators on Boards

Barring the case of Damodar Valley Corporation and the Reserve Bank of India, the membership of Boards in India is not closed to the legislators. However, the appointment of legislators on the Boards has generally not been favoured. Gorwala disapproves appointment of Members of Parliament "not only in order to avoid overlapping of responsibility but also from the point of view of maintaining the integrity of political life".[53]

To keep the Board submissive to his desires, the Minister may have a tendency to appoint junior party members on the Board ignoring the qualifications of ability and experience. The junior members will not be strong enough to act independently which would lead to an impairment of the autonomy and efficiency of the enterprise.

A legislator, who is appointed on the Board of a public enterprise, would hesitate to discuss in Parliament or in public the affairs of the enterprise concerned in the manner he would have done otherwise. In the words of Hanson, "...the job of a Member of Parliament is to supervise and critcise the Boards, to judge them on their performance. That task cannot be combined with membership of the Board. You cannot attempt to supervise the organisation of which you yourself are a member without placing yourself in an extremely invidious position".[54] The reason why Members of Parliament are denied membership on committees, where there is not only an element of profit involved but other elements are involved, is that "the position of members of Parliament in such committees is very undesirable because it is a position from which they can distribute favours and patronages. "When a person who has that opportunity or that position, naturally, though the individual himself may not try to make some profit out of it, he is in a position of influence, and that position is one which makes the ordinary man in the country to look to him as a person for favours. Therefore, the voter or any member of the public is thereby affected; thus, the public interest is affected. It is undesirable in the public interests that Members of Parliament should be occupying positions of this kind which are positions of embarrassment.[55] It is feared that the appointment of legislators may lead to their decisions being influenced by the interest of their constituency instead of that of the enterprise. In the words of Hanson, "The Member of Parliament's judgment of administrative and managerial questions tends to be deflected or distorted by constituency considerations and by party loyalties. From the very nature of his job, he is very susceptible to pressures from interest groups, from his constituency, and even from individuals who want jobs for themselves or their relations. To put him on a Board, therefore, is to give him a task which he is not very well qualified to perform".[56]

On the other hand, there is another school which believes that the Members of Parliament should be permitted to serve in all capacities except where it is incompatible with their duties as Members of Parliament. In developing countries, which are short of talent and public spirit, it is not proper to exclude Members of Parliament from opportunities of service on such vital committees. With the rapid expansion of public sector, there is danger of large public undertakings becoming increasingly bureaucratic unless the Members of Parliament take an active interest in them. Further, when there is no bar on Members of Parliament in participating in private concerns, there is no reason why they should be excluded from public concerns.

The Parliamentary (Lok Sabha) Committee on offices of profits summed up its considered opinion in its Report in 1955 by stating that, "The Committee are...of the view that ordinarily Members of Parliament should be encouraged to go on such committees which are of an advisory character and represent the local or popular point of view in a manner which will effectively influence the official's point of view. Members of Parliament by virtue of their membership are in a position to say and represent certain matters with some authority and confidence, and their views are likely to go a long way in influencing the viewpoint of officials. It is at the same time felt that consistent with the above view expressed, Members of Parliament should not be permitted to go on committees, commissions, etc., which jeopardize their independence or which will place them in a position of power or influence or in a position to distribute patronage".[57] After reviewing certain public enterprises, in which the Government have complete or substantial financial interest, the Committee reached the conclusion that the Directorship of such undertakings or Membership of the administration of such undertakings should be considered as an office of profit and hence be closed to the Members of Parliament.

The British Acts have more or less uniform provisions which disqualify Members of Parliament for appointment on the governing boards of the state enterprises.

Ministers on Boards

In many countries, Ministers sit on the Boards of public enterprises, sometimes as Chairmen. This practice, however, is not considered proper on their part. The Minister has to supervise and perhaps give direction to the Board of which he is a member. It is a misapplication of a Minister's valuable time, particularly if he has a large number of Boards under his jurisdiction. It would be more useful if the Minister devotes his time to policy matters instead of going round from Board to Board. Furthermore, "if a Minister serves as a Director, he may well be placed in the equivocal position of being made a party to actions which he will subsequently have to review in his supervisory capacity, or of dealing with fellow board members whose appointment and dismissal are within his authority. Furthermore, as chairman, he will be subject to detailed questioning in Parliament concerning the day-to-day operations of the enterprise".[58] The presence of Minister on the Board will impair the initiative of other members and the collective responsibility of the Board because one member, the Minister, will be in a position to veto any decision. In the words of Hanson, "The failure of a minister to realize what this means in practice often gives him, and the enterprise, the worst of several possible worlds. By allowing himself to be persuaded to intervene in matters which ought never to be allowed to reach his desk, he frustrates the people at the lower levels, renders the pursuit of consistent managerial courses very difficult, and hinders the growth of corporate responsibility among members of the Board. The effect on managerial initiative can be particularly serious".[59]

There is inherent weakness in the conception of such Boards. When Minister is the Chairman, the other Members are likely to feel complacent over their action being shielded by the sense of having Minister by their side. Very often the responsibility of other Members is shelved and there develops a tendency to "pass the buck" to the Minister since he is a party to the decision.

The above, however, should not be taken to mean that the presence of a Minister on Board is always undesirable. The

Minister's presence on the Board may be quite useful in case of enterprises which are very important for the national economy and have wider effects. "There are certain public enterprises which exercise such wide functions, and are so important for the whole national economy, that it is convenient to have Ministers as members rather than to have a situation in which the Board takes initial decisions and sends them up for confirmation to the Minister on whose desk they may repose for a long time, and then, perhaps come back to the Board with a note of rejection, with the result that the Board has got to take amended decisions, send them up to the Minister once more, and so on. A tremendous amount of time can be consumed in that way".[60] But the Ministers should avoid sitting on the Boards of ordinary public enterprises with limited responsibilities.

Class Representation

With a view to reduce the bureaucratic tendency of the management and to produce refreshing outlook, businesslike operation, scientific organisation and creative dynamism in the management, it has been suggested that the Board of Directors should be constituted on the basis of group-representation. The supporters of class-representation on the Board of Directors envisage a tripartite arrangement of selection which gives equal representation on the Board to the representatives of the state, of the workers and of the private enterprise although sometimes voice of consumers' representation is also raised.

All such suggestions are an indication of mistrust of parliamentary system of democracy and negation of one of the fundamental principles of the Indian Constitution, that is, equal opportunities and equal rights for all citizens. In fact, they emerge from the concept of "group-interest loyalty". The danger of such an approach cannot be overemphasized from the point of view of planned economic development on a national level and the growth of the enterprise itself. It would encourage fissiparous tendencies, group consciousness to the detriment of the organisation as a whole and aggressive designs in various components of management and organisation towards each other.

The group representatives may not be able to view things objectively and dispassionately in the interest of the nation as a whole. R.A. Thornton describes the Board of "interested persons" as "an ill-digested conception of democratic perfection which advocates control by a representative of every institution, from Learned Societies to Housewives, which could conceivably claim any sort of interest in the activities of the proposed undertaking".[61] An assemblage of diverse and conflicting interests not only impairs the harmony of administrative functions but occasionally "frustration and deadlock, log-rolling and jockeying for position are much more likely to result from juxtaposition of discordant elements".[62]

This is borne out by the experience of foreign countries, particularly of France. The policy adopted in France has been of equal representation of three groups of representatives of the state, the consumers and the employees. But the experience shows that "the conception of a Board as the meeting place for the representatives of interests" is wholly mistaken. "The members of the Boards in France are all part-time and unpaid representatives of interests except the chairman and they continue to work as industrialists, trade union officials, civil servants, etc., while serving on the Boards".[63]

Representation may be given to the various interests in a condition that the undivided allegiance of the Members is not impaired thereby. The Administrative Enquiry Committee appointed by the Government of Bombay in 1948 rightly suggested that "the members of the Board should be selected on the basis of competence and ability to administer the industry efficiently in the public interest. Subject to above qualifications being satisfactory, representation may be made to the various interests concerned in the industry".[64] A successful and efficient Board must be judged by the competence and ability of its members, unity of purpose in its directions, convenience in its administration, financial viability in its planning, capacity for future development in its execution of policies, successfully co-ordinating and adjusting the working and operation of the undertaking with the national plan, undivided allegiance to the organisation over which it presides and reflecting a national personality in its imagination and outlook.

A possible composition of the Board indicated by Prof. Robson is that it should consist of (a) a person with experience in industry and commerce, (b) an ex-trade union officer of standing, (c) a former civil servant of outstanding calibre, (d) a financial expert or accountant, and (e) an engineer or scientist, "with an occasional retired General or Air Marshall thrown in".[65] In India, the Krishna Menon Committee has suggested that "a Board should consist of financial talent, administrative talent, technical skill, representative of labour and personnel management".[66]

In fact, it is not possible to lay down any hard and fast rules for the composition of Boards and much would depend on the nature of the undertaking. In a defence industry, for instance, an Army personnel would occupy an important place. In a social insurance organisation, a Trade Union official would be important. In a river valley project, the dominant position would be held by an engineer. "It is clear", observes G.D.H. Cole, "what is needed in these cases is a combination of personal qualities and of special expertness in particular fields, and that is most likely to be secured by not tying the Minister making the appointment down to any fixed formula".[67]

As a part of the process of participative management, a system of Worker-Director has been commenced in a few companies such as Hindustan Zinc and some banks. This method of the appointment of a Worker-Director without a sensitive system of participation of all levels of management may not prove effective.

Conceding representation to State Governments in the cases of single unit companies established in particular states is found useful for the solution of problems related to security, labour and infrastructural support. However, representation to nominees of State Governments should not be given in the case of major multi-unit companies whose activities are spread over the entire country and are not confined to local regions.

Whole-time or Part-time Members

The Governing Board may consist of whole-time or part-time members. The private enterprises usually have on their Board of Directors several persons whose principal contribution is simply the addition of their names to the list of directors. Because of their reputation, they help in convincing the public about the soundness of an undertaking. The addition of such dummy names and display directors is not required in public enterprises. It is highly desirable that varied talents are present on the Board who possess administrative, business, financial, and technical abilities and work with a team spirit. Ability and experience in industrial, commercial and administrative affairs should be the primary consideration in the selection of Board members. The part-time members who have other jobs to do cannot do justice to their assignments. They do not have much time to study papers and to make up their minds to arrive at decisions.

Though a full-time Board is certainly superior to a part-time Member Board, part-time membership may become unavoidable in some cases because of dearth of competent personnel to man the Boards. Part-time appointments may be necessary if the persons considered most suitable for the job are not available whole-time. The people may also be appointed part-time in the initial stages of the enterprise but when the enterprise is in full progress, it would be better to have whole-time Members. Morrison advocated part-time members for Transport Commission for their "bringing in experience from outside to prevent the Commission becoming too monastic and to bring a breath of fresh air".[68] Prof. Robson observes, "the advantage of part-time members is that they bring an element of outside experience into the higher direction and ensure that the undertaking shall not determine its policy solely in terms of its own outlook and interests", whereas "the disadvantage of part-time members is that where the service is highly technical in character or surrounded with a mass of detail not easily mastered by a cursory survey of occasional memoranda, the part-time members are unlikely to possess an adequate knowledge of the subject matter or sufficient grasp of the main problems to be able to play a part of real importance in influencing policy".[69]

The Chairman should normally be a full-time competent and really able person with confidence and drive. In some cases, appointment on a part-time basis may, however, become necessary because the really competent person for the job is not available on a full-time basis. An instance of the same can be cited as the appointment of J.R.D. Tata, a reputed industrialist, as the Chairman of the Air-India International. The Chairman, though full-time, should not be made executive head of the enterprise. He should be assigned on the one hand the more important work of supervising and influencing the work of the executive authorities and on the other hand keep informed every Member with the problems to make the Board function as a team.

Theoretically, the whole-time Board is by far the best but such a Board will have to be very small in size and lose the benefit of valuable advice and service of competent persons who cannot offer whole-time services to the enterprise. Hence, the best way is to have mixed Boards consisting of whole-time and part-time Members but the principle should be generally not to appoint any official on part-time basis with dual role to play because he must owe full allegiance to the enterprise.

Appointing Authority

The appointing authority is normally mentioned in the statute which gives birth to the enterprise. In the United Kingdom, all members of Board are appointed by the Minister. In the United States, the appointments are made by the President. In Canada, the appointing authority is the Governor-in-Council, i.e. the Cabinet. In India, the power of appointment lies with the Central Government which acts through the Minister concerned.

The Life Insurance Corporation and the Air Corporations Acts give absolute power of appointment to the Central Government. This power is slightly modified in the case of Damodar Valley Corporation where the Central Government appoints the Board after consultation with the State Governments of West Bengal and Bihar.[70] Statutorily, the Central Government is required only to consult the two Governments and is not bound to accept their recommendations. But in actual practice it becomes difficult to reject the recommendations made by the State Governments. The Central Government is the appointing authority in case of the Reserve Bank and the State Bank. Since the State Bank has also small outside participation, some directors are also appointed by the shareholders. In the case of Government companies, the Articles of Association of various companies empower the President to appoint all directors. Whether the appointment is made by the Central Government or by the President, it is, however, the concerned Minister who is responsible to the Parliament.

No doubt, the Minister has to play an important role in the field of public enterprises, it is disputable whether an individual Minister should have an absolute power to appoint and dismiss the Members according to his choice and desire. Instead of Minister's enjoying unfettered powers, it would be better if the appointments and dismissals are subjected to the approval of the Cabinet. But the purpose would be served only if the Cabinet assesses the position and justifiability of appointing or dismissing a Member and does not simply approve the actions of a particular Minister.

Appointing Procedure

As regards the procedure of appointing the Members of the Board, hardly anything is known. In the United Kingdom, the Fleck Committee recommended[71] that the Minister while appointing part-time Members to the Boards should consult leaders in various fields such as the President of the Federation of British Industries, the Chairman of the Trades Union Congress and the President of the British Employers' Confederation. The part-time Members in turn would, the Committee considered, by reason of their independent position and the knowledge they acquired of the Board's affairs, be of special help to the Minister in advising him on the appointment of full-time Members who will be drawn from within the industry itself. While it is desirable for the Minister to take maximum possible benefit of the knowledge and experience of such leaders, he should be under no statutory obligation to do so because these leaders represent sectional interests and as such in making their recommendations they may be guided by the interests of certain sections of the society and not those of the nation as a whole.

As regards the second part of the recommendation of the Fleck Committee, such a procedure would give part-time Members a privileged position as compared with full-time Members, who constitute a majority of the Board, to the extent they would have a special right of access to the Minister for this purpose which is denied to others. It would tend to divide the Board rather than unite it. This would imply that the judgment of the part-time Members concerning promotion to the highest positions is sounder than of those Members who are giving whole-time to the industry and who, therefore, have contacts with their colleagues on many other occasions than at Board meetings. Moreover, the full-time Members are expected to have a much wider and deeper knowledge of the leading executives and technical experts in the industry than the part-time Members who may rarely come into personal contact with them. This part of the recommendation of the Fleck Committee, therefore, does not appear to be very appropriate.

As less inappropriate suggestion made in a Labour Party Pamphlet is that the Minister should seek the advice of the Board in selecting a new full-time Member.[72] This pamphlet states that the Minister who appoints the Chairman and Members should have sufficient confidence in that Board to ask their advice before making a new appointment. That, however, may or may not be true. The Minister in office may not be responsible for any or some of the appointments in the Board. Even if the appointments have been made by him, he may not be satisfied with the result and in such a case he will not have much confidence in their advice. It would not be proper to bind the Minister to seek advice either from the Board or from any other body. He should be free to consult whoever he thinks can give him the best advice.

In India statutory procedure for appointments exists in the case of State Bank, where the Central Government has to consider the recommendation of the Central Board of the Bank and to consult the Reserve Bank before appointing the Chairman and the Vice Chairman.[73]

The dangers inherent in giving the Minister a completely free hand in selecting Board Members should not be ignored. In the absence of positive qualifications, the appointments may be made on the basis of other considerations like political patronage. The evil of political patronage is, at present, widely prevalent in India. The democratic governments, founded on the basis of the number of votes they can obtain at elections, are often compelled to bestow favours on those who have influence among voters and can help the government in retaining power at the event of elections. It is, therefore, essential that proper checks are devised to safeguard against the offices of public enterprises becoming places for "political favourites". In addition to evil of the political patronage, India suffers from evils of casteism, provincialism, communalism and religious fanaticism. Safeguards should be provided against such evils influencing the selection of Board Members.

In India, in the past sufficient attention has not been paid to the very important task of making appointments to the boards of public enterprises. Appointments have been made ad hoc, no effort having been made to look for persons of suitable calibre and experience before the urgent need to fill a vacancy arose. No systematic efforts appear to have been made to search all fields in which men of requisite competence and experience may have been found or to select the most competent men available for the job. It is only recently that the Department of Public Enterprises has been entrusted with the task of collecting information about the qualifications and experience of persons who may be considered for appointment to full-time posts in the Boards and at top management levels of public undertakings. Among other things, the Department is also tasked with formulation of Board structure, categorization appointment of non-official Directors and training of executives of public enterprises.

The Study Team of the Administrative Reforms Commission has suggested that a mixed type of board, having a full-time functional member, two Government representatives and a few part-time non-official members, should be adopted as the general pattern, except for the very small enterprises.[74] In regard to personnel, selections for appointment to a mixed type of board can be divided into the following three categories:[75]

1. Chairman and full-time functional members of the Board.
2. Government representatives.
3. Part-time non-official members.

Chairman and Full-time Board Members. In regard to the first category, the best situation will be one in which persons growing up from within the undertakings come to man the top posts. It is important from the standpoint of morale and incentive that every person in a public undertaking should have a reasonable expectation that if he works hard and well, he will have the opportunity to rise to the highest positions in the undertaking. The newly established public undertakings, however, would take time to produce an adequate number of experienced and senior men who are competent to take the top positions in the enterprise. Till such time, it will be necessary to draw persons from outside the public sector. This is also necessary to inject new blood into the enterprise. Men with the necessary aptitude and competence may be found from the body of government servants, leading industrialists and businessmen and professional managers and specialists in the private sector. In some of the foreign countries, particularly the United Kingdom, chairmen of public corporations are often appointed from amongst senior government servants, private businessmen and leading trade unionists; on appointment the person is required to sever his connections with his past organisation to varying degrees—the civil servants who become board members cease to be civil servants, the trade unionists give up their trade union jobs and private businessmen declare their business interests and dispose of such interests as the Minister may require. It would be useful to follow in India the practice of the

United Kingdom, particularly in case of government servants. A serving government officer will have interest at two places and will, therefore, not be able to discharge the duties of the head of an autonomous undertaking or a full-time member of the Board. At the time the government servants become eligible for such senior appointments, they would be nearing the end of their service career and, therefore, they would not be very reluctant to leave the government service on voluntary retirement terms.

Government Representatives: While appointing government representatives to the Boards of public undertakings, care should be taken that the persons nominated are not so burdened with the substantive work of the Ministry that they find it impossible to play a useful role in the Board meetings. It should not so happen that the Ministers' officials are appointed on a large number of Boards with the result that sometimes they find it impossible even to attend the meetings.

Part-time Non-official Members: While appointing part-time non-official members of the Board, care should be taken that the person selected for this purpose does not have any interest that conflicts with the commercial interest of the public undertaking on whose Board he is called upon to serve. Further, he should not be a person who has no faith in the value and role of public enterprise. The Board cannot be effective unless it functions as a team. For attaining team spirit, it is essential that the Chairman of the public undertaking should be consulted before the responsible Minister makes appointments to the Board.

Qualifications of Directors

Normally the Acts of the Corporations and the Articles of Association of companies do not prescribe any specific qualifications for the directors. This is considered to be a serious lapse and it is feared that this places excessive power in the hands of the appointing authority which may appoint persons who will always be submissive to its desires and directions.

Almost all the nationalisation Acts in U.K. provide that "Chairman and other members of the Board shall be appointed by the Minister...from amongst persons appearing to him to be qualified, as having had experience of and having shown capacity in industrial, commercial or financial matters, applied science, administration or organisation". In India also, in recent years, sufficient importance has been attached to this provision and the Articles of Association of the National Research Development Corporation of India provide that "The president shall appoint all the Directors from amongst persons having had experience in science, technology, industry, finance, commerce, administration or the acquisition or disposal of rights in inventions, but no person who is a member of Parliament or of any state legislature shall be so appointed". Such instances, however, are very uncommon and the qualifying provision has not become a normal practice of the basic Acts and the rules and regulations and articles governing state enterprises.

Instead of prescribing positive qualifications for appointment on the Boards, the Corporation Acts in India usually provide disqualifications for Membership. The D.V.C. Act, for instance, disqualifies a person for membership of the Corporation if he is a member of the Central or any state legislature. This disqualification, however, does not apply to any other corporation barring the Reserve Bank of India. Another important disqualification of a Member is the holding of any interest financial or otherwise that is likely "to affect prejudicially the exercise of performance by him of his functions as a member",[76] and if he is directly or indirectly interested in any subsisting contract with the Corporation, he is to disclose the nature and extent of his interest.[77] Most British nationalization statutes also provide that the Minister may declare the office of the Member to be vacant upon his engaging in any trade or business, becoming a director, etc., in a corporate body except in so far as the Minister may approve.[78] The D.V.C. Act, however, does not empower the government to exonerate a Member who may have a conflict of interest with the Corporation. The question of conflict of interest of the Members of the Board is, however, very delicate and difficult in the case of financial institutions. This is particularly so in case of part-time Members coming from trade and industry. This is evident from the case of the Bank of England which led to the investigation by the Parker

Enquiry Tribunal. In India also in the case of Industrial Finance Corporation, it was alleged that the interested Members on the Board expedited loan applications from some firms and provided loans to some others on insufficient security. These allegations led to the establishment of an enquiry committee.[79] The other important disqualifications are lunacy, unsound mind, insolvency, continued absence for a definite period from Board's meetings, conviction under some offence, etc.

Though there are cases of really competent persons for the job being appointed, the normal practice in India is that the majority of the Members of the Board of Directors are selected by the Minister concerned from the civil service itself without giving due weight to specific qualifications and experience in the fields of industrial activity.

It would be better if the essential qualifications for appointment are mentioned in a broad manner so as to provide some guidance to the appointing authority. If properly stated they may provide an adequately broad and well-defined sphere from which board Members may be chosen. The qualifications should not be too rigid or too vague. An instance of the latter arose in the D.V.C. At the time of the passage of the Corporation's Bill the Minister read out to the House the qualifications which in order of importance would guide the selection of the Corporation's board: (a) highest integrity and incorruptibility, (b) high intelligence, (c) clear concept of economic development of India on modern scientific lines, and (d) fairly wide experience of men and affairs. Evaluation of such qualifications largely depends upon the subjective judgment of the appointing authority and, as experience of D.V.C. shows, laying down of such vague qualifications will not serve much purpose.

In selecting members of the Board, the Minister should be guided more by consideration of their personality and ability than their party affiliation or allegiance to one or the other political group. The acid test of eligibility of a person for appointment on the Board is his successful performance in this particular line of enterprise or other fields in the past, having independent views and sense of personality not to become "the

Minister's stooge".[80] The Chairman of the Board should be not only a man of high calibre but of a towering personality to exercise the influence of his presence in the Board as well as to resist the informal ministerial views to prevail on his independent action performed in accordance with the policy of the Board. In this regard the advice given by Herbert Morrison is useful. He said, "we must insist upon all the members being persons of business ability and capacity", and "the people in charge, certainly the Chairman of the Board, must have great industrial and managerial ability, and we must be prepared to pay what is necessary in order to secure that ability, if the undertaking is to be efficient and if the ordinary work people are not to be let down by incompetent management at the top".[81]

There are, however, problems in India in selecting the right personnel not only because of shortage of talents but also because the businessmen of proved ability in the private sector are generally unwilling to work on the Board as it is believed that the Board is controlled and influenced by the Minister and Treasury to such an extent that it has hardly any autonomy. The sense of dominating position of the Minister keeps men of stature away from accepting any assignment in the public enterprises. The solution to this problem lies in broadening the outlook of the Minister in dealing with the Board, to repose confidence in the abilities of its Members and developing a free understanding between the Minister and the Board.

Appointment and Removal of Directors

In India, the right of appointing and removing directors usually vests in the Central or State Government as the case may be. In case of wholly state-owned enterprises, the directors are appointed by the President of India while in companies where the state holds a major share, this right is usually in proportion to the capital investment. In case of a mixed enterprise or joint-venture as between the Central and State Government or Governments such as the Orissa Mining Corporation (P) Ltd., the Chairman and some directors are usually appointed by the President and an equal number of directors are appointed by the Governors of the participating State Government or Governments.

For this purpose, the President as well as the Governors act through the Minister concerned. Where any private capital, Indian or foreign, participates, it may also be represented by one or two directors on the Board of Directors. The Chairman and the Directors appointed by the President or Governor hold office until removed by the President or the Governor, as the case may be, in his absolute discretion. In some cases, as the National Research Development Corporation of India, the directors hold office for a period fixed by the Articles of Association or such shorter period as the President may specify. The right of removal also lies with the appointing authority. If any Member fails in discharging his duties faithfully and diligently, he has no right to continue on the board of the enterprise. The circumstances of dismissal, however, are not uniform in different corporation Acts in India. In the Life Insurance Corporation, for instance, "the Central Government may remove any member, who, in the opinion of that Government, has so flagrantly abused in any manner his position as a member as to render his continuance as a member detrimental to the public interest".[82] In D.V.C. a Member may be removed inter alia if "he is held unsuitable to continue as a member."[83] A Member of Rehabilitation Finance Administration may be removed at any time by the Government "for any reason, which may appear to it to be sufficient."[84]

Tenure of Board Members

In regard to tenure of Board Members, there is no uniformity in the legislations creating public corporations. In the L.I.C, an official Member enjoys the office "during the pleasure of the Central Government" and a non-official Member for a period of two years "unless a shorter period is specified in the order of appointment".[85] In the State Bank of India, the Chairman and the Vice-Chairman hold office "not exceeding five years".[86] Similarly, the Reserve Bank of India Act provides for terms of office of the Governor and a Deputy Governor "not exceeding five years".[87] The terms of other Directors vary both in the State Bank and the Reserve Bank. Though the Acts provide for a term of four years, the actual tenures largely range from one to three years according to the source of their nomination. There is also provision for staggering of appointments which is helpful in maintaining a continuity of policy and administration".[88]

In government companies the directors hold office until removed by the President. In the case of the National Research Development Corporation, the directors appointed by the President hold office for a period of three years or such shorter period as the President may specify.[89]

The provisions in regard to tenure of office in other countries widely differ from those in India. In the Tennessee Valley Authority (T.V.A.), a federally owned corporation in the United States, the tenure of office is for nine years with the provision of staggering of the terms of office of the directors "designed to produce a consistency and continuity in policy which might not be possible, if the reappointment of all Directors fell at one time".[90] In contrast the D.V.C. Act does not fix any tenure and the practice is for a Member to continue unless he is withdrawn, transferred or dismissed by the government. The Members of the Air Lines Corporation in Britain hold office according to the "terms of the Instruments appointing them". Some of the Nationalisation Acts provide for the tenure to be determined by the ministerial regulations which have generally provided for the appointment to be "for such term, not exceeding five years as may be determined by the Minister before appointment of such members".[91] In Canada, the provisions in regard to tenure are not uniform. The Canadian Railway Boards provide for five-year term of office, while Members of the Wheat Board hold office on "good behaviour". The Directors of Crown companies "virtually endorse their discharge papers at the time of their appointment and the Minister is free to remove them at any time".[92]

The tenure of office of the Members of the Board should be determined judiciously. No doubt a fairly long period of tenure is necessary to provide a long range point of view to board members, a too long tenure has the disadvantage that the board may fall in a rut and may not adjust to changing conditions. The tenure of service should, therefore, aim at striking a balance between experience and new blood. While infusion of new blood from time to time is necessary, the process should not be so rapid that the past experience is not properly preserved and utilised.

In determining the term of office, one distinctive feature between the developing countries like India and the developed countries like the United Kingdom should be kept in mind. In Britain, by and large, state has acquired established and running enterprises through a process of nationalisation. But, as a matter of policy, developing countries like India have, by and large, to build new enterprises from a scratch, often, in entirely new and untrodden fields. The policies have to be evolved through a process of trial and error which takes time. Unless the Members are given a reasonable term of office to make sure of their success, they may feel shaky in their continuing in the posts over a short period or may be discouraged in experimenting with new ideas.

Some people have suggested that the Board Membership should involve a career appointment subject to good behaviour.[93] Career appointments have a serious defect that the removal of a member, if considered necessary, becomes difficult. A removal may become breeding ground for controversy which the Minister may not like to enter. In contrast, in case of a fixed term of appointment, it is easy to terminate the services of a person without creating bad blood.

A study made by the Harvard Graduate School of Business Administration shows that the Membership of boards in private corporations normally undergoes a more or less complete change within a period of about fifteen years.[94]

Closely related to the tenure of appointment is the question of eligibility for re-appointment. Absence of any restriction on re-appointment is quite useful but it is feared by some persons that this may create a false assumption and reappointments may be taken for granted. The Royal Commission on Broadcasting in Canada observed that if the practice is to re-appoint for a second and third term, it would become difficult or at least embarrassing not to offer to do so.[95] The Commission was, therefore, of the opinion that there should not be continuity for more than one term and a competent Member can always be brought back after a gap of one or two years. The Ullswater Committee on Broadcasting in the United Kingdom was also of the same opinion.[96] But if the re-appointments are made in a discriminatory manner, there is no reason to presume that the Board Members will take re-appointments for granted. Re-appointments should, of course, be restricted to exceptionally brilliant and competent persons.

Remuneration of Members

The provisions in regard to remuneration of Members are not uniform in all enterprises. Salaries and allowances paid to Members of the Boards generally vary according to the size and importance of the enterprise. Normally, non-official members hold their office in an honorary capacity. The Chairman and other Members of the Board are paid such salaries or honorarium and allowances from the funds of the undertaking as the government may decide from time to time. They are entitled to draw travelling and daily allowances for journeys performed for attending the meetings of the Board or for the purpose of discharging such duties as may be assigned to them by the Board, in accordance with the rules and orders issued by the government from time to time at the highest rate admissible to government servants of Grade I.

With a view to attract the best available persons on the Boards of state undertakings, the salaries and allowances to be offered to the Members of the Board should be sufficiently high. The salaries and allowances should be such that they provide inducement to the expert and competent administrators to join state undertakings, incentive for work, loyalty to organization, devotion to public service, uprightness and efficiency in operations and social prestige commensurate with the importance of the undertaking. The Herbert Committee Report on the British Electricity Industry observed, "If the Boards are to be run as a commercial enterprise (and we think they should) the remuneration, of the men who run these enterprises should be on a level commensurate with their abilities and their market value".[97] A.D. Gorwala has also remarked, "If good men are wanted, especially from business, there should be no objection to paying sufficiently high salaries".[98]

The salaries of chief business executives have everywhere and always been much higher than those of top government officials because of more attractive conditions of service of civil servants, e.g. security, right of pension, dignity and powers. Not only the Chairmen and the Vice-Chairmen but also full-time members of the Board (after some time) draw salaries higher than those paid to the topmost civil servants.

The entry of government as employer in industry and commerce has given rise to the problem of salary differential and the need for establishing some parity. The problem is more serious when a going concern is nationalised by the government and the salaries paid to the top executives of the concern have been much higher than those of top civil servants. If the substantially higher salaries of top officials are permitted to continue after nationalisation and top civil servants are allowed to join the same, there would develop unhealthy rivalries and competition among officials to go in for these posts and discontentment would prevail among those who fail to get them.

One approach to the problem suggested by the Estimates Committee (9th Report) is that the pay scales in the private sector should be ceiled. The argument put forward is that "should something better or more prosperous offer itself to them in private business or trade, they (top officials in the civil service) are in all probability likely to change their services for private employment. To that extent, therefore, there is depletion of competent and experienced men in the public services and those who do continue for one reason or another are constantly disgruntled or dissatisfied". The more appropriate approach would be to raise salaries of civil servants than lowering those in the private sector. In India, the pay scales even in the private sector are so low that many highly qualified and competent persons do not feel attracted to return to their country and continue serving abroad. During recent times, however, salaries in India have risen to international standards.

The best way is to establish an industrial service quite separate from the civil services. The pay scales at different levels should be fixed keeping in view the several factors affecting the willingness and efficiency of the most competent persons needed to hold the jobs. The civil service men should be free to join such a service if they are found qualified and competent and prove their worth in a field where nothing but creative ability and dynamic energy counts. Those civil servants who join the industrial service should resign from their original service.

Powers of Board

The Board occupies a mid-way position between the government and the Managing Director, who, subject to the general control of the Chairman and the Vice-Chairman of the Board, exercises such powers and performs such duties as may be entrusted or delegated to him by the Board. The Board of directors, in its affairs, is to be guided and directed by the government and certain general and specific powers have been conferred upon the directors by the statutes. Thus, the Board acts as a liaison between the government and the management. As such it has full authority for management and is responsible for the general superintendence and control of the day-to-day administration of the enterprise; but certain matters, clearly defined by the statutory regulations, are absolutely subject to the approval of the appropriate government, e.g. the borrowing powers, determination of the number of directors, appointment and removal of directors, appointment and direction of the office of the Chairman of the Board, appointment of Managing Director, convening of a general meeting of the company, and making of the regulations in accordance with the Articles of Association of the company.

Autonomy for the Board

A fairly large degree of autonomy for the Boards is essential for the efficient conduct of the public enterprises. Unfortunately, the state enterprises in India lack in autonomy. "The substance of autonomy is generally lacking and most of the defects due to that cause are present in greater or lesser degree. The best results can hardly be hoped for in these circumstances".[99]

Conclusion

The success or failure of a public enterprise considerably depends on the quality of its Board which is responsible for its direction and governance. The type of Board that would be more suitable differs from enterprise to enterprise, depending primarily on the nature of its functions and its size. In case of a finance institution like the State Bank of India, a policy Board may be more advantageous but a functional Board may be preferable in case of industrial or commercial undertakings where technicality of operation is involved requiring responsible handling of policy matters and execution thereof. For major public undertakings, a functional Board with full-time Members would be preferable while in case of small sized enterprises, the management may be carried on by a Managing Director and a policy Board may be set up to advise him on various issues of policy. In most cases a combined Board would be more effective than either an exclusively policy Board or functional Board.

The size of the Board should neither be too small to be dominated by a single man nor too large so that its members can become a genuine team. To avoid overlapping of responsibility and to maintain integrity of political life, the legislators should be excluded from the membership of the Board. Excessive representation of officials on the Board should be avoided because it often leads to control and interference from the back door which impairs the autonomy of the enterprise. The Minister's presence on the Board may be quite useful in case of enterprises which are very important for the national economy and have wider effects. But the Ministers should avoid sitting on the Boards of ordinary public enterprises with limited responsibilities. All members of the Board should be persons of high calibre and business ability. The Chairman of the Board should be not only a man of high calibre but also of a towering personality to exercise the influence of his presence in the Board as well as to resist the informal ministerial views to prevail on his independent actions performed in accordance with the policy of the Board.

With a view to attract the best available persons on the Board of state undertakings, the salaries and allowances should be such that they provide incentive for work, loyalty to organization, devotion to public service, uprightness and efficiency in operations and social prestige commensurate with the importance of the undertaking.

NOTES

1. E. Dimock Marshall, "Government Corporation: A Focus of Policy and Administration", *The American Political Science Review* (October 1949), p. 916.
2. Report, 1949, pp. 381-82.
3. Indian Institute of Public Administration, *Administrative Problems of State Enterprises in India: Report of a Seminar,* December 1957 (New Delhi, 1958), p. 21.
4. Marshall, n. 1, p. 916.
5. W.A. Robson (ed.), *Problems of Nationalised Industry* (London, 1952), p. 91.
6. A.D. Gorwala, *Report on the Efficient Conduct of State Enterprises* (Delhi, 1951), p. 19.
7. Action Society Trust, *The Men on the Board* (London, 1951), p. 2.
8. William A. Robson, *Nationalised Industry and Public Ownership* (London, 1962), p. 212.
9. National Coal Board, *Report of the Advisory Committee on Organisation* (London, 1955).
10. Sudhir Sen, "The Economics of Public Corporation", *Capital* (Annual Number, 1951), p. 71.
11. Gorwala, n. 6.
12. A.H. Hanson, *Public Enterprise and Economic Development* (London, 1955), p. 397.
13. A.H. Hanson, *Managerial Problems in Public Enterprise* (Bombay, 1962), p. 39.
14. J.E. Hodgetts, "Public Corporation in Canada", *Public Administration* (Winter, 1950), p. 289.
15. Shiro Okabe, "Public Corporation in Japan", *Indian Journal of Public Administration* (January-March 1955), p. 219.
16. Indian Institute of Public Administration, n. 3, p. 22. Also Gorwala, n. 6.
17. Robson, n. 5, p. 263.
18. Rangoon Report as reproduced in Delhi Seminar Report No. 81, p. 13.
19. National Coal Board, *Annual Report 1948,* H.M.S.O. 187/1948-49, para 432.

20. National Coal Board, n. 9, p. 11.
21. Robson, n. 5, pp. 228-29.
22. Hanson, n. 13, p. 42.
23. Robson, n. 5, pp. 100-01.
24. National Coal Board, n. 20, para 116.
25. R.H. Thornton, "Nationalisation—Administrative Problems Inherent in a State-owned Enterprise", *Public Administration* (Spring 1947).
26. Conference Board Reports, *The Corporate Directorship* (New York, April 1953), p. 4.
27. Estimates Committee, *Report on Organisation and Administration of Nationalised Industrial Undertakings* (New Delhi, 1955), para 7.
28. All India Congress Committee, *Report on Parliamentary Supervision Over State Undertakings* (New Delhi, 1959).
29. Lincoln Gordon, *The Public Corporation in Great Britain* (London, 1938), p. 325.
30. W.A. Robson, *Public Enterprise* (London, 1937), p. 93.
31. Laxmi Narain, "Constitution of the Governing Boards of Public Enterprises, *Indian Journal of Public Administration* (January-March 1962), pp. 1-14.
32. Section 8(1) of the Reserve Bank of India Act.
33. Section 19(1) of the State Bank of India Act.
34. Articles of Association of the Company, Article 66.
35. Articles of Association of the Company, Article 115.
36. Articles of Association of the Company, Article 70.
37. Articles of Association of the Company, Article 88.
38. Gorwala, n. 6, p. 19.
39. House of Commons Debate, Vol. 250, cols. 54-55.
40. 68th Report (2nd Lok Sabha) 1959-60 in Reply to 39th Report of Estimates Committee.
41. Estimates Committee, *Report on Administrative, Financial and Other Reforms* (New Delhi, 1954), pp. 16-17.
42. Estimates Committee, *Report on Rourkela, Bhilai and Durgapur Steel Projects* (New Delhi, 1958), p. 13.
43. Estimates Committee, *Report on Air Corporations* (New Delhi, 1956), p. 5.
44. Paras 51 and 52.
45. Speech in the Constituent Assembly on 7 April 1948.
46. Estimates Committee, n. 43, p. 5.

47. Appleby Report, *Re-examination of India's Administrative System*, p. 39.
48. Estimates Committee, n. 27, p. 3.
49. All India Congress Committee, n. 28, para 38.
50. *The Statesman* (Calcutta), October 26, 1961 and *The Statesman*, Editorial Note, November 9, 1961.
51. Hanson, n. 12, p. 404.
52. Estimates Committee, n. 42, p. 11.
53. Gorwala, n. 6, p. 19.
54. Hanson, n. 13, p. 53.
55. *Lok Sabha Debates,* 12 December 1956.
56. Hanson, n. 13, p. 53.
57. Government of India, *Report of the Parliamentary Committee on Offices of Profit, Part I* (New Delhi, 1955), p. 33.
58. Economic Commission for Asia and Far East, *Report of the Seminar on Organisation and Administration of Public Enterprises in the Industrial Field* (Mimeographed) (Rangoon, 1954), p. 24.
59. Hanson, n. 12, p. 378.
60. Hanson, n. 13, p. 54.
61. Thornton, n. 25, p. 10.
62. Robson, n. 5, p. 263.
63. *Ibid.*, p. 94.
64. Government of Bombay, *Report of the Administrative Enquiry Committee,* p. 56.
65. Robson, n. 5, p. 96.
66. All India Congress Committee, n. 28, para 25.
67. G.D.H. Cole, "The National Coal Board", *Political Review* (October-December 1946), p. 319.
68. *House of Commons Debates* (December 18, 1952), col. 1707.
69. Robson, n. 30, p. 371.
70. Section 4(1), D.V.C. Act, 1948.
71. National Coal Board, n. 9, paras 62-63.
72. Labour Party, *Public Enterprises* (London, 1957), p. 28.
73. Section 19(1) (a), State Bank of India Act, 1955.
74. Administrative Reforms Commission, *Report of the Study Team on Public Sector Undertakings* (New Delhi, 1967) (Mimeographed), p. 211.
75. *Ibid.*, pp. 211-16.
76. Section 4(2) of L.I.C. Act and Section 42(2) of Air Corporations Act.

77. Section 42(2) of D.V.C. Act, Section 4(3) of L.I.C. Act, and Section 4(3) of Air Corporations Act.
78. D.N. Chester, *The Nationalised Industry, An Analysis of the Statutory Provisions* (London, 1951), pp. 22-23.
79. Government of India, *Report of Industrial Finance Enquiry Committee* (New Delhi, 1953).
80. Thornton, n. 25, p. 12.
81. House of Commons Debates, Vol. 250, cols, 54-59.
82. Rule 6 of L.I.C. Rules, 1956.
83. Section 51 of D.V.C. Act.
84. Section 6(1) of R.F.A. Act.
85. Rule 3(1) and (2) of L.I.C. Rules, 1956.
86. Section 20(1) of State Bank of India Act.
87. Section 8(4).
88. Gorwala, n. 6, p. 22.
89. Article 89 (ii) of the Articles of Association of the Corporation.
90. Herman Finer, *The T.V.A.—Lessons for International Application* (Montreal, 1944), p. 129.
91. Robson, n. 32, pp. 105-06.
92. Hodgetts, n. 14, p. 286.
93. Lord Simon of Wythneshaw, *The Boards of Nationalised Industries* (London, 1958), p. 30.
94. M.T. Copeland and A.R. Towl, *The Board of Directors and Business Management* (Boston, 1947), p. 172.
95. *Report of Royal Commission on Broadcasting* (Ottawa, 1957), p. 95.
96. *Report of the Broadcasting Committee,* Cmd. 5091, 1936, para 13.
97. *Report of the Committee of Inquiry into the Electricity Supply Industry* (January 1956), H.M.S.O., Cmd. 9672, para 314.
98. Gorwala, n. 6, p. 22.
99. *Ibid.*, p. 29.

Public Accountability

6

The problem of public accountability comprises control of public enterprises directly by the Parliament and indirectly through the Minister concerned and also making the management responsible and answerable to the Minister and through him to Parliament. The primary objective of accountability it to define the relationship between various authorities so as to focus responsibility, to facilitate co-ordination with related programmes, to ensure consistency in the implementation of policy by the government, to conduct operations with maximum efficiency and economy and in accordance with laws, to provide adequate information so as to enable appropriate authorities and the public at large to evaluate the effectiveness of operations, and to apply from time to time the pressures and sanctions to remove inertia, friction, impediments, or obstacles in the way of the fulfilment of the objectives.

The public undertakings involve complete severance between ownership and management which results in the absence of any control or vigilance by the proprietors and shareholders. The management is placed in the hands of those who have hardly any stake in the enterprises they manage. This gives rise to the need for putting such enterprises under some suitable control and for making the management responsible and answerable to some authority. There could be no better authority than the Parliament which represents the shareholders and consumers and which is responsible for safeguarding the interests of the nation. The public undertakings have such an important influence on the total national income, capital formation and consumers of their services that the Parliament cannot afford to be indifferent to their working. There is also the risk that, if left free, the public undertakings may develop into powerful centralised monopolistic bureaucracy exploiting the community at large. This would lead to state capitalism which is worse than private capitalism. The public accountability, therefore, is very essential.

The problem has become particularly crucial in recent years because of two major developments. Firstly, the public enterprises have fast grown in number as well as in size. Secondly, the organisation of public enterprises has undergone important changes. Previously, the public enterprises were managed departmentally. The departments managing the undertakings were fully answerable and responsible to the Minister concerned and who in turn was responsible to the legislature. In recent years, the departmental system has been giving place to autonomous public corporations with a substantial degree of freedom of operation. The emergence of public corporations has given rise to the problem of safeguarding the national interest by exercising the necessary control and at the same time maintaining the freedom and independence of the Board of the corporation. "To balance the two", remarks Earnest Devis, "is no easy task, and the extent to which the right system of checks and balances has yet built up is a matter for debate".[1]

MINISTERIAL CONTROL

The Minister is the chief instrument of the state who controls the working of public enterprises and through whom public accountability is ensured. It would be interesting to examine his powers and responsibilities.

Powers of the Minister

In order to ensure public accountability, the government usually reserves certain powers which are exercised through the Minister. Though the powers vary from enterprise to enterprise in detail owing to the particular conditions of an enterprise, they are more or less same as to their nature and scope. The most important controlling powers of Ministers over the state enterprises as stated in the various Acts and the rules framed thereunder or in the Articles of Association pertaining to the state enterprises, may be summed up as below.

Administrative Control

(i) The appointment of the Board members and Chairman, the Chief Executive or the Managing Director invariably rests with the controlling government or governments. Sometimes the local authorities, though they do not provide any capital, are given the privileges of sending Members. In some other cases, even the appointment of top or key officials is subject to approval and prior consultation with the government.

(ii) The government may depute one or two of their officers to attend any meetings of the Board and take part in the discussion of the Board. Such officers, however, do not have the right to vote.

(iii) The government may remove from office any Member of the Board who in the opinion of government has failed or who has any financial interest in any subsisting contract made with the Company, Corporation or Commission or in any business undertaking dealing with goods or services or any other industries competing with the goods produced or services rendered by the state enterprise in the management of which he has been appointed.

(iv) The government normally reserves the right to supersede the Board or to appoint a new Board if it finds that the Board has failed to carry out the object for which it was set up or if it refuses to follow the direction given by the government.

(v) The government, in general, reserves the right to frame rules, prescribe the various activities to be undertaken and procedures to be followed, general forms to be adopted as to budgets, annual accounts and financial statements, reserves to be built up and distribution of profits. The government also reserves the right to institute enquiries into the working of the corporation if and when felt necessary and may also appoint an advisory council.

(vi) The most important power of the government relates to the giving of directives. The directives issued from time to time relate to such subjects which are considered necessary in regard to the conduct of business of the enterprise or directors thereof, and, in like manner, may vary and annul any such directive. The directors shall give immediate effect to directives so issued. The directives may relate to recruitment, conditions of services, training of employees, wages to be paid, reserves to be maintained and distribution of profits. But in these matters prior consultation with the Board is made necessary. An interesting provision found in selected enterprises is that "if due to government directions regarding certain particular matters, the public enterprise suffers a loss, such loss shall have to be made good by the Central Government".

Financial Control

(i) The government may appoint a person not being a Member to be the Financial Adviser to the Board. The Financial Adviser advises the Board on all matters relating to receipts and expenditure. He has the right to record his views on every proposal involving expenditure from the funds of the corporate body prior to consideration and approval of such proposal by the Board. He has the authority to advise the Board that a particular decision affecting the general financial policy of government should be referred to government for consideration.

(ii) The government provides funds to the company, corporation or commission and guarantees the shares, bonds and debentures issued by them.

(iii) The approval of the government is necessary in case of some of the public enterprises for their schemes and programmes.

(iv) The accounts of public enterprises have to be maintained in a form to be decided in consultation with the Government or the Auditor General, and the audit of the accounts is usually by auditors appointed by the Minister or by the Auditor General himself. In certain cases the accounts are audited by one or more auditors qualified under Section 144 of the Indian Companies Act, 1913 to act as auditors of companies, who are appointed by the Central Government.

The power of appointing and removing Members of the Board is very essential if the Board is to be made to effectively carry out the directives of the Minister. In the absence of this power, other powers would be rendered ineffective. It is argued that this power places the Members of the Board at the Minister's mercy which impairs their courage and initiative that are indispensable for successful management of any enterprise. The Minister is, however, normally given this power in the belief that it will not be misused.

The controlling powers of the Ministers in regard to the development and programmes of reorganisation involving "substantial capital expenditure" are no less in other countries than in India. The French Coal Nationalisation Act of 1946 requires prior approval for expenditure *inter alia* on "programmes of new works, production and working plans for the coal mines"[2] and "government intervention in the affairs of an enterprise is more far reaching in France than in the U.K."[3] In Canada, the Financial Administration Act 1951 provides[4] for approval of the Minister of Finance even in matter of maintaining bank accounts in the name of a Corporation. In the United States, the Congress has much greater control over the financial administration of public corporations than the Treasury over their counterparts in European countries. In Sri Lanka, the Minister has wide powers in financial matters under the State Industrial Corporation Act (No. 49).[5] It is thus evident that the Minister has got a controlling power over capital and finance of a public corporation in all countries and this is quite in keeping with the Ministerial responsibility to ensure that the national funds are best utilised for development purposes and not frittered away by reckless or injudicious administration.

The power of the Minister in regard to specific directives is essential because the ultimate responsibility for co-ordinating and planning the whole activity in that particular field and for fitting it in the national plan rests with the Minister. This power is also necessary to enable the Minister to safeguard the interests of the employees and consumers. Under the specific directives, the Minister also exercises financial control. These checks exercised through 'approval and veto' of projects and demands involving finance are necessary because the Minister, in consultation with the Government, it expected to bring the issue of stocks and debentures and borrowing by the state enterprises into balance with its overall financial plan. The Minister enjoys such powers in the U.K. as well as in other countries and these are quite reasonable.

The public enterprises generally enjoy a high degree of monopoly and their prices are managed prices rather than market prices. In managing prices in a basic industry consideration has to be given not only to the solvency of the undertaking but also to the repercussions of prices on the economy as a whole, and to the wider issues of public policy. The Ministers are better judges of the national interest as a whole than the Board of a public corporation. This view was forcibly expressed by Aneurin Bevan in the House of Commons debate. Once we deny to the Minister...responsible for a great nationalized undertaking, the right to determine what he thinks to be in the national interest, then we are erecting a species of the corporate society more familiar to Italian Fascist principles than to the British democratic constitution. I have always denied the right of these great corporations to decide such issues.[6] The concept of the national interest may sometimes point in a direction different from that indicated by the needs of a public corporation considered in isolation. In such a situation the Minister must be able to override the Board.

It would, however, be unwise on the part of the Minister to issue a directive on each occasion of conflict of opinions.

Herbert Morrison, the principal architect of the modern public corporation, is of the opinion that the Minister should maintain close contact with the Boards but "on an informal basis and the relationship should develop on the old boys" basis.[7] The experience, however, shows that such consultations behind the door have tended to bring greater influence to bear on the Boards so as to ensure that government policy is implemented without the Minister's admitting any responsibility for the same. "The consequence is that whereas behind the scenes they [Minister][8] have exerted a greater influence on the boards, they have not accepted public accountability for their actions. They have exercised their responsibility in private and not answered for it in public."[9] There are two major reasons for this state of affairs. In the first place, the Ministers do not want to make themselves liable to accept the blame or public odium for a particular policy which may turn out to be wrong. Secondly, the Board lacks the courage to refuse to execute a policy which the Minister is urging on them without giving a directive to that effect in writing.

Justice Chagla has recommended that "Government should not interfere with the working of an autonomous statutory corporation; that if they wish to interfere they should not shirk the responsibility of giving directions in writing".[10] To cite Robson, "Ministers must be prepared to face up to the responsibilities which they have assumed. They should not be permitted to remain in the twilight zone in which some of them love to dwell, flitting happily from one private meeting to another, talking things over with the chairman at lunch, in the club, in the House of Commons, in the department, without disclosing either to the public or to Parliament the real extent of their intervention. This is not the way to strike the right balance between governmental power and managerial freedom".[11]

There can be no hard and fast rules for deciding the occasions for issue of directives. Krishna Menon Committee rightly remarked, "It is neither possible nor advisable to lay down the occasions or the categories of occasions when a Minister should or should not issue a 'directive' or 'special directive'."[12] The provisions in this regard in the Nationalisation of Coal Act, 1946 in the United Kingdom may provide some guidance. The Act provides that "the Minister may, after consultation with the Board, give to the Board directions of a general character as to the exercise and performance by the Board of their functions in relation to matters appearing to the Minister to affect the national interest, and the Board shall give effect to any such directions". This statutory power is a reserve power and a potential action of the Minister under certain conditions that would contribute to the national interest. The provisions in this regard vary in different Indian Acts. The D.V.C. Act has no such words as "in the national interest" but limitation on direction has been placed by the word "on question of policy".[13] This provision in the L.I.C. Act is "in the matter of policy involving public interest".[14] The Air Corporations Act contained neither the phrase "on question of policy" nor "involving public interest". It provided that the Central government may give directions "as to the exercise and performance by the corporation of its functions"[15] which connotes directions for the purpose of efficient conduct of the enterprise and is much wider in scope that may lead to interference in day-to-day matters.

There may at times arise controversy over the occasions on which ministerial directives are to be issued and over a matter whether it falls within the ambit of policy or management. To resolve such situations the D.V.C. Act provides that "if any dispute arises between the Central Government and the Corporation as to whether a question is or is not a question of policy, the decision of the Central Government shall be final".[16] More or less similar provisions are contained in other Acts also. But when the dispute between the government and the Corporation becomes flagrant, it would be better to obtain a decision on the dispute from some superior authority, say the Cabinet.

There is, however, much evidence to show that the Ministers have a tendency to interfere in the affairs of the public enterprises to an extent much greater than that justified by statutes establishing these. Lord Swinton went to the extent of saying that "the Minister's day-to-day contact with the chairman of a nationalized board is very like one's relationship with one's own officials in one's Department".[17] This is a very misleading statement and such a relationship between the Chairman of a Corporation and the Minister would seriously impair the autonomy of the corporation. In fact, the position of a Chairman is very different from that of a Departmental Secretary of a Minister. In the words of William A. Robson, "To say that policy is to be settled between the Minister and the Chairman represents a gross infringement of the managerial freedom of the public corporation, and a severe down-grading of the status of the other members of the board".[18]

The Minister is empowered to appoint and remove the Members of the Board. The Members faced with a directive to which they do not agree have to undergo the risk of being removed. In case the directive is thrust upon them, the only way out for them is to show protest by resigning from the Board. Even in England the Members generally prefer to bow before the Minister than either taking the risk of being removed or showing the courage to resign. There are hardly any chances of such probabilities in India since the whole-time appointed Members are required to give up other sources of earnings. Further even if they agree to suffer, they are not sure whether their resignation would have any effect on the government policy. "Hence when the Minister starts with persuasion, gradually passing to influence, then to pressure, and ultimately holding out the threat of imposing the directive, the Board fully realising the consequences prefers to yield to pressure if not to persuasion".[19] It has, therefore, been suggested that at least a portion of the Members should be part-timers. Having alternative sources of income, it is thought that they would be able to follow a bold, courageous and independent policy without submitting to pressure from the Minister. This contention, unfortunately, is not supported by actual experience. The Minister and his lieutenants are in such a strong position that the Members of the Board cannot have the courage of measuring strength with them. Moreover, it is doubtful if they have so much interest in the enterprise as to oppose the Minister who nominates them.

The position of the Company Board is still weaker. Most of the Boards have top government officials as Members. The same Members appear again and again in different capacities. At one time they are Members of the Board and at the other government representatives exercising necessary controls. The question of such a Board not carrying out the desires of the Minister does not arise. Such Boards do not require even the methods of persuasion and influence. The position is, in fact, anomalous. The Chief Secretary, who briefs the Minister and by whose advice he is guided, is also the Chairman of the Board considering the government proposals and acting as an adviser and guide to the Board Members. The question of giving directives and the Board Members differing with the government does not arise when the Members come with predetermined plans. The Members in the capacity of advisers to the Minister would not question Board's decisions and actions because they themselves are a party to these. The question of public accountability, therefore, does not arise at all. The Minister has no alternative but to defend the actions of the Board in the Parliament.

While the powers to control are essential in the wider interest of the nation, it is also necessary to preserve the autonomy of the corporation in its day-to-day administration. To strike a balance between ministerial interference and corporate autonomy is the greatest problem which no country has been able to solve. The precise extent of ministerial interference or control would largely depend on the personality of the Minister and also on that of the Board, and the manner in which he interprets the power and the responsibility placed on him. It also depends on the nature and importance of the public undertaking, on the political sensitivity of its operations, and on its financial relations with the government. Since these factors vary from enterprise to enterprise, so will ministerial control, to the extent it is conditioned by these factors. A Development Corporation with terms of reference wide enough to influence a vital sector of the government's economic plan would, for instance, invite greater ministerial attention than a corporation for a comparatively small factory. Such a corporation may also become a focus for political controversy, in view of which Minister may not give it much liberty. Moreover, a Development Corporation or a river valley authority, by its very nature, absorbs funds on projects which are not expected to become self-supporting quickly, and, therefore, invites ministerial intervention in financial matters more strongly than does a profit-making or even-breaking enterprise. The status accorded to the Head of a public undertaking considerably influences the extent of informal control of Ministry over the public undertaking. In India, at present, the Secretaries are, generally, manifestly senior and superior to the heads of public undertakings. In fact, the government order[20] relating to the salaries of top management posts in the public sector lays down that an officer cannot draw a salary higher than that of a Secretary unless he resigns from government service. The position in the United Kingdom, in contrast, is that the chairmen and even vice-chairmen of large public undertakings draw salaries which are substantially higher than those drawn by the topmost civil servants in the government. Such a pattern has certain advantages over the position prevailing in India. In the first place, a senior civil servant having requisite prior experience will be more willing to render service in the public sector even if he has to sever his connections with the parent department. Secondly, being senior in service and status to the Secretary, he will be able to withstand more stoutly the informal suggestions and pressures emanating from the Ministry.

Herbert Morrison envisages the relationship between Minister and the Board as follows: "Clearly it is desirable that the Minister should keep himself familiar with the general work of the Board or Boards with which he is concerned. It is wise for him with his parliamentary secretary and principal officers concerned from time to time to meet the chairman and, indeed, the members of the Board, to discuss matters of mutual interest either formally or informally. On such occasion both the Board and the Minister will be conscious of their legal rights: the legal right of the Minister to give general directions or to withhold approval, and the legal rights of the Board within the field of day-to-day management; but it is also desirable that such discussion should be free, frank, forthcoming, and co-operative.[21]

The Minister should be careful not to impair the Board's sense of responsibility, which is not only a legal obligation but a public asset. The Board, on its part, should understand that the Minister is not bound to defend a public enterprise from criticism in the Parliament unless he agrees with its policy. Frequent informal discussions are useful but these should be without prejudice to the rights and responsibilities of either the Minister or Board.

Ministerial Control in Practice in India

It is difficult to reach any conclusion in regard to the use of ministerial powers and the extent of interference in the day-to-day administration of state enterprises in India. Since publication of any directive or prior consultation is not obligatory, controversy or fact relating to ministerial control is not made known to the public. Even in the United Kingdom things happen more behind the curtain and public controversy is avoided.

The possibility of any differences, however, is more or less ruled out because the key positions are occupied by the civil servants who ensure that the methods used and general working of the organisation continues to be similar to that of a government. In Morrison's phrase the relationship is developed on the 'old boys' basis. There does not appear to be much truth in the professed autonomy of the corporations and companies. The Estimates Committee in its Ninth Report, 1953-54 remarks, "The climax is reached when an officer on the Board of Directors, who is generally the Secretary or the Joint Secretary of the Ministry concerned, does not agree with a proposal or a scheme has the final right to get the whole thing shelved or vetoed when it comes to the Ministry for a decision, because the constitution of such undertakings provides in many cases that in cases of serious disagreement between administrative and financial authorities the matter should be referred to Government for a decision. In practice, therefore, an officer of Government, be the senior or junior, controls an undertaking either in his capacity as Member of the Board or Managing Director or as administrative Head of the Department where he has power to give advice to Ministers in which case he takes a decision in the name of Ministry, and Parliament and Government are asked not to take notice of these things because it may interfere with the autonomy of the undertaking".[22] This is not a healthy state of affairs. The government must publish some sort of report broadly giving the measures adopted to control and manage the enterprises. A democratic government should not refuse to make public the measures taken by them for controlling the public enterprise in the interest of the people themselves.

Another useful step would be to find more and more administrative skill outside the already over-burdened ministerial departments and independent sources of finance provided by independent capital markets.

To establish a sound relationship between the government and state enterprises, it is very essential that the nature and scope of ministerial control is clearly defined. Such a relation may profitably be based on the following broad principles: (1) The Minister should resist the temptation of invoking his residuary power of issuing directives as far as possible unless there is gross negligence of the Board or commission of an egregious mistake. (2) Petty-fogging ministerial control should be scrupulously avoided because "if the Minister is too pliable or too opinionated his frequent interventions deprive the Boards of initiative and drive them to shelter behind him from public criticism."[23] (3) The phrases "on questions of policy" and "in the public interest" should be interpreted a little widely, though it cannot be ignored that general principle of policy "may quite often arise from a host of small decisions of the day-to-day order, which collectively constitute something of a genuine public importance."[24] (4) Administrative conflicts or irregularities unless they affect national interests should be settled as far as possible by persuasion and informal approach on both sides. (5) All directives should be given in writing and in clear and unambiguous terms so as to avoid possibilities of differing and contrasting interpretations of the matters. (6) Disputes in regard to propriety and on occasions for issue of directives should be referred to and decided by the Cabinet as the "Central Government" in this context cannot be the Minister who is a party to the dispute. (7) Since the Board is bound to carry out the directives of the Minister, he should assume full responsibility to face Parliament for public accountability.

Ministerial Responsibility

The ministerial responsibility falls into three categories. In the first place, the Minister is responsible to the Parliament. Keeping in view the national security, national interest and the welfare of the state, the Minister should place on the table all information and data sought by the Honourable Members of the House. He should not answer questions in an evasive manner.

Secondly, the Minister has the constitutional responsibility for the actions of his subordinates in pursuance of his policy. There are generally four types of constitutional and executive responsibilities of a Minister, viz. (1) Where the Minister has given clear-cut orders in writing obviously the Minister is responsible and he must cover his subordinates. (2) The subordinates have to take action but it falls within the broad purview of the government policy; here again, the Minister has to bear responsibility. (3) Where there may be slight error of judgement on the part of the subordinates which may not really do much damage; in this case also Minister will cover his subordinates. (4) If the subordinate goes out of the way, does something outside the policy, does something which is dishonest or corrupt, even then the Minister cannot escape his responsibility to Parliament for the actions of such subordinates, although he is free to punish them. While enunciating the principles which should govern ministerial responsibility, the Chagla Commission stated, "It is clear that constitutionally the Minister is responsible for the action taken by his secretary with regard to this transaction. It is clear that a Minister must take the responsibility for actions done by his subordinates. He cannot take shelter behind them, nor can he disown their actions. The doctrine of ministerial responsibility has two facets. The Minister has complete autonomy within the sphere of authority. As a necessary corollary he must take full responsibility for the actions of his servants. It is true that this may throw a very great burden on the Minister, because it is impossible to expect that, in a highly complicated system of administration which we have evolved, the Minister could possibly know, leave alone, give his consent to, every action taken by his subordinates. But it is assumed that once the policy is laid down by the Minister, his subordinates must reflect that policy and must loyally carry out that policy. If any subordinate fails to do so, he may be punished or dismissed. But, however, vicariously, the responsibility of his action must be assumed by the Minister. It may be said that a Minister is merely part of the Government as a whole, and if the Minister should take the responsibility for his subordinates' actions, equally so must the Cabinet. But it is well established that the Cabinet only takes the responsibility for the Minister's action if the Minister reports the matter to the Cabinet and obtains its sanction before he puts into effect this policy. Then the policy becomes the Cabinet policy and not only the Minister but the whole Cabinet must take the responsibility for whatever might have been done by a subordinate".[25] But whether he should resign or not, is a matter to be decided in individual circumstances depending on the merits of each case. It will be too harsh to the Minister to hold that he is responsible for all actions of his subordinates and should resign on every occasion but not to resign on any occasion whatsoever would be failing in duty.

Then there is personal responsibility of a Minister. A Minister is personally responsible when he does not approve of any action of his subordinate but does not repudiate it or when he connives at his own orders or does not take any action after having known that certain things have been done wrongfully and improperly within his departmental charge. In case of personal responsibility the Minister must resign from the government.

The matter was debated in the House of Commons on 26 December 1950 and the principle was laid down that the Minister could not escape his constitutional responsibility for any mistakes done by the officials working directly under his control. This principle has been accepted in India in Lok Sabha debate on constitutional responsibility of the Minister held on 19 February 1958. In pursuance of this principle,

Lal Bahadur Shastri resigned from office of the Minister of Railways in 1957, when a serious railway disaster occurred at Ariyalur, Madras. In L.I.C.-Mundhra deal, the Chagla Enquiry Commission observed, "The Minister must fully and squarely accept the responsibility for what Shri Patel did and if the transaction is improper and unjustified although Shri Patel may be actually responsible for the transaction, constitutionally the responsibility is that of the Minister".[26] As a consequence of this T.T. Krishnamachari resigned from his office as Finance Minister. But the assumption of personal responsibility by a Minister depends to a large extent upon the Minister himself, attitude of Parliament and pressure of the public because in similar circumstances some Ministers did not offer to resign. The next Railway Minister Jagjivan Ram, for instance, did not offer resignation though the number and magnitude of railway accidents were greater during his tenureship than during the ministership of Lal Bahadur Shastri and also there was public demand for his resignation following the Ranchi Express disaster. Similarly, in the United Kingdom, John Strachey did not resign his office for failure of "groundnut scheme" of Overseas Food Corporation.

Resinging on the grounds of constitutional responsibility is a morally sound policy, but for practical reasons, however, caution should be exercised in urging a Minister to offer resignation. In a developing country like India, talent and calibre for a ministerial rank are limited. If Ministers have to resign for mistakes of their subordinates in the Ministry or Board Officials for which they are not directly responsible, it would be difficult to have a stable Ministry because frequent change and reshuffling would be necessary. The practicable policy, therefore, would be that a Minister should be urged to resign only when serious losses are involved as a result of the direction given by him or as a consequence of gross negligence in his duty.

As seen above, the Minister wields vast powers of supervision and control over public enterprises. To safeguard against misuse of these powers, he must be held answerable to the Parliament for his actions. "The Public Corporation must not be thrown into the arms of a Ministerial father unless a fond Parliamentary mother is available to restrain the excessive application of paternal discipline".[27]

Parliamentary Control

The parliament as the trustee of the nation has a right to assure itself that in broad terms the financial and managerial policies followed by public enterprises are sound and promote the ends of public policy underlying their establishment. This is particularly necessary because the Members of the Board or the chief executive having no financial stake in the concern and being, in no way, linked to the fortunes of the enterprise, may not otherwise care much for the efficient conduct of the enterprise. The evidence of Lord Harcomb quoted with approval in the Report of the Select Committee on Nationalised Industries in the U.K. very aptly sums up the matter. He states that there is a "very real problem ultimately of accountability to Parliament" arising "from the vast amount of capital and of income and expenditure involved in concerns which are under public ownership, the charges upon consumers and users of the necessities of civilised life which they provide and the Treasury guarantee of the interest paid on the stock issued in respect of the various Nationalised Industries".[28]

Although in deciding the ultimate extent of parliamentary control, political ideology and social sentiments play an important part, it is generally accepted that "...the legislature should not attempt too close a control, in particular that it should not normally interfere in day-to-day running of the industries, but confine itself to questions of major policy and exceptional circumstances. Detailed interference will lead to delays, overcaution and lack of confidence on the part of those running the industries".[29]

The nature and extent of parliamentary control over a public enterprise to a large extent depends upon its form of organisation. So far as the departmentally administered undertakings are concerned, there is hardly any difference between industrial or commercial enterprises and government departments in regard to the nature and scope of parliamentary control and the ministerial responsibility to the legislature. In case of such enterprises, the control is absolute because the capital and the operating budgets of the units are presented before the House in the form of demands for grants. This tends to impair initiative and boldness of the persons at the helm of affairs. To quote Hugh Gaitskell, "Anybody who has worked in a Civil Service department would agree with me that if there is one major thing which leads Civil Servants to be excessively cautious, timid and careful and to keep records which outside the Civil Service would be regarded as unnecessary, it is the fear of the Parliamentary questions".[30]

Turning to public corporations, each of them is set up under a special Act of the legislature. The Act governing a public corporation specifically defines and determines the relationship between the legislature and the corporation clearly setting out the rights and powers vis-a-vis the legislature and corporation. The Act also specifies the rights and powers of the Minister in regard to the working of the corporation and also his duties and obligations to the legislature. The statutes differ in provisions in regard to ensuring of public accountability. Some statutes make it obligatory on the corporations to submit Annual Reports to the Parliament while others do not require this. Auditing by the Auditor General is necessary in some while appointment of auditor is left to the government in others. The government is authorised under the statutes to issue general, and in some cases also specific, directive but reporting of the same to the legislature is not obligatory. Under some Acts the government is required to submit a full report to the legislature if it exercises the powers granted under the statute to supersede the corporation.

In regard to joint stock companies fully owned by the state, the matters can be raised in the Parliament but that is not of much use in the absence of any jurisdiction over them. The first report of the Public Accounts Committee emphasized: "We attach considerable importance to the necessity of safeguarding against any whittling away of parliamentary control by the participation of the Government in private companies".[31] The Committee returned to the question more thoroughly in their third report (1952-53) and quoted a very strong statement from the Comptroller and Auditor General who was of the opinion that "It was scarcely proper either to pretend that the President or Secretary of a Department were 'persons' as intended by Companies Act or to take money from the consolidated fund for such concerns".[32] The Comptroller and Auditor General further expressed the fear that his own control might be ousted because he would have no automatic right to audit the accounts of such companies and even if he got an invitation to do so, the invitation would be from the company and not from the Parliament. Moreover, his report would be submitted to the company, bypassing the Parliament and the Public Accounts Committee. This shows that the joint stock private limited companies are the least subjected to proper parliamentary control.

Major Instruments of Control

The parliamentary control is exercised primarily through (1) questions, (2) debates and (3) legislative committees.

Questions

The members of Parliament have a right to ask questions from the Ministers concerned. The question hour constitutes the most important part of the day's business in the Parliament. The questions asked on the floor of the House elicit both valuable information and certain assurances for action from the government. The government on its part gets an opportunity to explain its position on important matters. The questions also provide an opportunity to the government to feel public sentiments and to adjust its policies and actions accordingly.

There are three types of questions, viz. (1) starred questions, (2) unstarred questions, and (3) short notice questions. A starred question (indicated by an asterisk mark) is one which requires oral answer. An unstarred question is given a written reply.[33] While a member is entitled to ask any number of questions regarding written answers, he cannot ask more than three questions for oral answers on a particular day.[34] A question requires ten clear days' notice. The purpose of advance notice is to give adequate time to the Minister concerned to collect information on the problem under question. If the question concerns a matter of urgent public importance, it can be asked as a "sort-notice Question". Such a question has to be answered within a shorter period. A Member, if allowed by the Speaker, may ask a supplementary question for the purpose of further elucidating any matter of fact regarding which an answer has been given.[35]

If the questions are put intelligently and well directed, much information can be obtained on the basis of which a greater control can be exercised on the enterprise. Questions may also be asked to call attention to some aspect of policy to which a member or a group of members take exception. Several questions relating to state industrial and commercial enterprises have been raised in Parliament by the concerned Members during the question hour.

Some questions fall within the range of ministerial responsibility for policy and exercise or non-exercise of their authority to issue directives to the Boards of the undertakings. Others relate to day-to-day administration and often to trifling matters. Frequent questions relating to day-to-day management seriously impair the initiative of the managers and compel them to function in a routine manner. In the words of Herbert Morrison, "If these men are to live a life which is really a Civil Service life, and are liable to be abused across the floor of the House and subjected to questions attacking them and their commercial ability we shall not get the men to serve on these commercial undertakings, and we shall not get the best out of those who are there".[36] The Members as well as the Ministers should, therefore, as far as possible, avoid interfering in the day-to-day working of the public enterprises.

Several times the Members ask questions not to elicit information but for catching the eyes of the press and finding their names in print and showing to their constituencies that they are very energetic, capable and alert to their responsibilities. Such a practice should be done away with. The Members of the Parliament should maintain some standard and impose a "self-denying ordinance" as is the practice in the United Kingdom.

Unfortunately, the Members as well as the Ministers have not made best use of this opportunity. The Members have not taken sufficient interest in the working of the public enterprises while the Ministers have evaded giving information in their replies which they do not want to divulge. The admissibility of questions is decided by the Speaker but it is always open to the Minister to refuse to supply information on the ground that it is not in the public interest to disclose the information or that the information is not available. In fact, it is true, as remarked by the Speaker in British Parliament, he can allow a question but cannot compel an answer.

Because of the fairly wide powers of the Minister, few questions are barred by the ruling of the Speaker. But he has normally exercised his discretion to direct acceptance of questions only on matters which seemed to him of sufficient public importance to justify the occasion. Even if the Members can get their questions on the order paper, they may fail to get the answer. According to one of the Rulings, "It is a ministerial privilege to keep back from this House certain information which they consider to be secret".[37] In fact, the Ministers have reserved the right not to answer any question on the pretext of secrecy or to answer it in an evasive manner. While investigating into the affairs of the Life Insurance Corporation, Justice M.C. Chagla remarked, "Taking into consideration the national security, public interest and welfare of the state, it is essential that the minister while answering the questions in Parliament must place all the facts fully and frankly before the members of the House. It is not sufficient that the answers are technically correct. But they must assist members of the House in making true assessments regarding a particular problem".[38] In exercising its rights, the Parliament should distinguish between a departmentally managed enterprise and an enterprise under autonomous management since the Minister stands differently under these two circumstances. In case of a departmentally managed enterprise, the Minister has all responsibilities including day-to-day management and, therefore, he is answerable to Parliament for all aspects of the undertaking. But in case of a public corporation, the Minister has no responsibility for day-to-day management and as such cannot be held answerable to the Parliament for day-to-day affairs of the corporation. There, however, arises the question as to whether or not the Parliament's jurisdiction should cover cases of abuses or inefficiency detected in a public corporation. From all considerations, such cases should be brought within the scope of Parliamentary questioning. Grave abuses, involving loss of enormous public money, affect the Corporation as well as the public interest and, therefore, should not be excluded from the circle of the Parliament. While the Parliament cannot disown its responsibility to have checks and balances on public corporations where national economy is involved, it should preserve the autonomous character of the corporation and avoid undue interference in the day-to-day management of the corporation.

In fact, the ministerial responsibility depends to a great extent on the behaviour of the Members of Parliament who are expected to restrain from questioning the Minister on matters that are outside ministerial vigilance and are responsibility of the management of the corporation. The Members should realise that the Minister is not to be identified with the Corporation and indiscriminately attacked on all grounds. When the Minister finds himself much heckled by Parliament he may be forced to form a misconception of his duties and responsibilities to Parliament vis-a-vis the Public Corporation. At one time he may disown responsibility on the ground that the matter lies outside the scope of his functions and at another he may use all his force to defend the action of the Corporation though wrongly. In India there are instances where the Minister assumed more or less the position of the 'Managing Director' of the Corporation to defend the action. Dr. Krishnaswamy alleges, "Very often we find the spectacle of Ministers getting up to defend the Boards under the impression that it is they that are being criticised".[39] In the course of discussion over a Report of the Parliamentary Committee in the United Kingdom, Molsen was of the opinion that the Minister should keep a neutral line when the matter is debated but this approach was not approved by Herbert Morrison.[40] It is, in fact, difficult for the Minister to take a neutral position because he will naturally feel an urge to defend the action of the Board, the Members of which are appointed by him.

The principles which should determine Minister's liability to answer parliamentary questions about public enterprises have been stated by Herbert Morrison as follows: "A large degree of independence for the boards in matters of current administration is vital to their efficiency as commercial undertakings. A Minister is responsible to Parliament for action which he may take in relation to a board, or action coming within his statutory powers which he has not taken. This is the principle that determines generally the matters on which a question may be put down for answer by a Minister in the House of Commons. Thus the Minister would be answerable for any directions he gave in the national interest, and for the action which he took on proposals which a board was required by statute to lay before him. It would be contrary to this principle, and to the clearly expressed intention of Parliament in the governing legislation, if Ministers were to give, in replies in Parliament or in letters, information about day-to-day matters. Undue intervention by the Minister would tend to impair the board's commercial freedom of action".[41] In the words of Robson, "If once the parliamentary question were given free play over the whole field of activity of a nationalised industry, half the advantages of having a public corporation rather than a government department would, be lost".[42]

In England there was a great controversy regarding the Minister's right to refuse or his responsibility to answer a question. As a result of this, Herbert Morrison, Lord President of the Council, laid down that the Minister was not responsible for day-to-day administration but had responsibility to the Parliament for action which he may take in relation to the Board or actions falling within his statutory powers which he has not taken. The opposition, however, persistently continued challenging the Minister's right to refuse information on matters which appeared to the House of national importance until the Speaker gave his ruling somewhat extending the sphere of ministerial accountability. Questions can now be put to Ministers on matters where there is some ministerial responsibility and which are of sufficient public importance.

The position in this regard in India has been stated in a directive issued from the Speaker's office which reads as below: It is stated for the information of members that broadly speaking, admissibility of questions relating to statutory corporations and limited companies in which government have financial or controlling interest is regulated generally in the following manner on merits of each case:

(i) where a question (a) relates to a matter of policy, or (b) refers to an act or omission of an act on the part of a Minister, or (c) raises a matter of public interest, although seemingly it may pertain to a matter of day-to-day administration or an individual case, it is ordinarily admitted for oral answer.

(ii) A question which calls for information of statistical or descriptive nature is generally admitted for written replies.

(iii) Questions which clearly relate to day-to-day administration and tend to throw work on the Ministries and the corporation incommensurate with the result to be obtained thereof are normally disallowed.[43]

Keeping in view the autonomous nature of the public enterprises, the number of questions asked in Indian Parliament about the working of these enterprises is rather large. The scope of the admissibility of questions is much less restrictive in India than in other countries like the United Kingdom and Canada. In these countries, questions relating to matters that Parliament itself has placed within the competence of autonomous public corporations are not generally admitted. Even when such a question gets admitted or raised as a supplementary, the Minister makes it clear in his reply that the matter lies within the competence of the public corporations as provided by an Act passed by the Parliament itself and he should not, therefore, be held responsible for it. Sometimes the reply given by the Minister is prefaced by words like "I have been informed by the Board that...".

In fact, the present criteria for the admissibility of questions can be made more specific to exclude the matters that Parliament itself has, by an Act, placed within the competence of autonomous corporations. This will not dilute the essence of their public accountability since the Act of Parliament setting up the corporation has already embodied the autonomy that is consistent with accountability. The application of this principle should be extended to government companies as well.

The actual working of the rules and guidelines laid down for determining the admissibility of a question considerably depends on the initiative of the Ministry concerned. When a question intrudes into the area of autonomy, it can point out that the question does not qualify for admission. But the experience in India shows that the Ministry seldom moves for the disallowance of any question. Often questions falling within the purview of day-to-day administration get admitted and answered. Sometimes, detailed information had been supplied earlier in a slightly different form to an earlier question. The Ministries should be more vigilant in ensuring that what Parliament itself has excluded does not reappear due to oversight or neglect. They should insist on the strict observance of the rules governing admissibility. The admissibility of questions should be quickly examined first in the Parliament Secretariat and then in the Ministry. The Ministry should draw attention of the Speaker to questions which have been excluded from the purview of the Parliament by the Parliament itself. They should also check if similar information had not been supplied in reply to an earlier question. This would avoid waste of effort in the Ministry and the public undertaking concerned.

The main purpose of the questions is to obtain information. The Members of Parliament can directly obtain information by writing to Board Members, as is the case in England. If this method is introduced, the Members of Parliament shall come into close contact with state enterprises and shall better appreciate their difficulties and problems. It shall also provide an opportunity to public enterprises to explain their point of view and to remove the doubts of the Members of Parliament.

The Parliament has an unfettered right to ask questions on policy matters but not so about normal administration. The distinction between the two sometimes is too fine to distinguish and it is rightly said that "matters of policy merge imperceptibly into matters of day-to-day administration". The example given by Captain Crookshank in the course of the House of Commons Debate shows how there comes a moment when "day-to-day management merges into the larger question of administration" and becomes a subject of parliamentary question. He observes that one day's late running of a train is a matter falling within day-to-day management but if the same train runs late every day for a month it indicates something wrong with the administration somewhere, and the matter comes within the ambit of parliamentary questions and discussion.[44]

Debates

The debates provide an important opportunity to examine, discuss and review the working of public enterprises. The following are the opportunities available for this purpose:

(1) Raising half-an-hour discussion on any enterprise.

(2) Moving a motion for adjournment on a matter of public importance.

(3) Raising discussion on matters of urgent public importance for short duration.

(4) "Calling attention" of the House to matters of urgent public importance.

(5) Moving resolutions, and discussing any matter.

(6) Discussion on President's address.

(7) Discussing the report of the Enquiry Committee, if any.

(8) Amendment of the statute under which the public enterprise has been set up.

(9) Budgetary demands.

(10) Discussion on Annual Reports of the Public Enterprises can take place.

Half-an-hour discussion: A questioner, who is not satisfied with the answer given by the Minister and desires to pursue a little further, is entitled to request for half-an-hour discussion. "The Speaker shall allot half an hour for raising discussion on a matter of sufficient public importance which has been the subject of a recent question oral or written and the answer to which needs elucidation on a matter of fact".[45] For half-an-hour discussion, there is neither any formal motion nor voting in the House. The Member who has given notice may make a short statement, and the Minister concerned shall reply to it.

A Member desiring to raise a matter is required to give three days' notice in advance of the day on which the matter is desired to be raised and to briefly specify the point or points that he desires to raise. He has also to mention the reasons for which he wants to raise the discussion. The notice has to be supported by the signatures of at least two other members. It is the Speaker who decides whether the matter is of sufficient public importance to be put down for discussion and he may not admit a notice which, in his opinion, seeks to revise the policy of the government.

Such a discussion has a limited utility because only a few specific questions can be raised in a short discussion. It does not provide an opportunity for a thorough examination of the issue.

Motion for adjournment on a matter of public importance: A motion for an adjournment of the business of the House for the purpose of discussing a definite matter of urgent public importance, may be admitted for discussion with the consent of the Speaker.[46] This opportunity may be utilised by Members for discussing the working of a public enterprise whose affairs may have taken a serious turn, e.g. labour trouble in an enterprise.

Discussion on matters of urgent public importance for short duration: A Member wishing to raise discussion on a matter of urgent public importance may give notice in writing to the Secretary of the Lok Sabha specifying clearly and precisely the matter to be raised. He should also mention the reason for it. The notice should be supported by at least two other Members. If the Speaker admits the notice, he may allow the maximum time of two and a half hours for discussing the matter. There shall be no voting and no formal motion before the House. The Member who has given notice may make a statement, and the Minister shall reply to it.[47]

Calling attention to matters of urgent public importance: A Member may, with the previous permission of the Speaker, call the attention of a Minister to any matter of urgent public importance, and the Minister may make a brief statement or ask for time to make a statement at a later hour or date. There shall be no debate on such a statement at the time it is made. By this method, some information can be obtained, some doubts can be removed and some clarifications can be made.

Motion: A motion may be introduced with the consent of the Speaker, for the discussion of one definite issue of a recent occurrence, and the Speaker may, after considering the state of business in the House and in consultation with the Leader of the House, allot a day or days or part of a day for discussion of any such motion.[48]

Resolutions: A discussion may take place on resolutions. A Member wishing to move a resolution is required to give fifteen days' notice of his intention. A resolution may be in the form of a declaration of opinion, or a recommendation; or may be in a form so as to record either approval or disapproval by the House of an act or policy of government, or convey a message or command, urge or request an action, or call attention to a matter or situation for consideration by government, or in such other form as the Speaker may consider appropriate. A resolution may also be moved relating to a matter of general public importance.[49] A copy of every resolution which has been passed by the House is forwarded to the Minister concerned. When a resolution has been moved, the sponsor makes a speech, other Members participate in discussion, and amendments to the original resolution may be moved. Resolutions provide an opportunity to Members to scrutinise and properly review the working of state enterprises.

Discussion on President's address: This opportunity can be utilised by the Members for discussing matters relating to public enterprises. President's address contains the general policy of the government concerning national and international problems. State enterprises are an important national problem today and while discussing the address on a Motion of Thanks, the Members can refer to their working.

Discussion on Enquiry Report: The government is empowered to appoint an Enquiry Committee to enquire into the affairs of a particular public undertaking. Such reports are naturally laid on the Table of the House and if the House desires, it can discuss these reports.

Amendment of the statute under which the public enterprise has been set up: The Members of Parliament get an opportunity to discuss, review or criticise the working of a particular corporation, when the statute, under which it has been established, is amended.

Budgetary demands: These are the important occasions for invoking debates on the working of departmentally managed organisations, demands for which are included in the general budget. But the occasion has not been much availed of because of scarcity of time and lack of interest. The budgets of the joint stock companies and corporations do not come before the Parliament for sanction and, therefore, do not provide an occasion for debate on their working.

Annual Reports: The annual reports on the working of each government company are made available to the Members of the Parliament. Section 619 of the new Indian Companies Act requires that all government companies must, in addition to their balance sheets and profit and loss accounts, also submit annual reports on their working to Parliament. This provides an opportunity to the legislature to take stock of operations of the government companies. Similar provisions are also made in the Acts of various statutory corporations and their annual reports are laid before the legislature, Central or State, as the case may be.

The annual reports, as these are prepared at present, unfortunately are not of much use. The reports are very short and only glorify achievements without making any mention of the defects, shortcomings and failures. It is not possible to form an objective and balanced idea about the working of public enterprises from such scanty and one-sided reports. The reports should honestly state the working of the public undertakings without concealing mistakes and failures.

There is a tendency to herald profits and to push aside unprominently losses. Such a tendency is not very appropriate and the Board should not fight shy in making correct position known to the public through annual reports.

Practice in reporting on matters is not uniform. For example, directives issued by the Minister are important matters for which he is responsible to the Parliament and these, therefore, must be published in the annual reports. The reports should also mention the circumstances necessitating the issue of the directive and the differing views of the Board, if any, for public information. This would help towards an illuminating parliamentary debate on the reports.

There is no standard form of accounts and the reports are heterogeneous in character. Some reports, for instance, give comparative figures of the last few years while other reports do not give such figures. The Estimates Committee suggested that the government should initiate a study of the nationalised industries and public corporations of other countries to evolve "a common pattern" of reports of public enterprises in India.[50] It is very necessary that the reports are published in a standard form. It would be better if a proforma is prescribed for the publication of a fully documented annual report and each public enterprise is instructed to strictly adhere to it. It should be adequately detailed and exhaustive and describe every aspect of the functioning of the enterprise, e.g. organisational, operational, productive, financial, personnel, etc.

The Administrative Reforms Commission had recommended that the Bureau of Public Enterprises, in consultation with the Ministries and public undertakings, should work out a model form for the Annual Reports of public undertakings. Standard operational indices should also be prepared for use by the public undertakings so that essential information relating to their working is brought out in the Annual Reports in a readily intelligible form.[51] The Annual Reports should cover, *inter alia*, the following points:[52]

(1) Information about the adequacy of the quantity and quality of output and reductions in cost.

(2) Information relating to the utilisation of the principal ingredients of production, viz. labour, materials and

installed capacity; in the case of undertakings not concerned with manufacture like transport and trading concerns the corresponding information should relate to factors relevant to such concerns.

(3) Comparative performance between different sections of the undertaking, between one undertaking and another, and in relation to similar undertakings abroad.

(4) A brief report on future plans indicating the extent of demand for the product proposed to be met, the variations in the quantity and quality of supply and the steps planned to reduce costs.

(5) A brief summary of the past operational results with comparisons of the results achieved during a specified period in order to bring out long-term trends.

Until a few years ago, the reports were generally made available with a time-lag of two to three years. B.L. Bansal remarked on this situation that "naturally when you receive the report in respect of a company or a corporation for a period which is two years behind, all the topical interest goes. Whatever you might have heard about the mismanagement or about the shortcomings of that particular undertaking goes out of your mind, that freshness no longer remains there, the urgency is not there and all the piquancy of your criticism goes away and it becomes a purely post-mortem case which you do not like to indulge in because you are already busy with so many other things".[53] If the reports are to serve any useful function, these must be submitted within a reasonable period after the end of the year. The views in regard to the time-limit, however, differ. For instance, the Company Law Administration issued instructions to companies to lay the reports within three months of the Annual Meeting and Section 166 of the Companies Act provides for the Annual Meeting within nine months from the closing of the year which may be extended by further six months by the Central Government which means a maximum time limit of 1½ years. The Comptroller and Auditor General suggested that "the Reports of the statutory corporations should be presented before the Budget for the next year is discussed in the

Parliament". It is very necessary that this divergency of views is resolved and a time-limit fixed on adequate consideration of facts and keeping in view the practice prevalent in other countries. The time-limit is, for instance, 6½ months in the United States. The conventional time-limit ranges from five to six months in the United Kingdom. Normally, a period of six months from the close of the accounting year should be considered adequate for laying the reports before the Parliament.

The effect of parliamentary debates on public enterprises depends to a large extent on their quality. If the debates lack substance, mere vituperation may not have any healthy influence on the Ministry and the Board. But for a skilful debate a Member must be well-informed and expert in the particular field. This, unfortunately, is lacking in Parliaments, particularly in developing countries. The result is that the quality of debates has not been very satisfactory. "The general debates have on the whole been disappointing. They could and should provide an unequalled opportunity for searching analysis, comparison, contrast, criticism, and constructive proposals. Unfortunately, too many members have tended to use them as occasions for rehashing stale arguments in favour of, or against, nationalization, and some of the speeches would have been more appropriate on the second reading debate of a nationalizing Bill".[54] Cohen also observes, "Hitherto debates in Parliament have shown that very few members have devoted the necessary effort to acquaint themselves with the facts of these industries. They cannot be blamed for this because they are busy men and have many preoccupations but too many Members, unfortunately, approach these industries with a political bias. In the eyes of the Labour Members they can do no wrong, and any criticism of them is an attack. In the eyes of the Conservative Members it is doubtful whether they can do anything right, and most probably anything they do is wrong. The records, therefore, of the nationalized industries and their elaborate statutory framework never receive the impartial, careful and thoughtful scrutiny they require".[55] Debates over public enterprises have become a party issue. Points are brought in by the Members either to defend or attack the principle of Nationalisation as such. Supporters of private sector make all efforts to highlight the drawbacks of public undertaking to prove their thesis that the public sector cannot be as efficient as the private sector while the supporters of public enterprise challenge their arguments. Further, there is a tendency on the part of the Ministers to act as advocates of the enterprise whose boards are appointed by them. Whatever be the occasion for, or nature or scope of, debate, it ultimately turns into "party dog-fights", with the Ministers and Parliamentary Secretaries defending stubbornly and the opposition attacking with an eye on a not-too-distant election. This is not the way to discuss the working of public enterprises. The Members should be more objective in evaluating the working of public undertakings and offer constructive suggestions for improvement.

Another reason for unsatisfactory quality of debates is that the Parliament is overworked and does not get adequate time for this purpose. To remove this defect, it would be better if the Parliament can set apart two or three days during every session for reviewing the working of public enterprises, as is done in case of foreign affairs and other important matters.

Committees

The inadequacy and limitations of the methods discussed above left the Members agitating for finding more suitable measures of establishing the desired parliamentary control. This led to an extension of the scope and sphere of the Public Accounts Committee and the evolution of the Estimates Committee. In May 1964, the functions of both these Committees were taken over by the newly set up Committee on Public Undertakings. In answering questions or in the case of a debate, it is the Minister who speaks on behalf of the public undertaking. The examination by a Committee of the Parliament has the advantage that the Chairman and other officers of the undertaking get an opportunity to appear before the Committee and explain their point of view across the table. Since the Public Accounts Committee and the Estimates Committee have done useful work in the field of public enterprises for a fairly long period, we shall briefly study their working before we go to study the functioning of the Committee on Public Undertakings.

Public Accounts Committee

With a view to ensure that the money granted to the executive government is spent economically and for the purpose for which it was granted, the Parliament exercises its control over expenditure, first by the provision of audit of public accounts by an independent and statutory authority—the Comptroller and Auditor General of India—and thereafter an examination of his report by a parliamentary committee—Public Accounts Committee.

The chief functions of the Comptroller and Auditor General are to examine the annual accounts in order to satisfy himself that the parliamentary grants have been used for the purpose for which they were meant and in amounts intended and that they have been spent according to law, rules and regulations; to certify the accounts as correct, subject to whatever reservations he chooses to make; to submit his report to Parliament; to report on any waste and inefficiency; and finally, to comment on important occurrences of topical interest, on disputable matters involving accounting or financial principles, on transactions where heavy losses have occurred or might occur, on expenditure of new services, and on departures from settled precedents and procedures.

The report of the Auditor General is presented to Parliament for examination. In most of the countries the usual practice is to entrust examination of this report to a special committee of the House, designated the Public Accounts Committee. There are three main reasons for this practice. In the first place, the Parliament cannot find enough time to scrutinise the report in detail. Secondly, it is a highly technical matter which can best be undertaken in the committee. Thirdly, a debate in the House may destroy the non-party character of the examination and distort it from its proper perspective.

The Public Accounts Committee consists of twenty-two Members of which fifteen are from Lok Sabha and seven from Rajya Sabha. The Chairman of the Committee is always an elected member of the Lok Sabha and is appointed by the Speaker from amongst its own members. In case the Deputy

Speaker is a member of the Committee, he shall be appointed as the Chairman. As a convention, starting from the Public Accounts Committee of 1967-68, a member of the Committee belonging to the main opposition party/group in the House is appointed as the Chairman of the Committee.

In addition to ascertaining that the money granted by Parliament has been spent by the government 'within the scope of the demand', the examination of the Committee extends 'beyond the formality of the expenditure, to its wisdom, faithfulness and economy'. The objective of this comprehensive review is to ascertain whether the executive has observed the principle of 'prudent house-keeping' in national expenditure.

The scrutiny of the Committee extends to the calling of the officers of various Ministries and putting questions to them to seek clarifications. The Committee scrutinizes cases involving losses, nugatory expenditure and financial irregularities brought out to the notice through the Report of Comptroller and Auditor General. It examines the executive actions of the Ministry of Finance in regard to its compliance with the law. It discusses points of financial order and principle. The Committee also examines cases involving expenditure in excess of voted grants or appropriations. It has, however, no power, even after the most minute examination and on the clearest evidence, to disallow any item of expenditure. It can only comment on that item.

To enable the Committee to discharge its functions effectively, it has been given sufficient powers. It has the authority to send for persons, papers and records to record evidence and to report its opinions and observations on matters coming under its consideration. The Committee has the power to ask questions relating to expenditure whether or not these matters have been mentioned by the Comptroller and Auditor-General. It has a right to intervene in matters of administration and to examine the working system of any department, if necessary, in order to check unwise methods of expenditure. When any case of proved negligence resulting in loss or extravagance is brought to the notice of the Committee, it is authorised to call upon the

Ministry or Department concerned to explain what steps, disciplinary or otherwise, it had taken to prevent a recurrence. But the Committee is in no way a punitive authority. "It does not award punishment, but considers the question of adequacy or otherwise of the action taken by the executive with a view to seeing that the public interests are safeguarded in future and a high standard of public morality is maintained in all financial matters. It must be remembered that in the case of delinquents the Committee adopts an impersonal attitude. It is concerned with the system and not with the individual".[56]

The Ministries or Departments concerned furnish their comments direct to the Committee. The recommendations of the Committee are invariably accepted and implemented by Government. Where the Government has reasons to differ from the recommendations made by the Committee, such reasons are placed before the Committee which reconsiders the matter in the light of Government's views and either modifies its recommendations or adheres to it. If the executive and the Committee disagree on certain matters, they are placed before the Parliament.

Public Accounts Committee has brought out many financial irregularities concerning public enterprises. It has developed a non-party character and has suggested several improvements in the financial working of state enterprises. While many speeches may be made in the House to gain publicity or headlines in newspapers, in the Committee room, the few members, who are there, work with a sense of seriousness, which is very essential for reviewing the working of public enterprises. The Committee is assisted by technical experts who help it in understanding the technicalities of public enterprises and pass correct judgements on them. Officers of public enterprises have to appear before the Committee members for giving evidence or for answering questions. These meetings between Committee members and officers of the public enterprise help in removing doubts and suspicions of the former. Committee members understand the viewpoint and appreciate difficulties of Board Members. The information and experience which the Members of the Committee gather in meetings with the officers of the public enterprise is very helpful to them when they discuss matters pertaining to public enterprises in the Parliament. They can provide first hand knowledge to other Members and their views will be valued because they have studied the enterprise on the spot. The Reports of the Committee have great educative and publicity value. They provide valuable information for the newspapers and journals. In the absence of the Public Accounts Committee, the Comptroller and Auditor General would be less effective.

The general criticism levelled against this Committee is that its work is only post-mortem. It does not serve much purpose because once money has been wrongly spent, it cannot be recalled. This is, however, not true and the postmortem has its own utility. "The very fact of consciousness, that there is some one who will scrutinise what has been done, is a great check on the slackness or negligence...of the executive. The examination, if it is properly carried out, thus leads to general efficiency of the administration. The examination by the Committee may also be useful, as a guide for both future estimates and future policies".[57] Similarly, Asoka Chanda observes, "The committee's power is indirect and lies nominally in the potential results of its reports and in the publicity which it is able to give to the questions it investigates and in the moral effect of its criticism".[58]

The Public Accounts Committee works on the Report of the Comptroller and Auditor General, who also acts as its adviser and expert guide. The approach and conclusions of the Committee, therefore, are not much different. The work of the Committee starts only when the Report of the Comptroller and Auditor General is out and placed before them. The Committee, however, is empowered to call for any papers or persons from the ministry concerned as and when felt necessary for reaching its conclusions. This normally results into long delays in bringing out a report and by the time the report is available, the conditions change so much that the findings of the Committee lose much of its relevance and are thus rendered useless.

There is, however, one consolation that the very existence of the Public Accounts Committee serves to remind the management that their actions are subject to scrutiny on behalf of the Parliament. It is argued that this has impaired initiative and incentive rather than assuring public accountability in regard to efficiency in administration and economy in working. The Committee bothers more with financial procedures and regulations than with efficiency and economy. No doubt, financial irregularities cannot be tolerated but these alone should not be the basis and final test of public accountability.

Estimates Committee

Before the establishment of the Committee on Public Undertakings, this was the most powerful committee which critically reviewed the operations of most of the public undertakings and offered constructive recommendations for attaining greater economy and efficiency.

The Estimates Committee was set up on 10 April 1950. The then Finance Minister, John Matthai, remarked that "the Committee would act as a continuous economy committee, that is to say it would not be concerned with specific proposals but the question of economy over the whole range of Public Administration. They would examine the estimates of the various departments not with a view to changing the expenditure already undertaken for that year but to give guidance to the Government as to the proposals to be made for the following year. The Committee would not be concerned with matters of policy which were the responsibility of the Government; rather within the frame of the policy they would see that only the minimum expenditure is incurred for fulfilling the objectives of the Government".

The Estimates Committee consists of 30 members, all of whom are from the Lok Sabha. The Members are elected by Lok Sabha every year from amongst its members according to the principle of propositional representation by means of single transferable vote. Members of the Rajya Sabha are not permitted to become members of the Estimates Committee because under the Indian Constitution the Rajya Sabha is not authorised to interfere with or cut down any item of the Budget.

The Estimates Committee is the watchdog of the finances of the country. The main function of the Committee is to suggest 'economy consistent with efficiency'. It examines in detail the estimates after they have been voted by Parliament with a view to securing possible economies in the execution of plans and programmes consistent with the policy implied in those estimates, and to make suggestions and recommendations which may, to the extent acceptable, be incorporated in the estimates for the subsequent years.

The recommendations of the Committee are by convention as good as resolutions of Parliament which are binding on the government. If the government wants any modifications in the recommendations, that is possible only through the assistance of, and satisfaction to, the Estimates Committee. Soon after the Report is submitted, the government or the particular department is required to report to the Committee as to how far they have been able to implement it. If the Department does not find it possible to carry out some of the recommendations, they have to take up the matter with the Committee giving full reasons for that and it may modify its recommendations, if necessary.

It is not difficult for the Estimates Committee to move from economy to efficiency and from administration to policy. The terms of reference of the Committee are flexible and the members have not found it difficult to extend their probe deeper and wider. The Committee claims that, although it cannot question approved policy, it is its duty to comment on a particular policy provided it was not fulfilling its purpose or that it was leading to a waste of public funds. It also maintains that while examining estimates, economy is linked with efficiency and efficiency with organization. This emphasis on review of the policies of government and of the structural basis of departmental organization has substantially changed the character and purpose of the Committee which has not been liked by the government officials. In the words of A.K. Chanda, "These activities of the Committee have not been gracefully regarded by the Secretaries to Government. A geat deal of their time is certainly taken up in trying to defend the policies of Government and the structure and functions of their Ministries. The practice of the Committee has created an embarrassing situation for the permanent officials of the departments who are required to defend before a parliamentary committee the policies of Government. But in a democracy it is the responsibility of the Ministers to justify on the floor of the House the policies of Government, if challenged by the opposition. The Estimates Committee cannot be the forum of discussion, nor can officials be counsels for defence. Parliamentary functions must be distinguished from that of Ministers. Further, a committee with a floating membership can hardly be sufficiently familiar with the minutiae of administrative processes and problems to be able to make any significant contribution towards administrative organisation. Its activities thus encroach indirectly on the policy-making functions of Government and its reproaches undermine public confidence in the administration. At the same time, the Committee is arrogating to itself a role which, constitutionally, is that of the House. The Committee makes many recommendations on matters of administrative reorganization, reconstitution of departments and redistribution of functions. This may perhaps have publicity value, but in most cases hardly any practical utility. The Government may have perforce to reject many of these recommendations. This creates a most undesirable situation, detracting as it does from the prestige and authority both of the Government and of a parliamentary committee".[59]

The Committee, since its establishment in 1950, has submitted a number of reports on the working and management of almost all public undertakings. These are valuable documents giving critical reviews of activities, highlighting drawbacks in the planning of projects, defects in various contracts, and suggesting improvements needed in the administrative set-up, directions of economies in working, reforms in finances, and problems of appropriation of profits. They are the only sources of objective and critical information about state enterprises. In the absence of these reports some serious and sensational facts involving losses through inefficient administration or wasteful working would not have come to light.

Committee on Public Undertakings

The question of setting up a Parliamentary Committee on Public Undertakings was initially raised in 1953 on a resolution tabled by Dr. Lanka Sundaram, and subsequently discussed during debates in 1954, 1955 and 1956. The inadequacies of parliamentary supervision over public undertakings attracted greater attention after the L.I.C. case. Soon after, the G.V. Mavalankar, the then Speaker, addressed a letter to the Prime Minister emphasizing the need for appointing a separate committee of Parliament for supervision over public undertakings. This led to the appointment in 1958 of a sub-committee of the Congress Party in Parliament which recommended the setting up of a separate committee of Parliament to supervise public undertakings. The government accepted this recommendation and a Motion constituting the Committee on Public Undertakings was passed by Lok Sabha on the 20 November 1963 and concurred in by Rajya Sabha on the 2 December 1963. The Committee was constituted on the 1 May 1964. The functions of the Committee are:

(a) to examine the reports and accounts of the Public Undertakings.

(b) to examine the reports, if any, of the Comptroller and Auditor General on Public Undertakings,

(c) to examine, in the context of the autonomy and efficiency of the Public Undertakings, whether the affairs of the Public Undertakings are being managed in accordance with sound business principles and prudent commercial practices; and

(d) such other functions vested in the Public Accounts Committee and the Estimates Committee in relation to Public Undertakings by or under the Rules of Procedure and Conduct of Business of the Lok Sabha as are not covered by (a), and (b), and (c) above and as may be allotted to the Committee by the Speaker from time to time.

The items specifically excluded from the Committee's purview are:[60]

(i) matters of major government policy as distinct from business or commercial functions of the public undertakings;

(ii) matters of day-to-day administration; and

(iii) matters for the consideration of which machinery is established by any special statute under which a particular public undertaking is established.

The rules of procedure followed by the Committee on Public Undertakings are for all purposes similar to those of the Committee on Estimates.

The Committee selects for examination such undertakings/ subjects whose comprehensive appraisal appears in the Audit Report (Commercial) presented to Parliament by the Comptroller and Auditor General of India. The Committee also selects on its own certain other undertakings/subjects for independent examination. The Committee may also select one or more aspects of working of various Public Undertakings for comprehensive study. The observations/recommendations of the Committee are embodied in their reports which are presented to Parliament.

The Ministry or Undertaking concerned is required to take action on various recommendations and conclusions contained in the Report. Since its inception in May 1964, the Committee has presented more than 500 Reports so far. From November 2000, the Committee has started presenting to Parliament the Study Tour Reports pertaining to the functioning of individual undertakings with full-fledged recommendations/observations. More than 50 Study Tour Reports have been presented by the Committee. The examination covered several undertakings including the Airports Authority of India Ltd., Hindustan Aeronautics Ltd., Bharat Petroleum Corporation Ltd., Power Grid Corporation of India Ltd., Housing and Urban Development Corporation Ltd., IRCON International Ltd., National Thermal Power Corporation, New India Assurance Company Ltd., Oil and Natural Gas Corporation Ltd., Mahanagar Telephone Nigam Ltd., Bharat Sanchar Nigam Ltd., Mahanadi Coalfields Ltd., and Central Coalfields Ltd.

Since the number of public undertakings is quite large, the Committee found that it would not be possible to cover all of them within the period of one Lok Sabha. The Committee, therefore, decided that, in addition to the individual undertakings taken up for examination, a horizontal study of one or more common aspects or problems of all the Undertakings should be taken up every year.

In addition to the examination of Central Government Undertakings, the Committee also examined in 1966 the working of the state-owned Public Undertakings in Kerala State. This examination was made on the basis of a suggestion made in December 1965 by the Governor of Kerala, upon which the Speaker directed that the Kerala Undertakings be examined by the Committee. The Committee submitted eight Reports on these Undertakings.

The setting up of this Committee has met a long-felt demand for a separate Committee to examine the working of Public Undertakings. The Reports of the Committee have enabled the Members of the Parliament to keep themselves well-informed of the working of various Public Undertakings and the Undertakings themselves have benefited because the examination by the Committee has pinpointed several shortcomings in their working.

In conducting the enquiry, the Committee has considerably depended on eliciting information through detailed questionnaire. The meticulousness with which such detailed questionnaires emanating from a Parliamentary Committee have to be answered have often imposed a heavy burden on the management of the public undertakings and sometimes resulted in the enquiry gravitating towards the area of day-to-day management. In this connection, it is useful to draw on the experience of the United Kingdom. Although the scope of inquiry by the United Kingdom Select Committee on Nationalised Industries was left to the good sense of the Committee, it was made clear during the debate that preceded its constitution that the Committee should not trespass in matters of day-to-day administration or on matters of major government policy. The Select Committee has not considered it necessary to issue a detailed questionnaire as a preliminary step to examination. The Committee follows a quite different mode of enquiry. It first selects a few subjects and frames the issues that it would like to take up for examination.

The Chairman and officers of the concerned undertaking then prepare and submit memoranda on the issues. After this the enquiry takes the form of "across the table" discussions with the Chairman and the officers on the basis of the memoranda that have already been submitted. Generally, the UK Select Committee takes up one subject for examination during the course of a year. It examines the representatives of the undertaking, the controlling Ministry and the Treasury separately and does not undertake any on-the-spot study tours. The more important aspects considered by the U.K. Select Committee, according to its former Chairman, are:[61]

(i) the attitude of the Chairman and the Board on the question whether they were carrying out a public service or doing a commercial job;

(ii) the degree of ministerial interference; the direct effect of this upon the financial accounts and results; and the indirect effect through blurring the lines of responsibility;

(iii) the provision and continuance of uneconomic services; and

(iv) the control of capital investment.

In India, the reports of the Committee on Public Undertakings show that the Committee has been keenly interested in the control of capital investment. In other matters, the Committee have up to now tended to favour the laying down of rules and regulations and attaining uniformity in matters like service rules and conditions, expenditure on township, scales of accommodation, etc. The Committee does not appear to have yet directed their inquiry towards the area of ministerial interference which has been a very important area of inquiry in the United Kingdom.

The Administrative Reforms Commission have recommended that the Committee on Public Undertakings should take up for examination, instead of individual undertakings, a group of undertakings falling within one area of enterprise and bring out consolidated report thereon.[62] Such a procedure would have a number of advantages:[63]

(i) It would enable the Committee to cover, within the time at its disposal, a larger number of undertakings and to examine their problems more deeply.

(ii) It would enable the Committee to avoid having to reconsider similar issues of different undertakings operating in the same field of industry. It would also make possible a simultaneous and comparative appraisal of the performance of different units in the same field of enterprise.

(iii) It will make the enquiry move away from matters of day-to-day administration and gravitate to those of overall general importance.

(iv) A consolidated report will also enable Members of Parliament to acquaint themselves better with the problems on which Parliament should focus its attention.

The Committee on Public Undertakings has consistently taken up horizontal studies during the last few years. For example, in 2005-06, the Committee constituted during the fourteenth Lok Sabha undertook a study on Health Insurance which comprised an evaluation of health schemes of five public sector insurance companies. Topics for other such studies included aspects of disinvestment, industrial safety, etc.

Conclusion

The Minister should have adequate powers of control over public enterprises because the ultimate responsibility for planning and co-ordinating the whole activity in that particular field and for fitting it in the national plan rests with him. But actual experience shows that the Ministers have a tendency to interfere in the affairs of the public enterprises to an extent much greater than that justified by statutes establishing these. For efficient functioning of a public enterprise, it is very essential to preserve its autonomy in day-to-day administration. Frequent informal discussions between the Minister and the Board are useful but these should be without prejudice to the rights and responsibilities of either the Minister or Board. The Minister should resist the temptation of invoking his residuary power of issuing directives as far as possible unless there is gross negligence of the Board or commission of an egregious mistake. The directives, when considered absolutely unavoidable, should invariably be in writing and published in the annual reports of the enterprise.

The Parliament as the trustee of the nation has a right to assure itself that in broad terms the financial and managerial policies followed by public enterprises are sound and promote the ends of public policy underlying their establishment. But it should confine itself to questions of major policy and exceptional circumstances, and avoid unnecessary interference in day-to-day working of the enterprises. An unnecessary interference will lead to delays, overcaution, lack of confidence and impairment of initiative and drive on the part of those running the enterprises.

NOTES

1. Earnest Davis in W.A. Robson (ed.), *Problems of Nationalised Industry* (London, 1952), p. 110.
2. Robson, n. 1, p. 306.
3. Economic Commission for Asia and Far East, *Report of Seminar on Organisation and Administration of Public Enterprises in the Industrial Field* (Rangoon, 1954), p. 306.
4. Section 81(1).
5. Section 8.
6. Aneurin Bevan, *House of Commons Debate,* February 25, 1952, 496, 5s., col. 818.
7. Action Society Trust, *The Powers of the Minister* (Claygate, Surrey, 1951), pp. 4-7.
8. Words within parenthesis added.
9. Earnest Davies, "Government Policy and Public Corporation", *Political Quarterly* (June 1955), pp. 115-16.
10. M.C. Chagla, "Government Policy and the Public", *Political Quarterly,* October-December 1955, p. 111.
11. W.A. Robson, *Nationalised Industry and Public Ownership* (London, 1962), p. 162.
12. Krishna Menon Committee, *Report on Parliamentary Supervision over State Enterprises* (New Delhi, 1960), para 60.
13. Section 48 of D.V.C. Act.
14. Section 21 of L.I.C. Act.
15. Section 34 of Air Corporations Act.
16. Section 48(2).

17. *House of Lords Debates,* 5s; col. 1504 (March 12, 1953).
18. Robson, n. 11, p. 145.
19. R.C. Agarwal, *State Enterprises in India* (Allahabad, 1961), p. 224.
20. Cabinet Secretariat's Office Memorandum No. 72145/CF-65, dated 13 October 1965.
21. Herbert Morrison, *Government and Parliament* (London, 1954), p. 264.
22. Estimates Committee, *Report on Administrative, Financial and Other Reforms* (New Delhi, 1954), pp. 17-18.
23. "Parliament and the Corporation", *The Times* (London), 3 March 1948.
24. A.H. Hanson, "Parliamentary Questions on Nationalised Industries", *Public Administration* (Spring 1951), pp. 52-53.
25. "Chagla Commission Report", *Hindustan Times* (14 February 1958), p. 13.
26. Government of India, *Report of the Chagla Commission on the Life Insurance Corporation* (New Delhi, 1959), p. 23.
27. Ernest Davies, *The Development of the Public Corporation* (London, 1946), p. 81.
28. House of Commons, 235, 23 July 1953, as quoted by C.O. Keyes, "Public Corporation", *Political Science Quarterly,* Vol. LXX, p. 55.
29. United Nations, *Some Problems in the Organisation and Administration of Public Enterprises in the Industrial Field* (New York, 1954), p. 6.
30. Cf. N.V. Gadgil, "Accountability of Administration", *Indian Journal of Political Quarterly* (January-March 1955), p. 195.
31. Public Accounts Committee, *Report on the Accounts of 1947-48 (Post-Partition)* (New Delhi, 1952), p. 5.
32. Public Accounts Committee, *Report on the Account of 1947-48,* Appendix I.
33. *Rules of Procedure and Conduct of Business in Lok Sabha,* 1957, Rule 36.
34. *Ibid.,* Rule 37.
35. *Ibid.,* Rule 50.
36. House of Commons Debates, 5s. (March 3, 1948), col. 456.
37. Chairman's Ruling in Lok Sabha Debates, 17 December 1964.
38. "Chagla Commission Report", *Hindustan Times,* 14 February 1958.
39. *Lok Sabha Debates,* 11 December 1953, col. 1963.
40. Herbert Morrison, "Public Control of Socialised Industries", *Public Administration,* 1950, p. 8.

41. *House of Commons Debates,* ds. (December 4, 1947), col. 566.
42. Robson, n. 11, p. 176.
43. Lok Sabha Secretariat, *Bulletin Part II* (New Delhi, 1958), pp. 1431-32.
44. *House of Commons Debates,* Vol. 447, 3 March 1948, col. 456.
45. Rules of Procedure and Conduct of Business in Lok Sabha, 1957, Rule 55(1).
46. *Ibid.*, Rule 56.
47. *Ibid.*, Rules 193-95.
48. *Ibid.*, Rule 190.
49. *Ibid.*, Rules 170-72.
50. Estimates Committee, *Report on Preparation of Budget Estimates of Public Undertakings and Presentation of Their Annual Reports and Accounts to Parliament* (New Delhi, 1960), para 29.
51. Administrative Reforms Commission, *Report on Public Sector Undertakings* (New Delhi, 1967) (Mimeographed), pp. 57-58.
52. *Ibid.*, p. 58.
53. G.L. Bansal in "Parliamentary Democracy", Report of the First All India Seminar, 1956. The Indian Bureau of Parliamentary Studies (New Delhi), p. 143.
54. Robson, n. 1, p. 318.
55. R. Kelf Cohen, *Nationalization in Britain—The End of a Dogma* (London, 1958), p. 157.
56. V.B. Gandhi, M.P., Chairman of the Public Accounts Committee, "Parliamentary Democracy", *Report of the All India Seminar* (1956), p. 139.
57. G.V. Mavalankar, "Speech to P.A.C., April 10, 1950", in G.V. Mavalankar, *Speeches and Writings* (1953), p. 79.
58. Asoka Chanda, *Indian Administration* (London, 1958), p. 183.
59. *Ibid.*
60. Rule 312 of the Rules of Procedure and Conduct of Business in Lok Sabha—Rules relating to Committee on Public Undertakings.
61. Sir Taby Low: "The Select Committee on Nationalized Industries", *Public Administration,* Vol. 40, Spring 1962.
62. Administrative Reforms Commission, n. 51, pp. 56-57.
63. Administrative Reforms Commission, *Report of the Study Team on Public Sector Undertakings* (New Delhi, 1967) (Mineographed), p. 95.

7

Management—Goals and Measurement

Goals for Management

Formerly, it was common to distinguish between public and private enterprise by reference to the motivations of their respective managements. Both served the public by way of producing goods and services as economically and efficiently as possible, but while service was direct and conscious objective in public enterprise, it was a by-product of profit-making in private enterprise. Thus, in public enterprises, there could be no conflict between social purposes and managerial objectives, while in private enterprises such a conflict could arise to the extent the maximisation of profits did not automatically lead to maximum public benefit, particularly if the enterprise was operating in a field that was short of fully competitive.

It would not be correct to maintain that this contrast has entirely lost its validity, but, today, it is subject to so many qualifications that it no longer has its former clarity. The well-known divorce between ownership and control has made the motivation of private management much more complicated than it used to be. The very conception of profit, when analysed, tends to become ambiguous. The pursuit of long-term profitability has very different economic effects and social implications from the mere search for immediate rewards, and profitability itself, in the sense of material gains accruing to individuals, may be of secondary importance to the expansion and consolidation of the concern, or in other words, to the pursuit of economic power. On the other hand, a public enterprise, while in theory having no other motive than that of service, may conspicuously fall short of this ideal, and may grow into a kind of managerial 'empire', in which officials, enjoying the security of tenure characteristic of the civil service, ignore the purposes they are supposed to pursue and behave in a dictatorial manner with the public. Finally, the very concept of public service can be interpreted in different ways. For instance, none has succeeded in attaching an agreed meaning to the well known statutory injunction to British nationalised industries "to serve the public interest in all respects", and it is inconceivable that any court of law can give any specific interpretation to this clause.

If we reject the distinction between 'profit' and 'service' as too imprecise and ambiguous for purposes of analysis, the question arises as to whether there are certain other general principles which can serve as a guide to the behaviour of public enterprise managements. Some analysts are of the view that there is no fundamental distinction between the private and public sectors in regard to the principles of management. Managements in both sectors, to the extent they are permitted to do so, are expected to behave in accordance with sound and well-established commercial principles.

From the point of view of the actual running of the individual enterprise, 'sound commercial policy' carries a very definite meaning. It almost goes without saying, for instance, that the management of a public enterprise, like that of any other enterprise, should try to minimize cost of production, should make efforts to make the concern "pay its ways", and should constantly adapt production policy to the changing requirements of the market. Principles of this type provide reasonable guides to managerial policy. If they are consistently ignored, there would occur wastage of precious productive resources. But they are by no means absolutes, and have to be considered in relation to other requirements which may be applicable to both public and private enterprise, but which are particularly applicable to enterprises deliberately set up by the state as agencies of economic development.

Costs of production, for instance, may be minimised by methods which, although immediately economical for the enterprise concerned, are not at all economical for the country as a whole. Labour welfare activities, though raise the costs of the enterprise, may be justified in order to preserve industrial peace and to attract and maintain a stable labour force and also on social considerations. Expensive training and apprenticeship schemes, the benefit of which rarely accrues exclusively to the enterprise providing them, may be very important for the general improvement of skills.

From the point of view of economic development, sometimes enterprises might have to be run at a loss, even over a considerable period. Such losses have to be balanced against actual or potential gains to the economy as a whole. It would not be in the interest of the country, for instance, to close down or contract the operations of a fertilizers plant simply because the peasants were not in a position to purchase its products at a price which covered its costs of production. Similarly, it would be wrong to expect that, in all cases, the supply of electricity to a rural area or the operation of a railway line to 'open up' an underdeveloped region could be conducted on a profit-making or 'break-even' basis.

Even "adaptation to the requirements of the market" is not a principle of absolute validity. No doubt, many public enterprises have not done well because of their constant neglect of consumer preferences. But the 'lumpy' nature of economic development frequently requires that an enterprise should adapt itself not to existing demand but to a future, planned demand, in a manner that the ordinary profit-minded entrepreneur would consider as commercially hazardous—and rightly so.

It appears thus reasonable to assume that a public enterprise may be required, in the interest of planning for economic development, to operate in a manner which appears 'uncommercial' from the point of view of management. This is likely to happen rather more frequently in a less developed country than in a comparatively highly developed one.

It might be contended, however, that the 'non-commercial' considerations, examples of which we have cited above, are matters for the government, and not for the management, which is supposed to operate according to strict commercial principles within a frame of reference provided by legislation and by directives from higher authority. But it may be emphasized that the more important considerations of 'national interest', as distincts from 'strictly commercial' considerations, become the more desirable it is that the management itself should be aware of the role that the enterprise is expected to play and convinced of the validity of the objectives that it is enjoined to pursue. Such objectives cannot be formulated *in vacuo*, at a high political level. These can best be formulated only in co-operation with the enterprise itself because if there is constant conflict between managerial policy and 'higher' policy, the performance of the enterprise is likely to be adversely affected.

It nevertheless remains true that within the frame of reference which has been framed in consultation with them, managers must constantly endeavour to minimize costs and maximize revenue on the basis of a product or service which satisfies certain quality specifications. It is probably in regard to the 'quality' factor that some of the most difficult problems may arise, particularly when a choice has to be made between (i) a comparatively large quantity of comparatively low quality and therefore low priced products, and (ii) a comparatively small quantity of comparatively high quality and therefore high priced products. Here management may possess considerable discretion in regard to the fulfilment of its general objectives, and here, also, 'commercial' considerations (that is minimization of total costs and maximization of total revenues) may not be the decisive ones.

Final stress must be laid on the clarity of objectives. In collaboration with those concerned, it is essential to break down the over-all national plan into a series of goals, or terms of reference, for each individual industry and plant, so that the managers clearly know the object of the exercise and have before them a series of well defined targets. It is equally essential that these are laid down in such terms as can be grasped by all the categories of personnel. In the absence of clearly formulated goals, the organisation is likely to change its policies in response to all kinds of stray influences, both internal and external.

Coordination of effort also suffers, and in the extreme case may become almost impossible when no one is certain what the object of the exercise is. In such a situation, spontaneous, contradictory and predominantly self-interested objectives soon begin to predominate among the various people concerned. Further, clarity of objectives is very essential for the proper delegation of responsibility. In the absence of this, the ever present tendency towards centralisation is strengthened since those in the lower ranks of the managerial hierarchy have no criteria for taking decisions independently. Every question becomes 'difficult' and as such has to be referred to someone higher up.

However clearly defined, realistic and attainable the goals may be, they would not be of much use if they are simply embodied in a document which the top manager keeps in his drawer to consult occasionally. The twin requirements of proper coordination and adequate delegation becomes possible only if a thorough understanding of the goals is diffused among personnel of all levels.

Measurement of Management[1]

'Measurement' as consciously applied to management is a recent phenomenon. Earlier the management was considered to be an 'art' pure and simple, the successful application of which depended completely on the inherent capacity of the person who was entrusted with the task. But with the expanding size and growing complexity of business enterprises, the necessity was felt for tools which would enable management to discharge its duty by methods other than purely personal knowledge and observation. The scientific method came to be applied to the problems of management and this naturally led to efforts towards the formulation of objective and precise criteria for helping and evaluating the performance of management. This was particularly so because the management function in a modern business enterprise came to be exercised by different persons operating at different levels and in different capacities, instead of by a single person as in the past. The divorce between ownership and operational management required the owners to perform the function of selecting managerial personnel and evaluating their efficiency of operation. The actual management itself became so complicated that it was not possible for a single person to perform it. It became necessary for the head of the management organisation to delegate several management functions to subordinates specialised in particular functions or individual parts of the whole enterprise; and such delegation led to the creation of multiple tiers in the management hierarchy. This made it necessary for the higher level of management to lay down definite objectives for the lower levels to pursue and to try to evaluate the extent to which these objectives were being effectively achieved. All this has led to an increasing use of "measurement of management".

The criterion of effective management can be considered from two points of view:

(i) that of an outside controlling authority which wants to evaluate whether the management that it has set up is functioning efficiently. In public enterprises this would mainly be the controlling Government and the Legislature; in case of private enterprises it would be the shareholders;

(ii) that of the higher management of the enterprise itself which may find itself essential to provide for internal checks of various types. These should enable it to carry out a continuous examination of the levels of efficiency at which each of its component parts are operating and so to rectify inefficiencies and ensure a high level of performance for the enterprise as a whole.

Thus there are two points of view in the evaluation of the efficiency of management. Some of the criteria formulated may happen to be commonly useful for both types; some may be more useful for one or the other category; and some useful exclusively for either the external authority or the higher management.

The criteria for measuring management efficiency can be broadly divided into two categories: (i) general indices which are based on a money measure and provide some over-all index of efficiency; and (ii) particular indices which indicate efficiency in respect of particular parts of enterprise or the use of a particular input.

Profitability

This criterion has the great advantage that it is simple to calculate and understand. It provides a common standard with which the controlling authority can compare the efficiency of management in different enterprises under its control. Further it is a general criterion which provides an over-all indication of efficiency combining all the different operations together. This is useful for the outside authority, whether it be the government, the Legislature or the public.

It is generally accepted that in private sector, profitability provides a rough and ready measure of managerial efficiency, particularly if the enterprise is operating under competitive conditions. This measurement, however, is not entirely satisfactory. A rise in profits need not always be the result of improved efficiency, nor a decline in profits of deteriorated efficiency. Nor does a comparison of the profitability of different enterprises operating in the same field necessarily reflect differences in managerial efficiency, because it may be extremely difficult, and sometimes impossible, to separate the effect of the latter on the over-all result.

It may be assumed, however, that in a privately-owned enterprise, run for profit is keenly competitive, and there exists a continuous incentive to raise the level of managerial efficiency. This incentive is weakened to the extent the enterprise becomes protected from competition, whether by accident or by design. It is weak in a public enterprise which generally enjoys such protection. Since most of the public enterprises are, more or less, in this type of situation, it becomes very important to provide alternative incentives. To provide them, it is helpful that some reasonably reliable and objective method of measuring managerial efficiency should be devised.

In the first place, we must try to distinguish between the various kinds of factors which influence the performance of an enterprise. These may be classified into three categories, viz.

(i) "objective" socio-economic conditions, e.g. the 'stage of trade', both internal and external, the condition of the labour market, the availability of various types of skill, the general social and ideological environment, (ii) decisions taken externally to the enterprise, e.g. the law which lays down its constitution and governs its relationship with higher authority, the laws which impose on it obligations in regard to labour relations, employee welfare and personnel practices in general, the directives which it receives from the responsible Minister, and the general economic policies which determine the scope of its operations and (iii) the internal organization and procedure of the enterprise itself. Unless the effect of the third of these can be separated, to some extent, from that of the other two, it would not be possible to measure the specific contribution of managerial behaviour to the over-all result.

Such separation is easiest when the enterprise is operating under competitive conditions, is comparatively free from political interference, and is subject to legal controls not much different from those which govern its competitors, with whom it shares the same socio-economic environment. But in the case of a public enterprise where the elimination of other factors is not easy, it is not possible to attribute with confidence a particular result to managerial virtue or vice because a lot depends on the personal qualities of top management. A genius may produce good results from a rather inferior managerial set-up merely by communicating his dynamism 'down the line' and using his authority to short-circuit rules and conventions which stand in his way. But the results attained in this way cannot continue beyond the tenure of office of the person responsible for them, and provide no index of efficiency of the managerial system, which is likely to reveal its defects when a normally able manager takes over from the genius in the top-level position.

Such complications caution those concerned with the measurement of managerial efficiency to avoid short-cuts and to approach the problem in a logical and systematic manner. The first step obviously is to compile data which measure, not the performance of management specifically, but that of the enterprise in general. It may then be possible, by a process of step by step elimination of the extraneous factors (necessarily, however, an inexact and approximate action), to form an estimate of the contribution of management to the over-all result.

Cost Reduction

In public enterprises where maximization of profit is not desirable, a good alternative to the measure of profitability may be that of cost reduction. This is also a general measure covering the whole enterprise. If standard norms regarding the cost of production are laid down for all the main products of the enterprise, the efficiency of management can be evaluated by the management's success in keeping actual costs within these limits. Obviously, the extent of the usefulness of this measure will depend upon the care with which the norms are set up. If they are based purely on historical costs, they may provide only a rough measure of management efficiency. Even so, cost norms based on historical cost may have to be used in the earlier stages of an enterprise before other norms based on detailed study are built up, since the latter process may take time. They would be possible only after some experience in regard to the actual working of the enterprise. If prices of most of the inputs remain unchanged, such norms would provide a rough basis for measuring efficiency; in case the prices do not remain stable, costs at fixed prices of inputs can be specially calculated to provide a basis for comparison. There are generally some reserves in any production process which provide opportunities to an efficient management to improve upon its performance. The success of the management can, therefore, be evaluated fairly by its capacity to reduce costs below the norms established on the basis of previous history. The problem is that as management succeeds in utilizing these reserves and thus eliminating waste, such efforts will yield progressively diminishing returns, particularly as year after year the norms themselves will be brought down according to the cost levels actually attained. If cost reduction as compared to cost norms historically established is to be the sole measure of management efficiency and every achievement in cost reduction is to lead to a further lowering of norms, the management may be induced not to attain too much cost reduction in any given year.

While cost norms based on purely historical data may be useful in the initial stages, an early effort should be made to calculate standard costs for the various inputs, based on a proper study of the processes of production. The general cost norms will then be a total of these with allowance for overheads. Obviously, this will be useful for the external controlling authority for measuring over-all management. The itemized standard costs will be more useful for measuring efficiency for the purpose of bringing about improvements.

An important disadvantage of any over-all measure of efficiency like profitability or cost reduction is that in a complex enterprise, where several different products are produced and there are a large number of constituent parts of the enterprise, the over-all measure may conceal the state of efficiency or inefficiency of particular sections of the enterprise. This shows the need for maintaining separate accounts for the different parts of the enterprise.

Other General Norms

In the case of a regulated or planned economy, there may be certain other objectives which the controlling authority desires the management to pursue. For instance, the supply of certain commodities may be particularly scarce. For various reasons, it may be decided not to raise the prices of these commodities to a level commensurate with their actual scarcity. Economy in the use of such commodities may then be considered as an important criterion of efficiency. In a developing economy, the supply of foreign exchange may be taken as an example of the commodities belonging to this category. It may be decided not to change the exchange rate to show the actual pressure on foreign exchange. In such a case, reduction in the use of imported goods may be set up as an objective and therefore as a criterion of efficiency.

In this context, it may also be stated that the measures of efficiency must generally be based on the objectives which the management is asked to pursue. In a planned economy the expected outputs of different industries might be so dovetailed that a shortfall in the output of one enterprise would have serious consequences for the economy as a whole, particularly if the dovetailing does not leave much of a margin. In such a case the attainment of the target output may become a very important criterion of management efficiency.

Internal Norms

The methods mentioned above, while of some use to the management itself, will mainly be useful to the outside controlling authority. But the management should also provide criteria which can be used by the higher management of a production unit to check on the operational efficiency of the operating units under its control and to indicate the correctives necessary to improve their efficiency. For this purpose, a large number of norms, standards and so on, will have to be formulated keeping in view the needs of the particular production unit. Through a detailed study of operations, a series of norms in regard to input-output relations can be formulated for every workshop, for various definable parts of a workshop, and to a certain extent for small groups of workers or even individual workers. The formulation of such norms is obviously a complicated problem. Technical studies are necessary for formulating standards in regard to the use of raw materials, power, spare parts, and so on. Formulation of these for labour utilization involve greater complications. Studies are being conducted in regard to the whole process of production, the flow of material, division of operations, and the manner and technique of carrying out various production processes. This requires a considerable degree of co-operation from the personnel operating at various levels. In many enterprises there is a tendency to look down upon the man with the stop-watch and unless the management takes care to see that the workers adopt a positive attitude towards such a study of operations, it may be difficult to conduct such a study. It is now widely recognised that it is essential for the management to take the workers into its confidence and obtain their consent if labour norms are effectively to be set up and used for improving efficiency.

It is encouraging to note that the importance of measuring managerial performance has been widely recognised. But there appear to be limitations to what the less developed countries can accomplish, or should try to accomplish, in this regard. The two limiting factors are (i) non-availability of adequate and reliable statistical data of the required type and (ii) shortage of personnel qualified to interpret such information and to conduct the "follow-up" investigations.

The second limitation is more serious than the first. To attain results, an efficient investigating unit needs to be staffed with competent experts—adequately trained management engineers working under the supervision of people possessing wide experience in the fields of industry, commerce, finance, and administration. In less developed countries, there is an acute shortage of such personnel and to employ the available personnel in investigatory capacities does not appear to be very economical. The services of the experts should be used for running the enterprises rather than for checking their efficiency. To cite Hanson, "An effectively staffed organisation for checking the efficiency of public enterprises is a 'western' luxury which an under-developed country simply cannot afford not because it costs too much money, but because it represents a misapplication of scarce and valuable manpower".[2]

NOTES

1. Also see chapter on Efficiency.
2. A.H. Hanson, *Public Enterprise and Economic Development* (London, 1959), p. 387.

Personnel Management 8

The public enterprises constitute the largest employer employing lakhs of persons doing different types of work throughout the length and breadth of the country. As an employer of such large personnel, they are expected to perform a dual role. On the one hand, they are expected to ensure that the efficiency of the staff is maintained at the highest possible level; and on the other hand, they have also to ensure that the directive principles of state policy laid down in the Indian Constitution are applied to their staff. In other words, they have to fulfil conditions of efficiency consistent with economy and of 'model employer' in their operation. In order to attain a high level of efficiency, it is essential that the right type of persons are recruited for the jobs, that they are given the proper type of training, and that a sense of discipline is maintained among them. The public enterprises should also try to create just and human conditions of work.

Some people hold the view that the management of public enterprises should have complete freedom to employ, promote and dismiss staff, and fix grades and pay scales. Their autonomy in this regard is quite wide in some countries. However, the tendency to assimilate employment conditions in public enterprises to those in the civil service is very wide-spread; and even where it is non-existent or weak, the demand that all public enterprises should be subject to certain common standards, enforced by external authority, is quite strong. The important reasons for this are: (i) the prestige and security enjoyed by the civil service, in which public enterprise employees are anxious to share; (ii) the view that wide dissimilarities of conditions in different sectors of government employment are not fair and justified; (iii) the need to restrict competition for scarce personnel as between the civil service and the enterprises, and among the enterprises themselves; and (iv) fear of corruption and nepotism in personnel practices if the enterprises are left completely free. To the extent that such considerations influence public opinion and government policy, management may find itself severely restricted in its attempts to provide the enterprise with a system of personnel management in accordance with its specific requirements. An effort should be made to find the best balance between autonomy and control.

One of the way out is to set up a special Personnel Commission for public enterprises, to which each enterprise should submit for approval its own personnel regulations. If such a commission, consisting predominantly of persons with industrial and commercial experience, uses its powers wisely, the resultant compromise between the public interest and the interests of the enterprises can work out satisfactorily.

Internal Organisation

The performance of an enterprise largely depends on the quality of its top-level organization. Generally, the supreme authority (within the limits set by law and ministerial directive) is vested in a Board. Various types of relationship between Board and General Manager are possible. In some cases, he is not even a member of the Board and merely attends its meetings, as and when required to give advice and to report on his stewardship. This arrangement, however, is not satisfactory. A General Manager, being the key man in the organisation, should be a member of the Board, and there is a strong case for giving him the chairmanship. If the chairmanship and the general managership are occupied by different persons, unnecessary and energy consuming conflicts may develop between them, unless their personalities and policies happen to be particularly well attuned. It is very important that the prestige and authority of the General Manager is enhanced in every possible way. The worst situation is one when the Board constantly looks over the shoulder of the General Manager and tries to concern itself with matters of day-to-day administration which should be his exclusive responsibility. Such a situation would lead to very unfortunate results. It is likely to arise when the Board (i) has frequent meetings and (ii) divides itself up into a large number of committees for the supervision of particular aspects of the enterprise's work. Full Board meetings more frequently than at monthly intervals require very special justification, and if the Board wants to give itself a committee structure, it should do so on the basis of the broadest possible allocation of responsibilities.

Regarding the structural organization below the Board level, no uniform pattern can be laid down because the form of organization best suited to a given enterprise necessarily depends on its special needs and requirements. In planning the organizational structure of an enterprise, a number of factors have to be taken into consideration, e.g. the objectives of the enterprise, its size, the nature of the product or products manufactured, geographical location of the enterprise and its markets, skill of available personnel, need for co-ordination with other public agencies, and the degree of public scrutiny and control, etc. For instance, if an enterprise is subject to constant public scrutiny and criticism, its organization is likely to be highly centralized even though a decentralized structure might be more conducive to efficient working. The problem of devising a sound organization is much more complex than that of designing a machine. Sir Charles Renold, Chairman of the British Institute of Management, has cautioned that there is a tendency for organisation to attach excessive importance to "things to be done" and underrate the importance of establishing suitable relations among the human beings who are to do the work. He is of the view that "care for the well-being of the team or community is just as important as concern for the things to be done. It is, in fact, a condition of doing them successfully".[1] While no single pattern of organization can be laid down for public enterprises, there are certain common principles which should be kept in view in planning organization structure.

L. Urwick summarizes the generally accepted principles as follows:[2] (i) a clear division between administrative and executive functions; (ii) provision at every level of a centre of energy, direction and administrative management; (iii) adequate decentralization of executive responsibility and initiative; and (iv) channels at every level for the expression of individual responsibility and the exercise of leadership.

The two most difficult problems are co-ordination and delegation. They become more difficult with the expansion of the size of organization. The larger the organization, the more specialized do managerial functions become and the greater is the number of 'levels' in the line of command. The more difficult, therefore, becomes the task of ensuring that everyone knows what everyone else is doing and that all are working to a common policy.

Co-ordination requires an intelligent and imaginative use of all available management tools and must be secured at every level of operations. Formal co-ordinating machinery, whether it takes the form of staff agencies or committees, cannot be a substitute for the day-to-day informal co-ordination which is necessary for the conduct of any enterprise. Formal co-ordinating machinery should not impair or delay the informal processes of co-ordination, nor dilute the individual official's responsibility to co-ordinate his work with those engaged in related activities. Care should be taken that the committees themselves do not hinder co-ordination by encouraging needless debate and delays in resolving issues. Formal co-ordinating machinery may be necessary, however, in developing the basic programme and determining over-all policies. In large enterprises staff agencies may be used in the fields of planning, budget, finance, and organization and methods, to review and co-ordinate programme proposals and to prepare such analyses as may be necessary to assist top management in making sound judgments. It may, however, be stressed that these devices provide no recipe for success, and there is always the risk that the General Manager, frustrated with the delays that the use of committees and staff conferences appear to involve, may decide to override them. Going to the opposite extreme, he may sit at his desk, issuing orders without consulting anybody, and trying to obtain co-ordination by insisting that all but the most routine matters be brought before him. This will generally lead to even worse consequences. The machine becomes clogged; subordinate managers, deprived of any responsibility, cease to exercise authority and experience a lowering of morals; and the General Manager, overburdened with a mass of detail, all of it 'urgent', has no time for making those broad strategic decisions which are the essential basis of effective co-ordination. Good committee work and good discipline are equally necessary, but neither can be a substitute for what F.C. Hooper calls "keeping touch". "Paper contact", he states, "is no substitute for personal contact. Nor can the latter be regarded as adequately secured by periodic round-table conferences. A head of a great business will commonly make a practice of seeing every one of his principal departmental heads, perhaps numbering 200 or 300, man to man at least twice a year, and many of them far oftener. At these meetings, which will be private and personal, the whole results of the subordinate's activities will be 'on the table' with the fullest opportunity to discuss in principle and in detail. Similarly, a director, or departmental head, will spend the minimum time possible at his office desk, and as much as possible in the department, the factory, or the branches.... The initiative in keeping touch should come from the top. It is the head who should seek the subordinate and not the subordinate who should be left to seek out the head, for in practice he will seldom do so".[3]

As regards delegation, this is the very essence of the line and staff concept. The top management can free itself for the essential duties of policy formation and over-all control only by a well-defined and adequate scheme of delegation. Only thus can subordinates enjoy an authority commensurate with their responsibilities, become genuine leaders within their spheres of jurisdiction, and obtain the experience necessary for promotion to higher and more responsible posts. Yet at the same time control must be maintained. It is not safe to delegate a function and then forget all about it. Periodically, the subordinate must have his performance checked and be held to account. It is not easy to build into the system adequate checks and at the same time avoid excessive interference with the performance of delegated functions. It is probably particularly difficult in a country where excessive governmental centralization tends to be reproduced in public enterprises, and where managers, both top-level and subordinate, are inexperienced and nervous. A General Manager who finds himself minutely accountable to higher authority will obviously hesitate to permit his subordinate a larger freedom than he himself enjoys, particularly if he is not sure of their capacities and powers of judgment. Yet a bold scheme of delegation is very essential if the clogging of the managerial machine is to be avoided, and if the subordinates are to learn—as, in the last resort, they only can learn—by making mistakes and taking responsibility for them.

Procedural and Supervisory Problems

The function of management is often considered to be simply as the making of decisions which, expressed in the form of orders, are communicated, verbally or documentarily, to subordinates who are expected to obey them without question or comment. No doubt, this type of management would work, but it is not likely to yield good results. The essence of good management is leadership, and leadership means not simply issuing orders but convincing those to whom they are issued that on the basis of their own experience the orders are the right ones. Obedience then becomes both willing and informed, and it would be more so if the recipients of the orders have been associated with their formulation. When this happens, the need to think in terms of orders becomes less and less. In a sense, the "government of persons is replaced by the administration of things". It is, however, not easy to attain this ideal; but a progressive management must work in this direction.

Even if we continue to think in terms of a flow of orders downwards, it may be stressed that these are not likely to be good orders unless there is an equally vigorous flow of information and suggestion upwards. Subordinates should not only be permitted but positively encouraged to offer constructive criticisms. If they disagree with certain matters, they must have opportunities to express their views, and if possible to suggest a better way of doing things. Otherwise, they will merely grumble unconstructively among themselves. But this freedom of criticism must be combined with firm discipline. While there should be maximum amount of discussion about what should be done, there should be maximum discipline in the doing of it.

The public enterprises in developing countries urgently need a new conception of the role which a "subordinate" should play. In civil services of these countries, there is a tendency to consider him as the passive recipient of directives, whose performance is judged by his 'correctness' in carrying them out. He is not expected to show initiative, and any suggestion from him is often considered as approaching impertinence. To cite A.H. Hanson, "The young man is not usually expected to think critically about his country's administrative system or to develop ideas for its improvement. Superiors do not normally expect suggestions from him, and are liable to resent them, as implied criticism, if they are made".[4] Such attitudes are not very congenial to the efficient working of public enterprises. The job of the superior is not that of periodically "catching out" the subordinate, but that of helping him to attain higher standards of efficiency. This can only be done if the subordinate considers himself free to bring his problems and suggestions to the notice of his superiors, and is assured of a sympathetic and constructive response from the latter.

What is being emphasized above, in short, is the importance of communications, upwards, downwards and sideways. Good and flexible communications not only facilitate the widest possible participation in policy formation but also ensure that all concerned know what the enterprise is trying to do and enable each worker to see why he is performing a particular task in a particular way.

Recruitment

Public enterprises have so far enjoyed almost complete autonomy in regard to the recruitment of their staff. The Government did issue a circular on the subject in April 1961 but it did not have the force of directive, nor was it in the form of model recruitment rules. The Estimates Committee in their 52nd Report (March 1964) noted this fact and pointed out that many undertakings had not even framed any recruitment rules of their own. Accepting the recommendations of the Estimates Committees, the government, in November 1964, laid down the general principles which it desired government companies to follow in regard to recruitment of staff. Together with these general principles the government also formulated a set of model recruitment and service rules. The government should take steps to ensure that every public enterprise formulates and adheres to properly framed recruitment and service rules along the lines laid down by the government.

An important shortcoming in recruitment so far has been the inadequate attention paid in most enterprises to the task of job analysis and the laying down of precise job specifications. This has led to unnecessary qualifications being prescribed for certain jobs and the recruitment of more qualified persons, e.g. degree holders for jobs which can well be done by diploma holders. Another important shortcoming has been the poor phasing of recruitment resulting in promotion bottlenecks and over-staffing resulting from the inadequate attention that was paid to the need for regulating the staff strength in the beginning.

One of the suggestions which have been put forward is that a Personnel Commission on the pattern of the Union Public Service Commission should be set up for discharging similar responsibilities in regard to the recruitment in the public sector. This has been recommended by the Estimates Committee from time to time. Reiterating their earlier recommendations, the Estimates Committee on National Coal Development Corporation stated, "The Committee consider that the problem is one of reconciling the requirements of public responsibility and regularity on the one hand and adequate business and commercial freedom to the greatest possible extent on the other. They feel that the solution lay in establishing a Personnel Commission similar to the UPSC for public enterprises staffed by people with business experience who understand the personnel needs of the public sector".[5] The Estimates Committee again made recommendations in this regard observing that "such a centralised recruitment for higher posts would enable uniform standards of selection, eliminate competitive bidding for scarce personnel and ensure fairness, besides saving the time and work of the public undertaking".[6]

It is, however, felt that establishment of such a Central Commission independent and outside the public enterprises will seriously affect their autonomy and tend to increase the lead-time in obtaining the personnel urgently required by the enterprises. The delays involved in going through a Central Commission would have adverse effects on managerial performance.

The position in regard to the recruitment of staff for operating public enterprises in developing countries like India is very much different from that in advanced countries. The plants or factories are generally situated in areas with no readily available supply of labour, no ready familiarity with mechanical appliances, no idea of standards of output or productivity and no appreciation of the exacting standards of mass production or even of the occupational hazards. The educational system of the country does not fulfil the requirements of an industrial society. There are problems of cultural adaptation; the workers for industry have to be recruited mostly from the agricultural community life. "In the early stages of industrial development, deficiency of skilled personnel in the new enterprises can hardly be made good by recruitment from others, and even if a few outstanding individuals are available to form the nucleus of a directing staff, or can be borrowed for a time from other countries, there will be a dearth of immediate managers and supervisors able to carry out the policy and train operative workers. The specialized skills of the accountant, the draftsman, the typist, the designer, the production and the maintenance engineer are likely to be in very short supply".[7]

It is not possible to secure immediately a high standard of skilled operation. It is very difficult to recruit senior staff. The available supply of recruits is much below the required standard. The selection of a wrong supervisor has sometimes adverse effects both on the immediate working group and beyond it, and poor supervising staff do not make good recruits for important junior ranks of management. A good recruitment policy should ultimately aim at a scheme of advancement within the organization to give adequate encouragement to good workers; of exploring the possibility of attracting outsiders, even foreigners, permanently or with short or long contracts; of stimulating vital action in the recruits of basic grade; and of persuading individuals to remain with the organization for a long period.

Appointment at the Senior Levels: At the most senior levels, three types of personnel are mainly required: a directing group which needs administrative aptitude; senior management, which should be familiar with the technology of the enterprise and should be able to organize its operations; and senior technical staff, whose professional advice is crucial to the success of the organization. But the problems of recruiting the senior personnel are extremely difficult because of a general lack of experience even amongst the better-educated members of the community. The civil service is occupied with its own problems and also lacks experience of commerce and industry. It is difficult to find men with required experience, technical knowledge and ability to fill up the constantly increasing number of senior posts. They lack the qualities essential for appointment at senior levels, viz., required qualification, leadership, financial experience, good judgment, organizing ability, technical knowledge, competence in the management of personnel and in dealing with conference and delegations, willingness to make bold innovation and sometimes of the pioneering spirit, etc. The only solution, therefore, is to select the best available persons with the greatest combination of these qualities.

Appointments at the Junior Levels: Most of the younger administrators of junior ranks are fine men with fine instincts. They are full of promise, vigour and competence and are also not unequal to the job before them, although they are less experienced and get much less guidance and in-field training from their superiors than their predecessors got. This is mainly because the administration has expanded so fast that training and supervision have become less intensive at all levels. Shortage of proper personnel has also resulted into an unfortunate but temporarily unavoidable lowering of standards in some cases. The young engineers, technicians, scientists and administrators, who are engaged in this revolution, are men of purpose and determination, anxious to get on with the job under conditions which are not always favourable. They have a spirit of challenge and adventure and possess the calibre to learn quickly new skills and techniques, improve upon them and adapt them to Indian conditions.

But this is only one side of the picture. There is another side of the picture which is often clouded by the dust of inefficiency, nepotism and corruption and administrative 'scandals'. There prevails a feeling that the country is rudderless and losing direction and that there has been a failure of leadership. This sometimes tends to generate an atmosphere of cynicism and gloom.

In view of the urgent recruitment needs of the public undertakings, the present recruitment machinery needs thorough overhauling. The motto should be quick decisions, efficient administration and invest a rupee today in order to earn two rupees tomorrow. When several projects crucial for economic development have to be executed according to a strict time schedule and are to be run on commercial principles, a flexible recruitment policy in accordance with the constitutional requirements of ensuring equality of opportunity is very essential.

Recruitment on Regional Basis

A very unfortunate development in some public enterprises in recent years has been the deterioration of relations between the local population and management of such enterprises owing to sectional rivalries and communal feelings. Backward Orissa, for instance, has complained that the legitimate rights of Oriyas have been ignored by various industrial enterprises in favour of people from other states. The complaint, fanned by interested parties, is that Oriyas are being ignored in employment for the benefit of people from other states, particularly Punjab, West Bengal and Tamil Nadu. Similarly, in the recruitment of skilled and semi-skilled working force, the ratio of local and displaced persons is less. This raises the pertinent question as to what extent the recruitment should be made on regional basis.

Since most of the public enterprises are being run essentially by the Central Government, in the recruitment of staff for such enterprises, no preference can be given to any particular area or region or a linguistic group. Debarring candidates from other regions or areas for recruitment to such public enterprises in particular areas will be contrary to Article 16 of the Constitution of India.[8] But so far as state undertakings are concerned, it would be better if the staff recruited in Class III and IV categories is familiar with the regional language, economic conditions and social pattern. The Estimates Committee of the Parliament in its 16th Report recommended that the unskilled labour should be mainly recruited from the local people and that the semi-skilled labour should consist of both local people and others drawn from all parts of the country in keeping with the national character of the organization. It added that the supervisory staff should be representative of the country as a whole.

Shortage of trained manpower acts as a severe constraint on the efficient running of public enterprises and the growth of public sector. The top management have to be provided with highly qualified and expert staff groups in the field of planning, finance and accounts, and personnel and labour administration. This gives rise to demand for staff of the following categories: (i) economists and statisticians including experts in market research; (ii) actuaries, chartered accountants, cost accountants and experts in management accounting; (iii) personnel managers and labour welfare officers; (iv) experts in materials management; and (v) experts in work study and productivity. It is in these fields that the public enterprises experience great difficulty in obtaining suitable persons.

In more advanced countries, the educational system has grown up to meet the requirements of the social, industrial, economic, and political society. In these countries, the universities and colleges, with their greater experience of educational methods and techniques, play an important role in the supply of highly trained managers and specialists in various fields. The educational system developed there lays great stress not only on technology and specialization but also promotes in-service training schemes both in public enterprise and public service. In contrast, the educational system developed in India has not been very useful for the growth of professional managerial class. The leading universities, known for their contributions in the fields of humanities and law, have not paid adequate attention to the training of industrial and business managers and specialists in various fields. It is only in recent years that attention is being paid to teaching of business and management in regular curriculum of colleges and universities.

With the fast growing public sector in India, the need for competent managerial personnel at all levels is growing as much as for any other technical and engineering personnel. It is, therefore, recognized in high quarters that "courses for executive development need to be encouraged in order to ensure adequate supply of personnel who possesses the necessary ability, capacity, and expertness of managerial assignments at each level as the need arises".[9]

It may be stressed that since there is separation of risk-bearing and management in public enterprises, the training in management in order to produce professional managers is more important than what it is in private enterprise. Further, unless the public enterprises institute training programme in management, devolution of authority will be difficult and also the management cannot function effectively unless the individual members are entrusted with effective responsibility. Speaking at the Second Tata Management Conference, Mr. J.R. Tata, the Chairman of the Tata Industries, expressed the guiding philosophy of training in management as follows: "Today in judging management I certainly attach the greatest importance to the capacity that has been shown by a particular individual or group of individuals to train men under them. However efficient a manager may be in doing the work himself, I always feel that the man who is not only capable of doing the work himself, but who has shown propensity and enthusiasm in training men under him even to do the work that he himself does, is a more valuable member of management. In expanding industries and companies, the careful and successful training of understudies and of men to take your place does not mean that your usefulness will be diminished but, on the contrary, that you will free yourself for opportunities to undertake higher tasks in management".[10]

The first step for meeting manpower requirements and formulating adequate training programme is to have a proper assessment of the manpower needs of public enterprises over a projected time span. There is not enough awareness in this regard in public enterprises. Since most of the public enterprises do not have the necessary expert assistance to make fairly accurate estimates of requirements for the future, the Government should get the assessment made by public enterprises examined by a body of experts with the help of the Institute of Applied Manpower Research.

In regard to arrangements for training specialists in different fields, only a few enterprises have set up their own institutions and they too are facing the problems of expense and inadequate utilization of training capacity. The National Coal Development Corporation had to close down two training schools because of inadequate utilization. The Estimates Committee has suggested the formulation of a co-ordinated and integrated training programme for enterprises operating in similar fields of technology.

In recent years, training facilities have been set up by a number of agencies outside the public sector. A number of institutes have been set up for non-technical managerial personnel and experts and specialists in different fields. Several courses are offered by Indian Institute of Management at Ahmedabad and the Administrative Staff College, Hyderabad, among others. The Institute of Chartered Accountants has expanded its out-turn to meet the increasing requirements. Training programmes, seminars and discussions are being arranged by many other agencies like the National and State Productivity Councils, Institute of Industrial Engineers, and the Institute of Cost and Works Accountants. The Management Division of the Planning Commission has held a number of training workshops and seminars in recent years. The Ministry of Finance has established a school for the training of cost accountants. The public enterprises have been participating in their programmes in varying degrees. But their participation has not been to the desired extent.

A Co-ordinated Approach to Training: The subject of training of personnel can be divided into three major categories: (i) non-technical managerial personnel, (ii) specialists required by public undertakings to provide the necessary staff support to the management of public undertakings, and (iii) specialists and technicians needed by undertakings which are pioneers in a new field of industry. So far as the first two categories are concerned, it will probably be advantageous to take full benefit of the training facilities offered by agencies like Management Institutes and All-India Institutes of specialists in different fields. If public enterprises establish their own training facilities in fields of general management education or professions for which facilities are already available elsewhere, it would lead to duplication and waste of expert talent required for imparting training. Arrangements will, however, have to be made for in-plant training and induction of new recruits.

At present, while there is a lot of duplication in the programmes offered by the various training institutes, none of them provides the required training facilities in some of the more specialised fields. The Department of Public Enterprises, in co-operation with the Ministries concerned, should undertake a review of the existing training facilities. This would help in avoiding duplication of efforts and identifying areas where training facilities need to be extended or increased. The Department, along with the representatives of the Ministries concerned and the public enterprises, should examine the curricula of training offered by different institutes to evaluate the suitability of the curricula to the needs of the public enterprises and to ensure that the training imparted is of the required depth and quality.

So far as training of personnel of category III is concerned, the public enterprises themselves will have to assume responsibility for this. In order to make a fuller utilization of the training facilities, the enterprises operating in the same field of technology may co-ordinate their efforts. In the initial stages, the public enterprises should also take the help of various institutes in designing suitable training programmes. Continued dependence on facilities abroad is not in the interest of the country. It strains the scarce foreign exchange resources. The difficulty in obtaining foreign exchange and having to fulfil numerous formalities to obtain Government's approval make it difficult for the management to implement an efficient training programme. It would be better to have the trainers trained abroad and then, with the help of a few foreign technicians, establish the required training facilities within the country.

Promotion Policy

Public enterprises, particularly the Government companies, have been largely free in framing their own promotion policies. Though the Government laid down general principles and model rules in November 1964, the policies adopted by different public enterprises in this regard do not show a uniform pattern. In some, the promotions are made by an officer in his individual capacity; in other cases, they are made on the basis of recommendations of the Departmental Committee or Selection Board with or without associating representatives of the Public Service Commission; in some other cases promotion is made solely on the recommendation of the Public Service Commission. In some cases promotions are also made on the basis of seniority irrespective of qualifications necessary for the post to which promotion is to be made. This diversity of systems and rules leads to anomalies which result in discontentment, lack of team spirit, lowering of morale, and decline in efficiency.

The formulation of a satisfactory promotion policy is, therefore, very essential for raising the morale of the workers and efficiency of the enterprise. The promotion policy of an enterprise must satisfy two basic considerations, viz., (i) it should provide reasonable avenues of promotion to the employees at reasonable intervals and (ii) it should enable the management to select competent employees and promote them to responsible positions for which they are suitable. A sound promotion policy should leave no scope for the widespread and intense suspicion which generally prevails throughout the industry regarding the methods adopted for selecting men for promotion. Suspicion about methods adopted for selecting men for promotion is not peculiar to India and even in advanced industrial countries like the United Kingdom "it is widely believed that management deliberately and cynically favours certain individuals and, where matters are not as bad as this, that promotion goes to those who are fortunate enough or ingenious enough to catch management's eye rather than to those who by virtue of merit or long service have the prior claim on the appointment".[11] A proper promotion policy must ensure employee's demand for maximum opportunity for merit and complete impartiality in selection for promotion. It is, therefore, very essential that the avenues of promotion and the methods of selection for higher posts are clearly laid down and known to the staff, that the seniority lists of the staff are expeditiously finalized and circulated amongst them, so as to enable them to form an idea about their future prospects of promotion, that the enterprises must be able to forecast the number of people required for different posts to make the employees realize the opportunities lay open to them for improving their prospects if they equip themselves. Such a programme would also serve the interests of the management. Unplanned promotions which take place simply because a vacancy has occurred in the next higher scale are not very purposeful. They may even lead to resentment and jealousies when it is found that a person may have secured quick promotions in one enterprise because of fortuitous vacancies which have taken place at higher levels, while equally qualified persons holding equivalent jobs have had to mark time in other enterprises in which vacancies have not occurred to quicken the pace of promotion. No doubt that there have been some cases of rapid promotion in public enterprises, the fact remains that in spite of a fast rate of expansion, public enterprises have not been able to take full advantage of the promotion opportunities offered by this expansion. New projects have come up, but the top management posts have been filled either by deputationists or persons from the private sector. For several reasons, the persons already working in the public enterprises have failed to occupy the top management positions.

It is now widely recognised in all modern countries and business concerns that:[12]

(i) Promotion should be solely on the basis of merit, efficiency and good conduct, irrespective of the seniority of the persons concerned in service.

(ii) Persons should be judged for promotion by the people who have watched their work and conduct over a period.

(iii) Promotions should be made on the recommendations of a committee consisting of not less than three officers, one of whom at least is acquainted with the work of the person concerned. In each case, the committee should record in writing the grounds on which claims of persons, if any, senior to the person selected, were overlooked.

(iv) In judging the person on the basis of the confidential reports on him, it should be seen that he was warned in time of the defects noticed in his work and conduct and that if he did not show improvement, he was warned again.

(v) If no warning has been given to a person, it should not be presumed that the reports on him are so good as to justify his promotion.

Keeping in view the above principles, the promotions may be made according to the following rules:

(i) Promotion to the posts of General Manager, Senior Administrators and Junior Administrators should be on the basis of the record of services as reflected in the confidential reports and personal knowledge of the Appointment Committee of the Cabinet and, also on the ability, temperament, personality and character of the officer concerned.

(ii) The promotion from junior scale to senior scale within Class I posts should be on the basis of seniority subject to suitability and attainment of certain standards of efficiency and training.

(iii) The promotion from Class II Service to junior scale in Class I should be made from a panel of candidates suitable for promotion to Class I Service on the basis of quota laid down for them simultaneously with direct recruitment.

(iv) As regards promotion from Class III to Class II posts, sufficiently high standards should be laid down for selection and the requisite standard should, among other things, include confidential report and service record, seniority, professional ability and capacity to do a particular job, personality, address and leadership and the results of interview and oral tests of the person considered eligible and likely to be suitable for promotion. This is very necessary because of the substantial difference in the nature of work handled by the Class III and Class II staff.

(v) Regular and wide avenues of promotion should also be provided for competent men belonging to Class IV Service on the basis of the satisfactory and efficient service rendered by them. A uniform system of giving promotions from Class IV to Class III Service should be laid down for all the state enterprises and a minimum period of service should be prescribed before such promotion could be made. The age restrictions for the purpose of recruitment to any category of service should be suitably relaxed in the case of Class IV employees.

(vi) The workers belonging to lower classes should be allowed to compete for posts to the next higher class by direct recruitment, if they so desire, and the minimum age qualifications should be suitably relaxed for this purpose.

Lack of Career Development Schemes

The main reason for the unsatisfactory state of affairs in regard to promotions is the fact that public enterprises have not formulated effective career development plans. When the National Coal Development Corporation introduced a cadre scheme indicating the number of posts at different levels and laying down the minimum experience required for promotion from one level to another, it considerably helped the Corporation in attracting technical personnel. A few other public enterprises have also taken steps in this direction. But howsoever carefully such schemes are designed, their effectiveness in motivating the employees will mainly depend upon the quantum of promotion prospects which the enterprise can offer to them. Obviously, it is only the large enterprises committed to a policy of growth which can offer adequate prospects to enterprising employees who have the initiative and will to improve their qualifications and prospects. Career development schemes will not be of much use in small enterprises where the total volume of prospects is not adequate.

The employees of any commercial enterprise must have the confidence that the top posts in the enterprises are open to them and that they too can obtain these positions by sheer dint of merit and effort. While an enterprise should take advantage of the knowledge and experience of persons appointed from outside and of the periodic acquisition of new blood, it should see that most of the senior and top management posts are filled up by persons from within the enterprise. Every public enterprise should formulate and implement suitable career development schemes in which a phased programme of training at different levels is linked to a ladder of promotion.

Manpower Planning and Overstaffing

Overstaffing is believed to be a common malaise in the public enterprises. While most of the public enterprises admit that there is an element of overstaffing in their units, many of them have argued that the extent of overstaffing is often exaggerated. Some have pointed out that it is not proper to compare the existing staff strength with those given in the Detailed Project Reports because the original Reports, in many cases, did not include all the various departments which are now functioning in the project. It has also been argued that the labour norms adopted by the consultants have not been realistic in many instances. The government as well as the public enterprises have been aware of the problem of overstaffing, and measures such as Voluntary Retirement Scheme (VRS) have been implemented to reduce the staff in overstaffed areas.

Opportunities arising from expansion have not been fully utilized to absorb surplus staff. This has partly been due to the fact that new projects were generally set up as independent companies and not under the old running concerns. Only a few enterprises (e.g. SAIL, Fertilizer Corporation of India) have undertaken limited work study programmes to assess the extent and areas of overstaffing. Most enterprises do not possess qualified industrial engineers to do this type of work on a continuous basis. The costs of overstaffing are heavy and recurrent, and are largely responsible for the higher operating costs of public enterprises. The additional cost of maintaining an industrial engineering organisation would be fully justified by the economies which it is likely to bring.

The main reasons for overstaffing are: (i) lack of manpower planning on a scientific basis in the initial stages; (ii) lack of restraint in the initial stages to restrict recruitment to manifest needs and a tendency to go up in routine to the level of sanctioned strength; (iii) undertaking construction departmentally and trying to follow too fast a time-schedule of construction; (iv) emulating governmental pattern in staffing offices and recruiting clerical staff and Class IV servants on that scale; (v) failure to lay down appropriate working standards and following traditional and uneconomical practices like the employment of helpers; (vi) the tendency on the part of the managers and officers to play safe and the tendency on the part of all concerned to distribute favours; and (vii) the political and administrative pressures in the way of shedding surplus staff.

The causes as well as the solutions of the problem of overstaffing are commonly known. Difficulties arise at the stage of implementation where a variety of considerations start restricting management's discretion. The real need is to work out practical solutions consistent with the social obligations of the public enterprises keeping in view the circumstances of each enterprise. The adoption of proper standards and other control techniques is necessary from the very beginning. When the situation goes out of hand, it becomes very difficult for management to retrench staff.

Regarding the enterprises in which overstaffing has become chronic, it is essential to have work studies undertaken by industrial engineers. For this purpose, adequate organisations should be set up, particularly in the large multi-unit projects. Identification of the extent and areas of overstaffing facilitates the absorption of surpluses during the expansion stage and setting up of new projects. As immediate corrective steps, the normal vacancies occurring in overstaffed departments should not be filled up, employees should be encouraged to apply for jobs outside and offered lumpsum gratuities, ex-gratia grants, etc., as incentives to leave the enterprise, offices of the enterprise should be rearranged on an officer-oriented pattern to reduce clerical staff, and skilled workmen persuaded with the help of incentives, if necessary, to do without the assistance of helpers.

Flight of Technical Personnel

Most of the public enterprises suffer from flight of personnel, i.e. large-scale migration of their managerial and technical officers to other enterprises, particularly the private concerns. The main reasons for this are: (i) the general imbalance between demand and supply in the case of qualified engineers particularly those having some years' operational experience or certain kinds of specialised experience; (ii) lack of security in service, particularly amongst construction engineers; (iii) differences in the pay scales offered by enterprises within the public sector itself; (iv) inadequate opportunities for advancement and the greater weight that the public enterprises, as compared with the private concerns, attach to seniority as a qualification for promotion; (v) lack of personnel development programmes and the recruitment of a large number of engineers of the same age group in new enterprises, clogging the avenues of promotion; and (vi) reasons of moral arising out of dissatisfaction with the certain features of organisation and procedure and the public image of these enterprises.

In order to check flight of personnel, the trainees should be made to sign bonds for a minimum period of 5 years and, in the event of infringement, the bonds should be rigidly enforced. Further, the training programme should, as far as possible, be linked to a definite ladder of promotions so that a person has an added incentive to stay on after the completion of training.

Personnel Departments

The personnel departments in public enterprises have generally been placed under officers on deputation from the Central or State Governments. As such, the personnel managers in public enterprises are often not professionally qualified. Some enterprises, however, have had their personnel officers trained in training institutes. Another common characteristic of the personnel departments of the enterprises is the lack of expertise in fields like industrial engineering, labour relations, manpower planning, etc.

The consequence of these factors has been that the personnel departments as they exist today resemble, more or less, the establishment sections of Government departments, their activity often decaying into a lifeless routine. The status accorded to the department also varies from enterprise to enterprise. It deals directly with the chief executive only in a few cases. In most cases, it is attached to a 'line' functionary below the chief executive. For effective personnel administration, the personnel administration should be recognised as a staff function of the highest importance, and the department dealing with it should be properly equipped with the necessary expertise in industrial engineering, labour relations, manpower planning, etc. and attached directly to the chief executive of the enterprise.

Discipline

In recent years there has been a general deterioration in the standard of discipline amongst the staff of public enterprises. An important reason for this is that the conception of the term 'discipline' has not been modified so far to correspond changeover from Police State to the Welfare State and generally the governmental activities are still governed by those rules which were framed to suit a Law and Order State. It is very necessary to make suitable changes in the rules and regulations and to introduce a somewhat liberal conception of the term 'discipline'.

The term 'discipline' is understood to mean strict adherence to departmental rules and regulations. The traditional concept of discipline envisages superimposition of something from an outside agency on a person creating a fear-complex simply by the severity of law or under fear of punishment. This concept was best suited when the country had a Police State. But with the replacement of Police State by the Welfare State, the traditional concept has become obsolete. The new concept of discipline must be understood according to its dictionary meaning 'mental and moral training' and should lay more emphasis on creating a frame of mind which would voluntarily follow the recognized rules of conduct rather than on enforcing such rules by creating a fear-complex.

Many times the reason for indiscipline among workers is the existence of some grievances and also the feeling among them that they can get these grievances removed only by bringing pressure to bear somehow upon the officers. In other words, the workers feel that justice cannot be obtained through normal channel and it is necessary to bring to bear outside influence on matters which should, in fact, be settled through the normal channel. In order to create a sense of security and justice among the workers and to convince them that there is no need to seek justice outside, the following recommendations, made by the Estimates Committee in the context of Railway Staff, may be adopted by all public enterprises with advantage.[13]

(i) Justice should not only be done, but should appear to be done.

(ii) Whatever is due to a worker should be given to him as early as possible.

(iii) There should be no delay in the disposal of representations; a time-limit should be laid down, for the disposal of representations at all levels.

(iv) The Minister, Members of the Board, General Managers and Heads of Department should set apart some time

> to give a hearing to persons, who might desire to represent their cases and draw attention to matters, which might not otherwise reach them.

Education of staff in the matter of discipline would also go a long way in improving the standard of discipline amongst the staff. The members of the staff should be thoroughly educated in rules, regulations and procedures through lectures and by publishing literature on the subject in regional languages so that the entire staff can know the rules of discipline applicable to them. Indiscipline amongst staff also exists because of loss of confidence and absence of ideal before the employees. While giving evidence before the Estimates Committee, on the subject of discipline amongst Railway staff, Shri K.C. Bakhle, ex-Chief Commissioner of Railways, stated, "...anything that can be done to create esprit de corps, to raise the moral and bring the executive and the staff into closer contact will help. Of course, trade unions have come to stay. To some extent, I have a feeling that social legislation has gone faster than social education and there is not perhaps any ideal before the average man in the services for which he would be prepared to work without consideration of remuneration...".[14]

It is not because no ideal exists, in fact, we have the ideal of building a socialist society. But, unfortunately, this ideal has not been adequately publicisized and brought home to the workers. Cordial relationships between the management and workers can be built only by properly appreciating the human values by mutual understanding, goodwill and closer contacts. Every effort should be made to resolve differences of opinion between management and workers by methods of reasoning, mutual confidence and discussion. "It should be the constant endeavour of both of management and the staff to maintain a happy relationship. They are engaged in a great national enterprise and their interests are common and not mutually exclusive. One of the greatest assets of the corporation is the morale of the staff and no effort will be too much to keep personal contacts with those who have to be guided and organised by them, understand their problems and difficulties and infuse confidence in them. The staff, on the other hand, should realise their responsibilities and co-operate to the utmost so that the nation may reap the benefit of their services".[15] The executive officers can inspire the staff working under them with a new spirit of enthusiasm for the job allotted to them by maintaining close and informal contacts with them, by studying their various problems and grievances in a sympathetic manner and by guiding them properly as to what is reasonable and what is not reasonable in their demands. The employees' unions, on the other hand, should also assist the administration in improving the discipline among the staff by intensive publicity and education and by bringing real and authentic grievances, after proper scrutiny, to the notice of the administration for an early action. Good results are very likely to follow if the office-bearers of the employees' unions are themselves working in the public enterprises.

The present elaborate and complicated procedure of departmental enquiry which has to be undergone before removal or dismissal of a guilty employee is another cause of indiscipline among employees. Under the present elaborate procedure, it becomes often difficult to complete the enquiry quickly and to take effective action. Sometimes the accused takes undue benefit of this cumbersome procedure to obtain postponement of enquiry and hinders its early finalization. Such abnormal delays are unfair both to the employees as well as the administration. The disciplinary procedure in public enterprises should be simplified so that it becomes possible to take prompt action against the guilty employee. Definite time-limit should be laid down for the various steps to be followed in the course of departmental enquiries and the same should be rigidly adhered to.

NOTES

1. G.E. Milward, *Large-scale Organization* (London, 1950), p. 223.
2. L. Urwick, *Comparative Organization* (Manchester, 1947).
3. F.C. Hooper, "Management in the Public Services", *Public Administration,* Vol. XXVI, No. 4 (London, 1948), pp. 217-33.
4. A.H. Hanson, "Assistance to an Underdeveloped Civil Service", *Universities Quarterly,* Vol. X, No. 1 (London, 1955), pp. 38-45.

5. Estimates Committee, *32nd Report.*
6. *Ibid., 52nd Report* (New Delhi, 1964), para 185.
7. "Some Problems in the Organization and Administration of Public Enterprises in the Industrial Field", ECAFE Seminar held in Rangoon, 1954.
8. Equality of opportunity in matters of public employment: (i) There shall be equality of opportunity for all citizens in matters relating to employment or appointment to any office under the state; (ii) No citizen shall, on grounds only of religion, race, caste, sex, descent, place of birth, residence, or any of them, be ineligible for, or discriminated against, in respect of any employment or office under the state.
9. Estimates Committee, *Eleventh Report on the Indian Telephone Industries (Pvt.) Ltd.* (Second Lok Sabha, 1957-58), p. 60.
10. *Tata Monthly Bulletin,* Vol. XI, No. 5 (May 1956), p. 3.
11. Action Society Trust, *Nationalized Industry* (London).
12. Estimates Committee, Ninth Report, 1953-54, *Administrative, Financial and Other Reforms* (Lok Sabha Secretariat, 1954), p. 44.
13. Estimates Committee, *Twenty-fourth Report,* p. 41.
14. *Ibid.*, p. 44.
15. Estimates Committee, *Forty-third Report on Indian Airlines Corporation,* 1956, p. 58.

Financial Management

9

Budgeting

At present there is lack of scientific planning in the actual day-to-day work of the administrative authorities in the public enterprises. Most of the schemes are not scientifically conceived in all their aspects in advance and the administrative authorities develop, change and recast their ideas after the schemes are initiated to such an extent that they are almost unrecognizable during execution stage. Schemes are prepared on the basis of mere expectations and estimated on *ad hoc* basis which often results in inordinate delays and wasteful expenditure and make scrutiny by the financial authority very difficult. To cite the Estimates Committee, "There is at present a tendency to sanction or start work without preparing technical blue-prints and detailed estimates of cost. This has led to grievous losses in some cases. There are also instances where projects or schemes had been abandoned on account of the technical defects which were found much later after the work had been started and had made considerable progress. Such instances, though they may be on a small scale depict a tendency which may ultimately prove dangerous if it is not checked now. Schemes are started merely on the basis of guess work and approximate costs that they would involve. This necessitates frequent revisions of schemes and estimates, consultations and vexatious delays".[1]

Most of the provisions made in the various demands for grants are not based on scientific appraisal of the schemes and their execution possibilities and of the amounts likely to be spent during the year. They are just 'guesstimates' and as such lapse of large funds is thus inherent in the existing procedure.[2] Unspent appropriations lead to freezing of resources which could have been profitably used elsewhere. They also result in the imposition of certain taxes which could have been avoided and also in the extravagant expenditure which the administration is tempted to incur at the end of the financial year.

In case of departmentally managed enterprises, all proposals involving financial implications, as a matter of rule, are referred to the Ministry of Finance by the administrative ministry concerned, and a decision can be taken only after the advice of the Ministry of Finance has been obtained. The present budgeting and financial control suffers from serious defects, some of which are briefly mentioned below:

(i) The dominating position enjoyed by the Ministry of Finance within the executive sphere of the Government has led to an excessive concentration of financial authority in its hands. The Finance Ministry is responsible not only for allotment of funds, but also for satisfying itself in adequate details that the schemes for which the funds are alloted have no undesirable features from the financial point of view, that they are sound and fulfil their objectives. Thus the Finance Ministry attempts to assume authority, which should belong to the operating ministries, without responsibility for the consequences. This unnatural divorce of authority from responsibility has created anomalies in the fiscal administration of the country. The administrative ministries hesitate to make any dynamic changes in the system and look upon the Ministry of Finance to take decisions for them. This leads the Finance Ministry to develop a feeling that it is its duty to criticise and scrutinize each and every proposal irrespective of its importance or urgency. Further, since the administrative ministries in many cases do not plan in advance, they have a tendency not to supply full data and press their proposals in such a manner that it leaves very little time for the Ministry of Finance to examine the details or to give their considered views. A sort of suspicion has, therefore, developed into the relationship between the Ministry of Finance and the administrative ministries. This has naturally led to departmental bickerings, recriminations, mild sensations, Secretarial or Ministerial crises and consequently delay, bad planning, wasteful or infructuous expenditure and public criticism at Government's inability to proceed with the schemes according to schedule or efficiency.

(ii) The administrative ministries often have a tendency to deliberately inflate their budget demands at least for two reasons: (1) it is assumed that the Finance Ministry will allot funds less than those asked for and it is, therefore, better to demand funds more than those actually required; and (2) the inclusion of schemes and large provisions gives politically and administratively an impression of efficiency and energy.[3]

(iii) There is general absence of adequate and competent technical advice in order to examine the spending capacity of the project reasonably and accurately.

(iv) The Ministry has no special machinery to watch the expenditure and progress of the scheme as implemented by the agency concerned.

(v) As a result of excessive concentration of central control in respect of the schemes, there is inadequate delegation of authority by the operating ministries to all levels of executive officers, commensurate with their status and responsibilities with reference to the scope of the projects. This leads to lack of adequate local planning and hindering the growth of responsibility. "The heads of departments and other executive officers feel frustrated and hampered now as there has not been sufficient delegation of authority. Even in the exercise of delegated

> powers, there is too much interference in their work, which undermines their authority and, therefore, effectiveness".[4]

Thus the freedom and initiative essential for a commercial enterprise is sacrificed on the altar of appropriatory legislation and excessive control exercised by the Ministry of Finance. It is to avoid this situation that the annual estimates of expenditure of public enterprises organised as companies or corporations are not presented to the Parliament for its approval. The expenditure incurred by government by way of investment or loans to companies are shown only in lump sum in the demands for grants. But the parliamentary committees have desired that the Parliament should be supplied full information regarding plans, programmes and estimates of even those public enterprises which are organised as companies or corporations every year along with the budget documents and in advance of the annual reports which are generally presented long after the end of the year. To cite the Estimates Committee, "...the undertakings should prepare a performance and programme statement for the budget year together with the previous year's statement and it should be made available to Parliament at the time of the annual budget. Further, these bodies might also be encouraged to prepare business type budgets which would be of use to Parliament at the time of budget discussion. In addition, the latest accounts and balance sheets as well as the annual report should also be made available to Parliament at the same time".[5]

While state enterprises organised as companies or corporations cannot be subjected to budget-estimating and appropriating controls which are generally imposed on government departments, it would not be advisable to completely free them from parliamentary or ministerial control. Budget-estimating in public enterprises not only yields information for the use of Parliament but also devises, for the internal use of the enterprises, its own procedure of obtaining experience from past happenings, projecting forward to effect the future business and understanding quickly and clearly what is happening.

The budgetary forms and procedure adopted in public enterprises follow, by and large, the traditional pattern. They have, by and large, copied the bureaucratic procedures prevailing in the government departments, which are not attuned to the larger requirements of industrial and commercial enterprises. In most of the public enterprises, the system of classification of expenditure adopted in the budgets does not link expenditure to activities and end-results. The budgets are also not prepared in sufficient detail. Beyond serving as a basis for obtaining funds and an instrument for controlling expenditure levels, they serve no other management requirements. If the public enterprises are to function on business and commercial principles, it is very essential that they set up adequate finance and accounts organisation and adopt improved techniques of financial management.

An effective mechanism of financial management and control can be built up only on a sound budgetary system. The budget of a public enterprise has not only to serve the requirements of external accountability and internal control but also to provide a plan of action, a framework in which to review progress and a standard against which to review performance. It should be an integral part of the management dynamics which enables the members of an enterprise responsible for the use of resources to project their ideas into the future, and concurrently to look back and review the actual performance as compared with promises and intentions.

It is commonly believed that the budget need only be expressed in financial units. In fact, other units may sometimes be more effective and convenient, e.g. a manpower budget may be expressed better by stating the estimates as the number of men and hours of work required or a production budget may be prepared more intelligibly in physical terms such as numbers or quantity of goods to be produced or services provided. The public enterprises should prepare comprehensive budgets to embrace the entire organisation and to cover *inter alia* the following range of budgeting activities: (i) production estimates,

(ii) sales estimates, (iii) cost of production budget with its necessary sub-divisions, e.g. (a) material projects estimates, (b) labour and personnel estimates, (c) overheads estimates, (d) plant maintenance estimates, (iv) manpower budget, (v) township and welfare estimates, (vi) research and development estimates, (vii) capital expenditure budget, (viii) profit and loss estimates, (ix) cash flow estimates and (x) capital employed budget—fixed and working capital.

For examining the method of preparing budgets, the role of budgeting in policy formulation and the use of the budget as a management tool, the subject may be divided as follows: (i) Revenue Budgets—budgets of income and expenditure on revenue account; (ii) Capital Expenditure Budgets—budgets covering proposals of acquisition and disposal of fixed assets including the resources required; and Cash Budgets—budgets of cash receipts and disbursements in a given period.

Revenue Budget

The immediate and compelling need for a revenue budget is, of course, the requirement that income over a given period should be adequate to meet expenditure on the planned activities. But, in fact, revenue budget should have many more uses than this. In addition to being a forecast of income and expenditure, it should be considered as a plan and a base for the formulation of policy and for laying down the expected standards of performance. The revenue budget should, therefore, be prepared in a form which is intelligible to those who examine or approve the estimates and to those who utilise it as a standard for judging performance as compared to estimates.

The preparation of the budget should be viewed as an opportunity to make a comprehensive and forward-looking review of plans and standards. The budgetary process is a two-way process, the submission upwards of estimates for different units, and the transmission downwards of provisions decided upon at higher levels. The work on the preparation of budget should be started sufficiently in advance to enable every part of the enterprise to be associated in the preparation of the estimates and to have their own separate budgets within the overall budget of the enterprise. The budget thus prepared will represent a consistent and comprehensive programme of activities expressed in terms of their financial implications.

The budget papers and programme statements provide a very useful base for formulating policy because they induce the management to look forward and determine objectives and standards in advance. The budget should be viewed as the occasion for reviewing the various decisions taken in isolation, for evaluating them in the overall context of their total financial impact, and for making such changes as the review might indicate to be necessary and desirable.

Once made, the budget provisions should be considered as firm but not fixed. A fixed budget is not suitable for industrial and commercial enterprises because it is difficult to make a forecast of future economic conditions with any great degree of precision. It is, therefore, essential to introduce a certain amount of flexibility into the budgetary process to make possible modifications of the budget during its currency. These modifications should take care of changes in the assumptions made at the time of the initial preparation of the budget. The higher authorities to whom the necessary budget modifications should be reported for necessary authorisation should also be designated in advance.

Budgetary Control and Management Accounting

The technique of comparing results with estimates and finding causes of deviations can roughly be described as management accounting or responsibility accounting. It involves reporting information, suited to their responsibilities, to the different levels of management which can then take action or offer advice based on that information. The comparison of performance data with budget estimates should be undertaken periodically during the currency of the budget as well as after the closing of the accounts. A forward-looking finance organisation should carry out this exercise for making relevant reports to all levels of management entrusted with the responsibility for using resources. The frequency and volume of information will naturally depend upon the cost and time required to compile it, the extent to which deviations from the budget are possible and the probable cost of such deviations.

The expenditure budgets in general should be reviewed at least twice a year to enable the management to obtain some mid-year knowledge of how expenditure is faring and make corrections, where required, before the year has ended and matters are beyond repair. Monthly profit and loss accounts and balance-sheets should be prepared to indicate the profit earned for the month as well as the cumulative profit accruing up to the end of the month. Sales, production, consumption, and yield figures at each plant should be reviewed every month and at the earliest possible after the close of the month. If these reviews show variations, possible adjustments should be explored. This type of exercise will be particularly useful for reviewing the cost statement for each product and comparing actual cost figures with the anticipations or standards assumed in the budget. The monthly cost statements should be prepared for controlling the scales of materials usage, services and supplies, repairs, etc.

All management levels required to submit reports and returns should themselves be encouraged to analyse and make use of the data with the assistance which the finance and accounts organisation of the enterprise can provide. Periodical comparisons of results with the budget estimates are necessary to keep the estimates up-to-date, both for purposes of policy formulation and for keeping a regular check on performance. Investigations into the deviations from the results originally estimated, generally known as the technique of 'reporting by exception' or 'control by exception', makes possible effective and speedy control over subordinates, where necessary. Periodical reviews and 'control by exception' make possible greater delegation of powers to the various departments and management levels without dilution of the control of supervisory levels.

The data on budget performance comparison reported to higher management levels should be so put up as to indicate the causes of variations as well as the persons responsible. The main purpose of such information reporting and comparisons is to ensure that the policy formulated by the top management is being carried out most effectively. Thus management accounting goes much beyond the task of mere inspection because after finding the variations, and possible areas of faulty planning or mis-management, it enables management in due time to investigate into causes and to take the remedial action essential for improved financial efficiency. The purpose is not only to ensure that each item of expenditure provided in the budget is being adhered to, but also to assess whether, within the budgetary limits, the money is being put to the best possible use.

Capital Expenditure Budget

The capital expenditure budget also involves the same twofold process as mentioned earlier in case of the revenue budget. It is essential for every public enterprise to have a fairly long-term capital expenditure budget to serve as a framework within which individual schemes can be planned, approved by the government and taken in hand. This framework, in addition to the schemes for expansion or creation of new assets, should also include proposals for the improvement or replacement of existing assets.

The budgeting for capital expenditure in the public enterprises is inevitably linked with the procedures followed in the government since it is the government itself which provides funds. A very important requirement of long-term capital budgeting is the existence of at least a provisional indication of the funds and other resources likely to be available for capital investment for as far ahead as the capital project has to be planned. The problem arises from the fact that the government does not have a separate capital expenditure budget and the annual budget of the government includes both revenue and capital outlays. Since it is the government which provides the capital required by the public enterprises, long-term planning on a firm basis becomes a difficult proposition. The provisions indicated in the Five Year Plans are for a particular block of five years and do not give a five-year perspective in the latter years of the Plan. In the United Kingdom where a similar problem exists, the government each year discusses with the enterprise and approves the general lines of its plans for development and capital expenditure for the next five years agreeing to appropriate long-term commitments as well. A similar procedure should be adopted in the case of public enterprises in India to enable them to undertake long-term capital planning on a realistic basis. The controls required to keep public sector investment generally within the government's resources can always be prescribed. For example, the government may each year fix an upper limit on the amounts to be spent on investment by the enterprises during a shorter period ahead, say, two years, and retain the right to approve the annual estimate of capital expenditure.

Cash Budget

It occupies a less important position in the public undertakings because they are financed by the government and do not operate under that limitation which availability of cash imposes on a private enterprise. The cash budget in a public enterprise is more a reflection than a determinant of the revenue and capital expenditure budgets. The cash budget and the preparation of periodical budget comparison statements and cash flow statements should be considered as an integral part of the budgetary process. This is essential to ensure that adequate cash is available for making payments as they fall due without incurring the unnecessary liability of accumulated cash balances lying idle.

Improved Financial Control and Delegation of Authority

The preparation of a business-type budget, periodical budgetary reviews and the adpotion of management accounting practices for exercising budgetary control facilitates an increase in the delegation of powers. An important advantage of a comprehensive budget of the business type is the fixation of responsibility centres and the conferment of commensurate financial powers on the persons entrusted with responsibility for the use of resources. An adequate management information system and periodical budgetary reviews can further ensure that delegated powers are being exercised in a proper manner. Once these improvements are brought about, it would not only be possible to ensure adequate delegation of authority but also to reduce the need for prior financial concurrence and the dependence of line authorities like managers, purchase officers, etc. on the finance branch.

Improvement in budgetary and financial control should be accompanied by a greater delegation of authority as well as a reduction in the number of cases requiring prior financial concurrence. This can be attained by increasing the financial powers of managers, purchase officers, etc. and setting up inter-branch standing committees for such purposes as the view of tenders, the purchase of equipment and stores, etc. The views and advice of the finance branch should be available to the line authorities in these committees, and the need for prior concurrence should be dispensed with. The practice of obtaining prior concurrence may be useful in government departments, but it is not suitable in the case of public enterprises. Its elimination will make the line authorities feel really responsible, as, in fact, they should. At present, there is a common tendency among line authorities to try to avoid responsibility by referring cases to different departments, particularly finance, even when such a reference is not very necessary. Unless such tendencies are checked, industrial and commercial enterprises cannot operate on business lines.

Internal Audit

An issue closely related to financial control is that of internal audit. In a large and complex organisation the degree of control and supervision which can be exercised personally by the supervising officer is necessarily limited. Therefore, it becomes necessary to have an internal audit organisation which is continually engaged in inspection and internal appraisal of performance in the light of established policy and procedures. There often prevails a misunderstanding about the nature, scope and performance of internal audit in the context of public enterprises. Many times internal audit is confused with pre-audit or is viewed as an additional check exercised in advance of external audit. In fact, internal audit should be viewed as a service provided to the management organisation, intended only to serve certain management needs. The internal auditor does not directly participate in management decisions though his findings and observations may influence decision-making. This freedom from the responsibility for executive functions is very necessary if the job of internal audit is to be carried out objectively. In case it gets involved in management or operational decisions, even as a stipulated pre-audit function, it is bound to irritate the line authorities and create problems and interfere with the flow of regular work. The internal audit should be viewed as an independent appraisal activity within the enterprise. The objective of the appraisal should be to review accounting, financial and other procedures and the observance of rules and procedures by the line authorities, to insure against fraud and mistakes and to ensure simplicity and efficiency in procedures.

The internal audit function, organised as a staff function, should be attached to the top management if it is to acquire the necessary effectiveness. The internal auditor should be allowed, and indeed encouraged, to cut across organisational lines in his staff capacity in order to examine the reasons for weaknesses in different areas of management and the functioning of different departments in relation to one another. The major functions of internal audit should be: (i) to review the soundness, adequacy and application of accounting, financial and operational controls; (ii) to ascertain the extent of compliance with prescribed plans and procedures and the accuracy of accounts and other data developed within the organisation; (iii) to offer constructive suggestions for improvement; and (iv) to review and report the action taken by line authorities on the points brought out in previous audit reports, both internal and external.

The management can also use the internal audit organisation for discharging their responsibility for the protection and efficient utilisation of the assets of the enterprise. Internal audit can thus be asked to verify that proper authorisations exist for the acquisition and disposal of the assets of the enterprise and that the prescribed procedures ensure that disbursements are validly made, and that the liabilities are incurred only in respect of the legitimate operations of the enterprise. While examining the documents, verifying inventories, etc., the internal auditor can also help in detecting and preventing frauds, misappropriations and pilferage.

Role of Financial Advisor

In view of the functions of the finance and accounts organisation in public enterprises outlined above, it becomes imperative to review and re-orientate the role of the principal finance officer (Financial Advisor or Financial Controller) of the enterprise. It is very important that the Financial Advisor of an enterprise should consider himself to be an integral part of the management team and not an outsider representing the financial interests of the government. The latter type of feeling grows because most of the Financial Advisors of public enterprises at present are government officers on deputation. For proper relationships to prevail and for the finance organisation to have the proper forward-looking and helpful approach, the power to appoint the Financial Advisor should be vested in the management board and not reserved to government. The management boards may, however, be required to make this appointment after consultation with the government.

The role of the financial advisor should be viewed as that of the principal adviser to the chief executive in all financial matters. The primacy of the chief executive should be maintained in the management field; otherwise, the entire finance organisation becomes a burden on the operation of the enterprise and much of its utility as a vital management aid is lost. The financial advisors should be encouraged to lay greater stress on the management accounting aspect of their working rather than on maintenance accounting or insistence on checks, scrutiny and approval of proposals coming from different departments. It would be unfortunate if the finance organisation of a public enterprise begins to function as the finance department of the government functions in relation to other government departments.

In short, the management is charged with the responsibility of making the best use of the resources entrusted to it, and in the discharge of this responsibility, the financial advisor and his organisation have an important role to play. Good financial management, however, does not try to dictate to line management but aims at providing to management information on resources utilization and statistical analyses which reveal what the plans and performance data truly signify so that management may improve the efficiency of resource utilization and ensure greater profitability.

Efficiency Audit

The financial audit conducted by qualified chartered accountants according to the conventions and ground rules of audit evolved by the professional bodies controlling them is utterly inadequate for examining the working of public enterprises. The major purpose of such audit is to detect fraudulent transactions. But of more crucial importance in case of public enterprises is the need for critically looking into the quality of decisions which *inter alia* would cover the nature and direction of investments, production planning, costing, distribution, etc., and the long-term cost and effects of the decisions taken by the management.

Thus what is required in the case of public enterprises is the management audit or efficiency audit, the purpose of which is to show to the men in positions of management the errors of their ways and their far-reaching long-term effects.[6] The audit conducted by the commercial wing of the Comptroller and Auditor-General has a tinge of this type of audit. The Reports of the Estimates Committee on Public Undertakings seem to touch upon some features of the scheme of management audit or efficiency audit. Such partial probings into the quality of management decisions very often create misgiving and confusion as they tend to take the overtones of probing into the *bona fides* of management decisions. Such misgivings can, however, be avoided if the management audit or efficiency audit is conducted in a scientific and systematic manner by a body of trained personnel, competent to go into the vexed question of techniques and technology apart from those of financing, marketing, etc. The efficiency audit team should be technically equipped to comprehend and judge the problems of capital projects of public sector which are of the nature of expansion-development, savings-renewal, and savings-reorganisation. It should clearly understand the significance of these various types of projects. The expansion schemes, for instance, are those designed to increase the firm's productive capacity so that the main source of additional profit is an increase in revenue, whereas the saving schemes aim at effecting annual savings, usually but not always, in labour costs and that is the main source of additional profit. Such questions will require technological expertise. Furthermore, as problems concerning saving schemes aimed at minimising marginal costs and thereby influencing price-policy are involved, the knowledge of costing is also necessary in the audit team. In addition to these, the team would obviously have experts in productivity, marketing, innovation, personnel and general management functions. While the financial audit can be carried out by one or more persons with financial expertise, the efficiency audit will require the service of a group of experts ranging from engineers to social scientists.

Having discussed the significance of efficiency audit, we may now spell out the main features of such audit. The efficiency audit to be complete, would take up for investigation each of such management functions as production, distribution, development accounts and finance, legal and secretarial, personnel and industrial relations, general management, etc. In the production area, the investigation will cover project planning, buying, process work, storage, inspection, etc. each of which has great significance. In the distribution area, sales records, sales policy, service and publicity arrangements would be critically examined. In regard to development, the enquiry will have to be directed to know in what ways the existing selling lines of the company are being continuously developed and improved from the technical as well as from the commercial aspects and whether schemes of market research have been prepared and how drawn up and implemented considering the long-term interests of the firm. As regards market research, it will have to be seen if it has been built up on a knowledge of the products of the firm and of the activities of all competitors in those particular lines, competitors' price, trade terms, service conditions, etc. Investigations into accounts and finance will extend to an enquiry into the working of cost controls and proper and meaningful recording and presentation of financial information. Policies relating to personnel and industrial relations will be scrutinised. Above all, it will be ensured that the overall working of the enterprise achieves optimum utilisation of the various scarce resources placed as a sacred trust at their disposal.

It is important to emphasize that the proposed efficiency audit should follow a constructive approach. It should not be a source of harassment to the officials managing the public enterprise. The efficiency auditors should devise ways of obtaining information without constantly harassing managers and discouraging them to take decisions. If they have to win the willing co-operation of management, without which they cannot perform their task, their purely advisory status must be emphasized and realised. Their objective should be to help the management in arriving at correct decisions and implementing right policies rather than to impair the will, the drive and the initiative of those in whom community's confidence has been reposed by handing them over vast investments and substantial amounts of scarce resources of the country.

External Audit

The system of audit of accounts of a public enterprise depends upon the form of its organisation. The receipts and expenditure of a departmental enterprise constitute part of the Consolidated Fund, and are, as such, audited by the Comptroller and Auditor General (CAG) just like those of any other department of the Government. In the case of statutory corporations the position varies widely: the accounts of the Life Insurance Corporation are audited only by the professional auditors (private firms of chartered accountants), while in the case of the Food Corporation the professional auditors are appointed by the Central Government on the advice of the CAG. In the case of the warehousing corporations, the audit is done by professional auditors appointed on the advice of the CAG, who also is empowered to undertake such audit as he may consider necessary either of his own motion or on a request from the appropriate Government. CAG is the sole auditor for ONGC.

Under the provisions of the Companies Act 1956, the accounts of government companies are audited mainly by professional auditors appointed by the Central Government on the advice of the CAG. The CAG is empowered to direct the manner in which the company's accounts are to be audited and to give instructions to the professional auditors on the performance of their functions. The CAG is also empowered to conduct a supplementary or test audit of the company's accounts and comment upon, or supplement, the audit report of the professional auditors. Any supplementary reports or comments that the CAG makes are also placed before the Annual General Meeting of the company along with the report of the professional auditors. In this way, the government companies are subject to multiple audit, the audit of the professional auditors and that of the CAG.

The present audit arrangements have been criticised on a number of grounds. In the first place, the existing multiplicity of external audit results into considerable waste of time and effort for the management because it has to reply to the detailed questions and objections raised in successive examinations by the professional auditors and the government auditors. Secondly, the government auditors, particularly the lower staff, do not have adequate appreciation of the commercial nature of the public enterprises and often raise such questions and objections as may have some value in the case of administrative Ministries but appear irrelevant in case of commercial enterprises. Thirdly, unnecessary importance is attached to the audit function as a whole and to the observations made by the auditors after the event with the advantage of hindsight. Fourthly, a too detailed and continuous audit dampens the initiative of enterprising managers compelling them to adopt a more cautious approach and limiting the scope of delegation of powers. Fifthly, at present, the auditors do not possess the necessary expertise or experience to undertake an adequate and systematic appraisal of managerial efficiency.

In 1955, the CAG set up a special organisation called the Directorate of Commercial Audit to look after the work relating to the industrial and commercial enterprises of the government companies and the statutory corporations for which the CAG is responsible. Five regional officers were also set up each under a chief auditor, and in areas not covered by such offices, the Accountants General in the States were specifically entrusted with the work of commercial audit as well.

While it is generally believed that the existing multiplicity of audit and the duplication of effort which it involves should be eliminated, there exists a difference of opinion regarding the manner in which it should be done. Chief executives and general managers are of the view that government companies should be treated like joint-stock companies and their accounts should not be subject to audit by the CAG. It is argued by some that even under the existing provisions of the Companies Act, the CAG is empowered to give directives to the professional auditors and that it is, therefore, possible for the CAG to have the entire work done through the professional auditors. They contend that this can be done by the CAG revising and amplifying his directives to cover whatever area he considers it necessary to cover. In contrast, the CAG and his senior officers are of the opinion that the private firms of chartered accountants are not yet equipped with the requisite expertise to conduct what may be called efficiency-cum-propriety audit. In view of this, it is sometimes argued, particularly by some of the financial advisors of the public enterprises, that the entire audit should be the sole responsibility of the CAG. They point out that since government companies are financed wholly or mainly from public funds, their accounts should be subject to efficiency-cum-propriety audit by an agency acceptable to Parliament.

As regard the position in other countries, in the United Kingdom where public enterprises have been set up as statutory corporations, the Comptroller and Auditor General has not been entrusted with the responsibility for conducting audit. In contrast, in the United States and Australia, the government corporations are subject to government audit. In Canada, most of the state enterprises are subject to government audit, but private firms of chartered accountants are entrusted with the work in case of a few enterprises. In France, a special body has been set up by statute to verify the accounts and appraise the performance of public enterprises. In Italy, the two public corporations, ENI and IRI, have a Board of Auditors consisting of officers from the Government Audit Organisation and the Ministries concerned. There does not appear to be any example in any foreign country where the accounts of a public enterprise are subject to audit both by government auditors as well as private professional auditors. There are three major alternative measures which can be adpoted to reduce the existing multiplicity of audit and the duplication of work: (i) public sector enterprises may be excluded from the responsibility of the CAG, (ii) audit by professional auditors may be completely eliminated and the entire work entrusted to the CAG, (iii) the existing area of the audit conducted by the CAG may be reduced to the minimum by strengthening the internal audit system and by increasing the area covered by the professional auditors.

It does not appear to be advisable to do away with the CAG's audit altogether. In addition to considerations of public accountability, the fact remains that the Directorate of Commercial Audit has gained some experience of efficiency-cum-propriety audit. Entrusting the entire work to the CAG may not, however, be practicable. It would require huge expansion in the government audit organisation, which may prove to be more expansive than the existing set-up. Nor would it be proper to suddenly reduce the business that is going to the private firms of chartered accountants which have been doing this work for quite some time and which have acquired some experience and expertise in the process. The suggestion that the area of the CAG's audit may be reduced by increasing the area assigned to professional auditors is a desirable objective but this will not lead to a significant reduction in the existing multiplicity and overlapping because the CAG would always like to test the work done by the professional auditors and it is this which causes overlapping.

More important than reducing the avoidable multiplicity is the need to revise and re-orient the attitude of government auditors to conform to the special requirements of public enterprises. It has often been pointed out that government auditors are not adequately aware of the special circumstances and conditions under which industrial and commercial enterprises have to operate and that they do not distinguish between the procedural needs and operational exigencies of the public enterprises and those of the administrative Ministries. The government auditors, who have the advantage of hindsight and additional information which was not available to the management at the time of taking decisions, try to criticise individual transactions with great zeal. This tends to dampen the enthusiasm and initiative of enterprising managers and promotes an atmosphere of caution among the managers. The government auditors fail to take a broad view and to recognise the fact that the management several times have to take calculated risks some of which may result in losses on individual transactions. It is highly desirable that they take these factors into consideration before commenting on the transactions of such undertakings. It would, however, not be in the public interest to completely immune public enterprises from enquiries for the purpose of an efficiency audit. At the same time, it may be stressed that the audit should take an over-all rather than a narrow detailed view of performance. It should not miss the wood for trees. Its objective should not be to hunt out for faults for the sake of fault-finding, but look upon the undertaking's performance for the year as an achievement to be reviewed. It could, of course, point out, if the circumstances warrant it, that more could have been attained at the same or less cost. By adopting this role, the audit can render useful service to the management and come to be welcomed and respected instead of being feared and avoided.

In France, a statutory body called the *Commission de Verification des Comptes* (Commission of Verification of Accounts) has been set up for work relating to the verification of accounts and the appraisal of performance of public enterprises. The Chairman of this body is the President of a Chamber of the Cour des comptes. The work of the Commission is divided into five sections, each section covering a different area of enterprise, namely, fuel and power, credit and insurance, transport and communication, engineering, chemical and miscellaneous industries. Each section consists of three magistrates of the Cour des comptes (Audit Court) and two other members appointed by the Minister of Finance and Economic Affairs. All the members are of high rank and possess a substantial measure of independence. For verification the Commission has its own staff but includes a large number of officers on deputation from the Audit Court. It also utilises the services of part-time investigators (rapporteurs) employed for the purpose from different Ministries. The verification aims not only at checking the correctness and proper maintenance of the balance-sheets, inventories, etc., but also to bring out the financial position of the enterprise and its future prospects. The Commission also examines the commercial and financial management of the enterprise and suggests improvements including the changes required to be made in the organisation and structure of the enterprises.

The Commission has full powers of investigation. It submits two reports: one an annual report on detailed aspects to the Ministry of Finance and the other a general report to the Parliament, the Cabinet, and the Cour des comptes. The coverage of these reports extends far beyond the accounting sphere. The scope of the first report covers "the quality of the commercial and financial management of the undertaking", while the second deals with "the modifications in structure or organisation which it considers necessary and gives its opinion on the future outlook."[7] The work of this commission has been highly appreciated.

The French system of audit can be adopted in India with advantage after making certain suitable modifications. We have already stressed the need for bringing about a radical re-orientation in the attitude of the auditors so that their outlook and methods may conform to the special needs of the commercial and industrial enterprises in the public sector. The process of this reorientation will be certainly accelerated if a Board is entrusted with the efficiency-cum-propriety audit of these enterprises and two eminent outsiders with experience of the working of public enterprises are also nominated to serve as members of this Board. While the senior officers of the audit department appear to be sufficiently aware of the need for a different and broader outlook towards the audit of public enterprises, this awareness somehow does not percolate to the lower levels of the audit organisation. This appears to be mainly due to the hierarchical structure in which the audit department is at present organized. It is expected that the position will improve fast if the audit department is reorganized along functional lines, and a Board on the French pattern constituted at the top to provide direction and guidance of lower levels.

The work which is at present being done by the Directorate of Commercial Audit should be divided amongst four or five audit boards, each audit board dealing with a particular major area of enterprise like iron and steel, engineering, chemicals, trade and commerce and transport, etc. Each of these audit boards should have five members including three senior audit officers as common permanent members. For this purpose an Additional Deputy Comptroller and Auditor General should be designated the common Chairman of these boards; the other two common permanent members should be of the rank of Accountant General. The two part-time members of each board should be appointed by the Minister responsible for the development of that particular industry. These two members need not be serving officials of the Ministry, but may be selected from amongst very senior persons experienced in the work of public enterprises or from amongst experts in commercial or financial matters. It would be advantageous if one of the two part-time members has occupied senior managerial posts in the public enterprises.

The existing departmental set-up of the Directorate of Commercial Audit should be utilized for providing the secretariat and investigating staff to the audit boards. It would not involve any transfer of service or fundamental reorganisation of the department because the administrative control over staff and the responsibility for running the organisation can be vested in the three permanent members who will be officers of the CAG. It will be necessary, however, to provide reorientation and training to the existing staff and to recruit certain specialists and experts like statisticians, economists and cost and chartered accountants. If an organisation is to conduct efficiency-cum-propriety audit, it is essential that its staff should be similar in expertise and specialisation to the management organisation of the enterprise concerned.

The reports concerning individual enterprises should be discussed in the audit board in the presence of the representatives of the Ministry concerned and the public enterprise under examination. These reports should not be considered as confidential and should be presented to the Parliament through the controlling Ministry. It is not necessary for audit boards to conduct a comprehensive review of the working of each undertaking every year. The audit boards can so phase their programmes that they conduct this review in respect of each enterprise once every 5-7 years. The works of annual verification of accounts and the balance sheet need not be delayed to coincide with the comprehensive review.

A large portion of the audit work, mainly relating to regularity audit, may be got done by the audit boards through the professional auditors who are trained for this work and who have also gained experience of doing this work with regard to the government companies. The Audit Board would, of course, utilise its own staff for conducting efficiency audit. Multiplicity of audit would be avoided because professional auditors would be working as agents of the audit boards and will have a clearly defined area of work which need not be tested or re-examined by the permanent staff of the audit boards. The work assigned to the professional auditors should be confined to regularity audit as in the case of private joint-stock companies. For each undertaking, or class of undertaking, combined audit parties comprising the staff of Audit Boards as well as professional auditors should be formed so that their task may be carried on concurrently and collectively. Thus the chances of duplication will be effectively reduced.

NOTES

1. Estimates Committee, *Ninth Report* (New Delhi, 1954), p. 8.
2. Public Accounts Committee, *8th Report* (New Delhi, 1957-58), p. 2.
3. *Ibid.*, p. 15.
4. *Ibid.*, pp. 19-20.
5. Estimates Committee, *Twentieth Report,* para 25.
6. Raj K. Nigam, "Concept of Efficiency Audit and its Application to Public Enterprises", *Lok Udyog* (January, 1968), pp. 13-14.
7. W.A. Robson (ed.), *Problems of Nationalised Industry* (London, 1952), p. 110.